Excellence in Direct Marketing

Excellence in Direct Marketing

The International ECHO Awards

DIRECT MARKETING ASSOCIATION, INC.

Library of Applied Design

An Imprint of

PBC INTERNATIONAL, INC. ✦ NEW YORK

Distributor to the book trade in the United States and Canada:

Rizzoli International Publications Inc.
300 Park Avenue South
New York, NY 10010

Distributor to the art trade in the United States and Canada:

PBC International, Inc.
One School Street
Glen Cove, NY 11542
1-800-527-2826
Fax 516-676-2738

Distributor throughout the rest of the world:

Hearst Books International
1350 Avenue of the Americas
New York, NY 10019

Library of Congress Cataloging-in-Publication Data
Excellence in direct marketing : the International ECHO Awards / by
    Direct Marketing Association.
        p.   cm.
    Includes index.
    ISBN 0-86636-181-2
    1. Direct marketing—Awards. 2. International ECHO
Awards. I. Direct Marketing Association (U.S.)
HF5415.126.E93 1992
658.8'4—dc20   92-7166
                                                           CIP

CAVEAT—Information in this text is believed accurate, and will pose
no problem for the student or casual reader. However, the author was
often constrained by information contained in signed release forms,
information that could have been in error or not included at all. Any
misinformation (or lack of information) is the result of failure in these
attestations. The author has done whatever is possible to insure
accuracy.

Color separation, printing and binding by
Toppan Printing Co. (H.K.) Ltd. Hong Kong

Typography by
TypeLink, Inc.

Printed in Hong Kong

10 9 8 7 6 5 4 3 2 1

RICHARD HAUGAN *Chairman*	Richard D. Haugan and Associates
KATIE MULDOON *Vice Chairman*	Muldoon & Baer Inc.
JANICE BRANDT	Newfield Publications, Inc.
PAUL D'ANDREA	Mystic Color Labs
HOWARD FLOOD	The Schmidt Group International, Inc.
JOAN GREENFIELD	Joan Greenfield Creative Consultant
HENRY R. "PETE" HOKE	Hoke Communications, Inc.
DAVID IVENS	Brann Direct Marketing, U.K.
DOROTHY KERR	Equifax Consumer Direct
RAYMOND J. MARKMAN	Life Planning Co.
DOREEN McCURLEY	Columbia House
PIERRE PASSAVANT	Kobs, Gregory, Passavant
RONALD PERRELLA	DRS Inc.
SUTI PRAKASH	The Direct Marketing Group, Inc.
SUZANNE RIDENOUR	Ridenour & Associates
KAREN RIDINGS	Herring/Newman Direct
JOAN THROCKMORTON	Joan Throckmorton Inc.
STANLEY WINSTON	Ogilvy & Mather Direct

Often called the "Academy Awards of Direct Marketing,"
the ECHO Awards recognize each year's best efforts in
the field, cited by a jury of the industry's foremost
talents not simply for outstanding creative work,
but for superlative creative work that meets or
exceeds a particular marketing objective.

CONTENTS

FOREWORD

In 1991, advertisers and their agencies entered more than 1,200 examples of their efforts in the Direct Marketing Association's 62nd International ECHO Awards competition. From among these many entries, direct marketing professionals in six cities selected the very best and awarded ECHOs, the industry's Oscars, to 142 winners.

This book is a tribute to the winning campaigns and the inventive, ingenious people who created the work. It is also much more.

For many years, the Direct Marketing Association has maintained and made available to its members the complete and original winning entry portfolios. We will continue to do so. But, for the very first time, the winning ECHO case histories are now available in this informative and handsome book.

While the book, obviously, cannot include all the details and actual samples provided in the entry portfolios, we believe it will be a valuable reference work for our members and all practitioners of direct marketing. A convenient and accessible source of inspiration, ideas and possibilities for catalogers, consumer, business to business, and financial products marketers and publishers.

We believe, too, the book, like the ECHO competition itself, will help us learn from each other and, by example, raise the effectiveness and standards by which future direct marketing work is judged.

Finally, we hope that many marketing executives who have not yet embraced our unique and powerful discipline will be encouraged to explore its potential.

The extraordinary growth of direct marketing, as these ECHO winners illustrate, is truly an international phenomenon. One third of all the winning entries came from outside the United States. And equally gratifying, many of the entries represent the direct marketing efforts of the largest, most respected companies in the world.

As an expression of appreciation, we are dedicating this first edition to Bonnie DeLay, Director, DMA International ECHO Awards. Much of Bonnie's time and bright energy has contributed to the successful annual ECHO competitions and award presentations over many years. Many thanks Bonnie!

The publication of this book is planned as an annual event, demonstrating the variety, creativity and ability of direct marketing to solve an almost endless array of marketing and communications challenges. And, of course, it is also a celebration of the exceptional and innovative people who are leading the way.

JONAH GITLITZ
President
Direct Marketing Association

INTRODUCTION

The International ECHO Awards, unlike most advertising awards, not only reward creative excellence, but results as well. If it didn't work, then you can be certain it didn't win.

This book, then, celebrates not only the creative talents who produced the work, but the marketing strategists, product planners, media professionals, researchers and production specialists who contributed to the very best efforts in 1991.

For those direct marketers looking for innovative ideas, the following pages can be a source of inspiration. For those advertisers not yet seriously engaged in direct marketing, we hope it will be the spark that ignites their interest.

The 1991 ECHO winners demonstrate the amazing variety of solutions and techniques that direct marketers apply to marketing problems.

The media used include mail, television and radio, magazine and newspaper print, even take-ones. Mail, still the workhorse of direct marketing, is shown in an endless variety of sizes and materials from outsize cardboard boxes and tubes to wooden crates. Inside are architectural drawings, talking chips, interactive computer disks, buttons, bows, samples, examples, product demonstrations and more.

Part of the challenge and much of the fun comes from the fact that direct marketing creative teams are not limited by the measurements of the page or the 30-seconds of commercial time. Only the imagination limits.

It's well known that direct marketing has enjoyed phenomenal growth over the past decade. Among the many reasons is accountability. Direct marketing advertising is measurable advertising. Results can be counted. Dollars spent can be precisely weighed against dollars returned. Advertisers who succeed increase their investments and their ambitions year after year.

There is another reason for the global growth of direct marketing. Not too long ago its principal participants were those advertisers whose sole distribution channel was mail order. For example, the book and record clubs, catalogers, private mints, collector clubs, magazine publishers and promoters of unique products not available at retail. They lived or died with the morning mail.

These advertisers continue to contribute ideas, energy and innovation to the industry. And in recent years they have been joined by a new breed. As you look through this book, you will come across the names of the most prestigious companies in the world: AT&T, American Express, Xerox, IBM, Lufthansa, British Telecom, Mercedes Benz and Citroen.

These companies have discovered the unique ability of direct marketing to sell merchandise, generate sales leads, introduce services, add value to their products and cement relationships with their customers.

Once they tasted blood, they came back for more. They learned how to integrate direct marketing into overall advertising, marketing and communication plans. They launched new products, new services and marketing ventures as a result of their newfound confidence in direct marketing's unique abilities.

These blue chips and their challengers have had a dramatic impact on the reach, proliferation and quality of direct marketing.

Over the past two decades, direct marketing has been the fastest growing discipline in advertising. But, we ain't seen nothin' yet. Sophisticated use of databases will improve targeting of prospects and the economics of direct. New technology will provide new opportunities to communicate one-to-one. And very encouraging, universities are introducing direct marketing into the curriculum of their business and communication schools, assuring a welcome stream of bright, new talent.

The future is bright indeed. But that's tomorrow. On the following pages is the state of the art, 1991. The International ECHO Award winners who produced the best direct marketing in the world.

STAN WINSTON
Executive Creative Director
Vice Chairman
Ogilvy & Mather Direct

DIAMOND ECHO AWARD
The "Best of Show"

Award: Gold-Diamond
Program: Crying

Client: Ryder Truck Rental

Agency: Ogilvy & Mather Direct
Creative Supervisor: Bob Cesiro
Associate Creative Supervisor: Shelley Lanman
Art Supervisor: Janet Penello
Copywriter: David Evans
Broadcast Manager: Helen Carney
Business Affairs Manager: Gail Grubman
Account Director: Becke Karl
Account Supervisor: Eric Raff
Assistant Account Executive: Michelle Morris
Assistant Account Executive: Kristin Paulus
Production Manager: Barbara Aly Amer
Associate Media Director: Marion Somerstein
Associate Broadcaster Director: Robin Friedman

To sell its used trucks at a premium price in an increasingly depressed market, Ryder Truck Rental leveraged its reputation for superior truck maintenance with these humorous spots, depicting the Ryder mechanics sobbing as their well-cared-for vehicles find new owners. The results were nothing to cry about: more than 35,000 responses at a cost of $18 per response, beating the previous campaign by 173 percent.

STEVE: See what I mean? They look after these trucks like they were their own.
MECHANIC #3: They've got their whole lives ahead of them.
STEVE: You're going to be okay. Do you believe these guys?

STEVE: Ryder sells more kinds of used trucks than anyone. Trucks, vans, tractors, trailers. Even specialized equipment. Just call and they'll tell you where to get them. They'll even—
MECHANIC #1: Not the book!
STEVE: Eh, I have to do this. They'll even give you free advice before you look. It's in here: "How to Buy a Used Truck." You gotta get this. It's the inside story. What to look for, and avoid. Whether you're buying now or just kicking some tires.

MECHANIC #1: (VO) Steve!
STEVE: It's okay, relax.
MECHANIC #1: Don't give 'em the number, please.

STEVE: Just call for the free book: "How to Buy a Used Truck." Even if you're not buying now, you'll be an expert. But you gotta call.

MUSIC UP—SAPPY, SENTIMENTAL VIOLINS
MECHANIC #1: (*Tearful*) There goes my baby.
STEVE LANDESBERG: Here we go again. I knew it. Every time Ryder sells a used truck this happens.

MECHANIC #2: (*Sobs*)
STEVE: There, there. You didn't know Ryder sells used trucks? They do. They sell 'em. (*to Mechanic #2*) Excuse me.
The same quality trucks they rent and lease to businesses, they also sell to businesses. Makes these guys fall apart.
MECHANIC #2: (*Sobbing*) We've been caring for them since they were new.

STEVE: Course, with a Ryder used truck you know what you're getting into. See this tag, "Road Ready." It means this truck has been maintained at the highest standards since it was new. Ryder has the records to prove it. And a limited warranty to back it. Impressive stuff.
MUSIC UP
STEVE: How ya doin'?
MECHANIC #4: (*downcast*) Great.

STEVE: These guys put their hearts into these trucks. They even fix things before they go wrong.
MECHANIC #4: (*VO*) (*Sniffs*) Brakes. Steering. Engine.
STEVE: You'll love your Road Ready truck as much as they do.
MECHANIC #2: Oh please, I don't want to see you go!
STEVE: Only you get to keep yours. So call for the Ryder Road Ready Center nearest you. And ask about financing.

MECHANIC #4: (*Sobbing*) Please take good care of her.
STEVE: Don't worry. You'll get more trucks. Sorry I'm out of tissues. It's a new jacket. Get off me...

I'm not kidding.
MUSIC UP AND OUT.

13

GOLD MAILBOX AWARD
The Most Innovative Use of Direct Mail

Award: Silver
Program: Free Lunch

Client: Manor Hill Food Corporation

Agency: Trahan, Burden and Charles Direct
Creative Director/Copywriter: Tom DiJulio
Art Director: Philip Tang
Production: Michael Jones
Account Management: Moira McNulty

Manor Hill Food Corporation knew their new Gourmet Beginnings salad bases would be a hit at restaurants and grocery stores—if they could just get buyers to sample them. Rather than deliver samples which might sit unopened in a buyer's office, Manor Hill instead delivered a place setting with an invitation to a Gourmet Beginnings lunch, to be served at the buyer's convenience. The results were especially appetizing: a response rate of 45 percent, at a cost per response of $17.09.

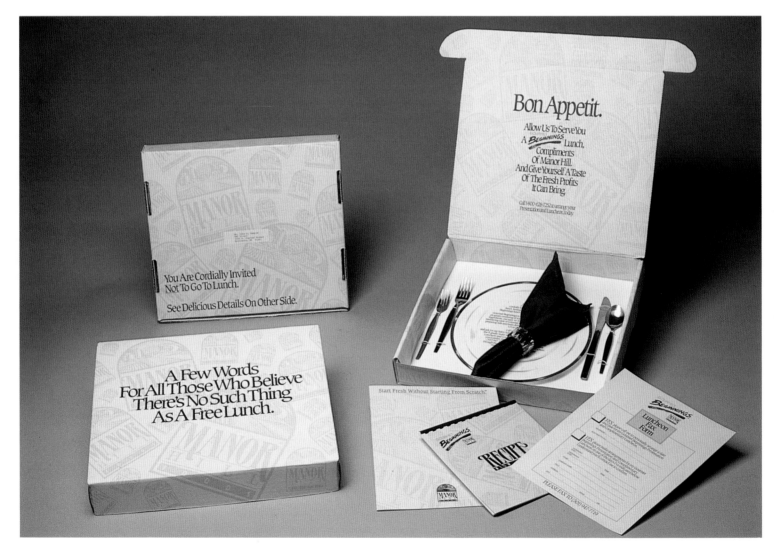

THE HENRY HOKE AWARD
The Most Courageous Solution to a Difficult Problem

Award: Leader
Program: EckerdCare

Client: Eckerd Drug Company
Director of Advertising: Betsi O'Neill
Manager, Database Marketing & Research: Mark Warren
Manager of Advertising & Marketing Services:
  Julie Gardner
Advertising Specialist: Sandy Krand

Agency: W. B. Doner & Company
Creative Director: Sande Riesett
Copywriters: Sandy Coleman, Jeff Rassmussen
  Dave Spivey
Art Director: Debbie Piccolino-Saag
Printing: Webcraft
Managing Director: Tony Everett
Account Supervisor: Holly Rich
Assistant Account Executive: Kathryn Brock

The Eckerd chain of drug stores was under attack from discount competitors. The company therefore decided to target three high usage groups—seniors, parents of children under four, and diabetics—and mail out a series of these informative newsletters, highlighting recent health tips of concern to each group, offering discount coupons, and identifying the location of the nearest Eckerd store. Each mailing cost just 30¢, with five mailings to each prospect a year, a small investment on customers who spend $300–$500 on prescriptions a year.

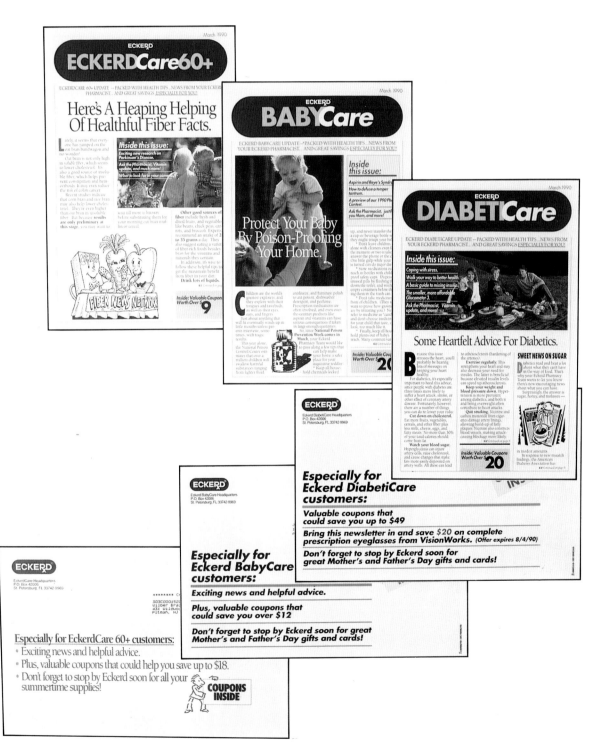

Chapter

Financial Services

NAUTILUS
Glassford Lines
P O Box 28916 Sandringham
2131 Sandringham Centre
SANDRINGHAM
2192

Tel (011) 640 3548

Only 25 captains
of industry will take the helm . . .

Dear Mr. MacLean,

I'm writing to make you an exclusive offer – personal participation in ownership of Southern Africa's largest private ocean-going luxury motor yacht.

The ownership participation plan for *Nautilus* spans five years and is available to a maximum of 25 industry leaders, top decision-makers and people in public life.

Nautilus was developed as an inspiring new venue for business and pleasure and offers you a range of invaluable marketing-related opportunities:

- a highly original and discreet venue for high-level talks and confidential negotiations
- the ability to offer top-level business prospects an irresistibly attractive invitation
- a refreshing and inspiring environment for your strategy planning conference or board meeting
- an intriguing way to launch a new product range and generate publicity for the event
- a top-class getaway for yourself, your family and guests

Nautilus provides luxury accommodation for 10 to 14 people plus 6 crew. There is television in each suite and the luxurious master stateroom also has a mini-bar. A formal cocktail lounge offers you further entertainment facilities, while the spacious aft deck and flybridge provide larger outdoor areas for product launches and larger gatherings. *Nautilus* has a fully-equipped cordon bleu galley, and our up-to-date presentation equipment includes a VCR with video enlarger and 2-metre screen.

Extensive leisure equipment offers a 4,5 m speedboat, jet and paddle skis, windsurfers, scuba equipment, water skis, fishing equipment, bicycles, board games and a small but tastefully fitted library.

Professional crew includes an experienced captain, engineer and 2 ratings. In addition a PRO is employed to assist with all your requirements whether they be catering for a seafood buffet for 100 or advice on coastal cruising.

The latest navigational equipment on the bridge, including weatherfax, radar and satellite navigation systems ensure your safety and guarantee problem-free cruising.

The Nautilus trust fund provides for the day-to-day running costs over the five year period, *so there are no levies to pay.* You will be billed for home port electricity, food and beverages, and, when cruising, fuel and crew.

A watertight legal ownership contract, with stringent conditions in the agreement of sale, including controls on the trust fund into which the purchase price is paid, *protects the rights and security of the purchasers.*

Comprehensive insurance cover protects you in any eventuality connected with *Nautilus.*

PRINCIPALS: Shipowner Fineline Aluminium (Pty) Limited Reg No 83/12748/07 Marketing & Management Co Glassford Lines
Members S Beaumont G Dryden M Hacker Tax Consultants Ernst & Young General Consultant A Menachemson
Attorneys Wertheim Becker Naval Architects Daggit Smit & Associates (Pty) Ltd Builder Ankou CC (Cape Town)

Mr. Clive MacLean
Grey Response
Marketing

The ultimate in oneupmanship.

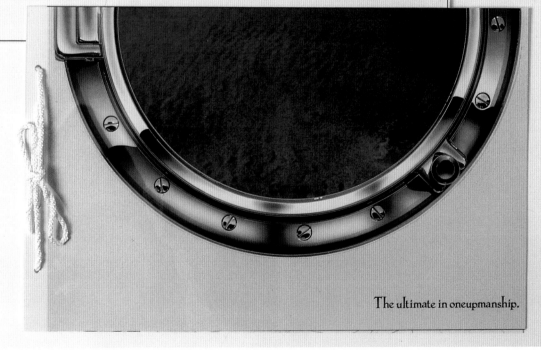

The ultimate in oneupmanship.

Award: Gold
Program: Nautilus

Client: Fineline Aluminium, *South Africa*

Agency: Grey Response Marketing (Pty.) Ltd.
Reprographics: Beith Process
Printer: Standard Press
Creative Director: Andrew Phillips
Client Service: Kaylene Wishnuff
Copywriter: Janine Pike
Art Director: Sue Edelstein

Key South African executives were offered "the ultimate in oneupmanship"—a time share in a luxury motor yacht designed as a unique venue for product launches, board meetings, client entertaining, and more. Thanks to this opulent, hand-delivered mailing—and despite the stiff price of R 250 000 per year for five years—the shares sold out completely, grossing $18.75 million and reflecting a response rate of 47 percent and a conversion of 15 percent.

Award: Silver
Program: Malta Affare

Client: Colonia Versicherung AG, *Germany*
Marketing Director: Werner Becker

Agency: Ogilvy & Mather Direkt
Creative Director: Michael Koch
Art Director: Birgit Schwarz
Copywriter: Andrea Arnold
Management Supervisor: Ulrich Haessner
Account Executive: Andrea Klever

To motivate part-time insurance sales representatives to learn more about the client's policies and improve their sales, this 6-part mailing series contained a murder mystery story with facts and a quiz about the insurance. Correct answers earned prizes, with the most policies sold earning a holiday in Malta. The campaign drew a 45 percent response rate and increased the number of policies written by 32 percent from the year previous.

Die komplette Filmkulisse haben sie einfach stehen lassen. Man kann in aller Gemütlichkeit im ganzen Filmdorf herum-spazieren. Macht man dann mal eine Tür auf, sind im Haus nur Stützbalken drin! Sehr witzig.

Die Fähre um 12 war leider schon voll, obwohl ich früh da war. Aber zum Glück gibt es an der Mole eine Bar.

Und zum Glück gibt's in der Bar SHANDY – dem Malteser Falken sei's getrommelt und gepfiffen!!!!

Original maltesische Bierlimonade.

Wieviel man davon wohl zollfrei nach Deutschland importieren darf? 15 Paletten wären das mindeste. Schließlich ist da kaum Alkohol drin.

Aha, da vorne taucht der Hafen auf. Ist ja richtig malerisch. Das rührt sogar einen hartgesottenen Schnüffler wie mich fast zu Tränen. Ach, hier müßte man mal Urlaub machen... Na, dann will ich mal mit meiner rechtsgesteuerten Mühle nach Xlendi fahren. Links, natürlich.

In Xlendi.

Diese kleine Hafenpromenade ist richtig nett. Gefällt mir immer besser hier. Die Leute sind freundlich, die Küche ist italienisch, und das Klima maltesisch...

15 Dosen Shandy.

und... plötzlich stand ich vor dem Süßwarengeschäft meines Lebens !!!

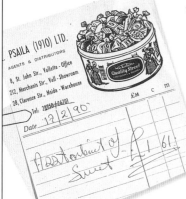

geschah........ und mir ist jetzt ganz schlecht vor lauter Gummibärchen, Schokonüssen und Kaffeebonbons.

Noch eine Entdeckung habe ich gemacht:

in Valeta gibt es eine sehr traditionsreiche Juweliersfamilie namens Azzopardi...

Unverblümt, wie ich nun mal bin, frag ich in dem Geschäft nach Marija Azzopardi.

Award: Bronze
Program: The Clear Choice

Client: National Financial
Vice President, Sales Administration: Robert J. Middleton

Agency: d.a.p. associates
Creative Director: Dorothy A. Pike
Art Director: Donald P. Reed
Copy: Robert J. Middleton
Fabricators: ALTEC
Coordination and Mailing: d.a.p. associates

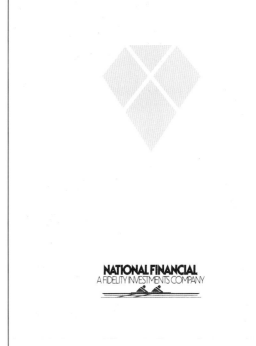

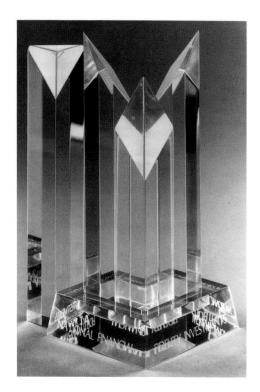

To develop awareness and appeal to the broker dealer firms for whom National Financial was offering clearing and execution services, the company sent out this series of mailings positioning themselves as the prospect's "clear choice," with a striking and unusual set of interlocking crystal prism keepsakes. The campaign clearly succeeded, generating 89 responses for a response rate of 35.6 percent.

Meet Olga.
In half an hour, she can ease the aches and aggravations
of a tough day at work. But chances are, they'll be back. And so will Olga.

What's the pain reliever travel executives recommend most?

Meet the Citicorp World Travel Payment™ system.
In minutes, it gives you fast, permanent relief from a pain in
the neck you've endured too long: those complicated international payments
to your foreign suppliers.
With the World Travel Payment system, the process is virtually
painless. Because you can issue checks and order payments in more than 40
currencies, right a...

quickly and comf...
acute foreign exch...

photocopy reque...
your shoulders. F...

as local items in t...
And you'll be pai...

details. You're su...

World Travel Payment℠

Dear Travel Executive,

Do you often feel exhausted at the end of your work day?

Are you bothered by headaches? Backaches? Leg cramps? A stiff, aching neck?

Most of us are sitting ducks for these executive ailments, because we spend much of our work day sitting. Hunched over a desk. Holding the phone. Tensing up. Until suddenly --

Ouch.

Fitness experts suggest you avoid these aches by standing up, walking around, even lying down on your office floor several times a day.

But for the recurring pain that bothers many travel executives, try this exercise:

Pain in the Neck Relief. Sit with a telephone directly in front of you. Lift receiver to ear with quick motion. Hold other hand above the keypad and press 1-312-380-5215. Say "Peter Andrews, please." Then say, "I'd like the facts about Citicorp's World Travel Payment™ system."

Unlike most exercises, this one never needs repeating. Because the World Travel Payment system is designed to eliminate the pain of making those irritating, time-consuming foreign currency payments to overseas suppliers. Permanently.

Imagine using custom software to make payments in more than 40 currencies, right in your office. Bypassing the usual paperwork. Saving valuable time. Outwitting the risks of foreign exchange fluctuations.

Once you learn how easy it is to use the World Travel Payment system, you'll never want to suffer through any other payment process again.

Call now or mail the enclosed reply card, and you may never again suffer from traveler's stiff neck, either. Because I'll send you a free travel pillow, just for responding.

It's simply one more way I can prove my basic point: You don't have to take a pain in the neck sitting down anymore.

Sincerely,

Charlene White

Charlene White
Sales Manager
World Travel Payment

CITICORP

Citicorp Global Payment Products, 8430 W. Bryn Mawr Ave., Chicago, IL 60631

Award: Leader
Program: Olga

Client: Citicorp Global Payment Products

Agency: Cramer-Krasselt
Creative Director: Maureen Moore
Associate Creative Director & Copywriter: Erica Silins
Art Director: Ron Randle
Account Supervisor: Donna Noonan
Product Manager: Jeff Kraft, Suzanne Dalmeyer

To promote the convenience of Citicorp World Travel Payment to travel agents, this humorous promotion was sent out offering "two ways to get rid of a pain in the neck." The first was a formidable-looking masseuse named Olga, the second was the product—and a bonus third was the premium with response, a travel pillow. The response must have eased a few tensions as well: 3.3 percent, beating the control by 120 percent.

Award: Leader
Program: Blue Chip Chamber Solicitation

Client: Connecticut Mutual
Client Contact: Tim Maurer

Agency: Ingalls, Quinn & Johnson
Agency Contact: Martha Bush
Account Supervisor: Harry Wellott
Copy: Evan Stone
Art Direction: Andre Cordella

Call this number today to get your Chamber involved in The Blue Chip Enterprise Initiative. You'll receive a complete "Turn-Key Kit" to help you implement this program, including prepared public relations materials.

You'll not only be helping your small business members, you'll benefit from substantial publicity opportunities. And everything's provided for you.

Help fine tune the engine that drives the American economy.

Connecticut Mutual
A Blue Chip Company of the CM Alliance

Endorsed by and *Nation's Business.*

THE BLUE CHIP ENTERPRISE INITIATIVE

Dear Chamber Officer:

We are pleased that the U.S. Chamber of Commerce is endorsing a major new Initiative to help small businesses compete more effectively in an increasingly competitive marketplace.

The name of this program is The Blue Chip Enterprise Initiative—and it is of vital importance in strengthening the fabric of American small business.

As the enclosed videotape explains, we are conducting a nationwide search for small businesses which have demonstrated an exceptional ability to survive the cyclical nature of business by overcoming formidable challenges and obstacles.

From this search, we will assemble tips on how to effectively manage resources to achieve overall success. These proven, real-world strategies will then be packaged and made available to small businesses—via participating local and state Chambers of Commerce.

We will recognize these exemplary businesses with The Blue Chip Enterprise Award and extensive publicity.

WE NEED YOUR PARTICIPATION.

To assure maximum benefit from this Initiative, we will need your Chamber's support and involvement. By participating, you'll be enabling your membership to enjoy the same important advantages that are being enjoyed by other members all across the country.

Specifically, you and your members can expect to receive the following benefits:

★ You can offer your Chamber members an important value-added service—namely, proven ideas for effectively managing resources and achieving small business success.

★ You will receive public relations support and promotional materials that allow you to increase your visibility in your market.

★ You may be instrumental in providing exemplary small businesses in your area with local and national media exposure in both print and television.

★ You can use the Initiative to enhance membership.

IT'S EASY TO PARTICIPATE AND ADMINISTER.

One of the best things about the Initiative is that you're provided with a wide array of prepared materials to help implement the program.

Additionally, virtually all of the program's logistical work will be handled at the national level.

For example, all applications for the award will be forwarded directly to an independent judging panel. And any questions you might have—or that area small business owners might have—can be answered via a dedicated 800 telephone number which will be provided after the program's launch.

TAKING THE NEXT STEP.

To find out more about participating, return the enclosed postage-paid Reply Card.

You can simply request a Chamber Turn-Key Kit—containing brochures, application forms, press materials, and all the other information you'll need to promote the Initiative to your membership—or you can request a special preview with a Connecticut Mutual Life Insurance Company representative.

As part of the Kit, you will also receive an additional video which can be shown as part of your presentation to assembled business groups.

To request your special preview or Turn-Key Kit even faster, just call our hotline at 1-800-AWARD-91. We look forward to your participation.

Sincerely,

Timothy F. Maurer
Director

Connecticut Mutual
A Blue Chip Company of the CM Alliance

Endorsed by and *Nation's Business.*

To reach the small business audience, Connecticut Mutual formed an alliance with the U.S. Chamber of Commerce to create a national small business recognition program. The trick was to get the local Chambers of Commerce to participate, which this ambitious two-part mailing accomplished, with a video message from the CEO of Connecticut Mutual and the Head of the U.S. Chamber endorsing the program and offering a turn-key kit to run the award program locally. The result was a 20 percent response, which beat projections by 250 percent.

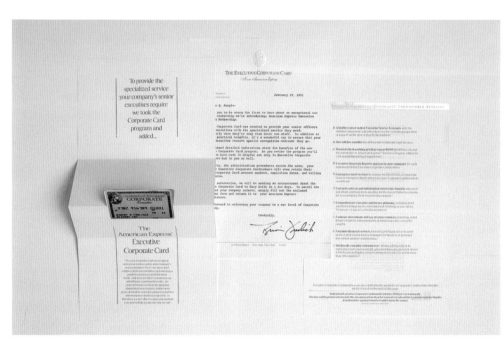

Award: Leader
Program: Launching the Executive Corporate Card

Client: American Express
Director: Wendy Brown
Manager: Vince Errico

Agency: Ogilvy & Mather Direct
VP, Creative Supervisor: Bob Adamec
Senior Art Director: Warren Godfrey
Copy Supervisor: Claire O'Brien
Art Director: Jeff St. Onge
VP, Account Director: Kathleen Solberg
VP, Account Supervisor: Marcy Q. Samet
Account Supervisor: Liz Deutch

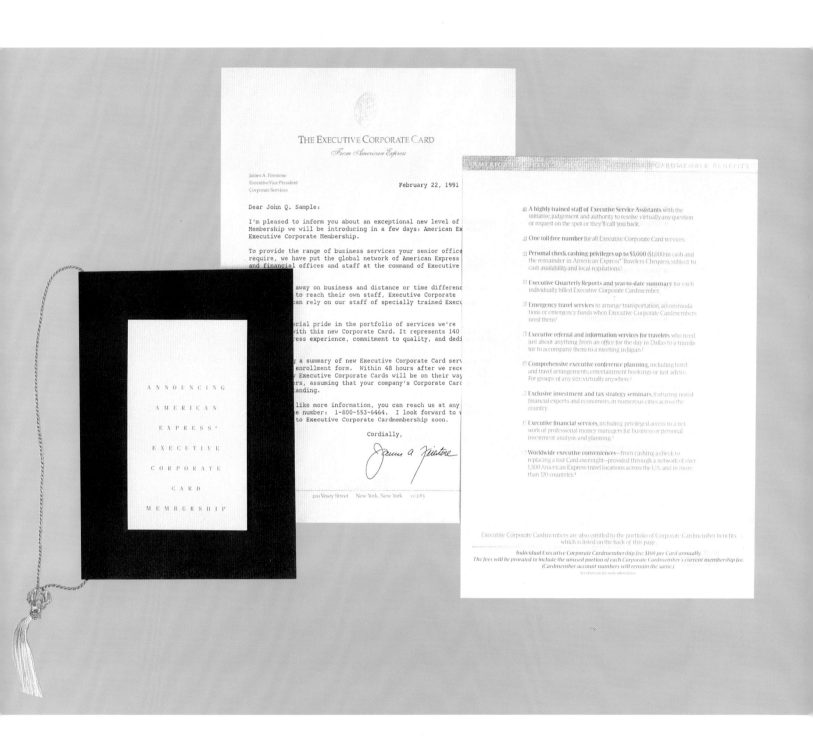

American Express faced the problem of introducing its new premium-priced Executive Corporate Card in a recession. The solution was this rich mail campaign, targeted to different levels within a large company, and relying on a handsome gift compass (representing a new level of global service) and beautiful embossed stationery to get past executive "gatekeepers." The results? A 4.3 response rate in just three months, plus intense sales force activity suggesting a record high conversion rate.

Award: Leader
Program: Dartboard Campaign

Client: DiMark, Inc.

Agency: DiMark, Inc.
Program Development: Rich Pocock
Copy Director: Rick Norris
Copywriter: Eric Ehrenteucnter
Designer: Ray Weinmann
Account Manager: Lisa Hanson Ruo

To dramatize their targeting capabilities to prospects, the direct marketing company DiMark sent out this clever and desirable dimensional mailing with a dartboard. The mailing hit its mark, with a 4.5 percent conversion that amounted to sales of more than $82,000 at a cost of just $5,589, including postage and materials.

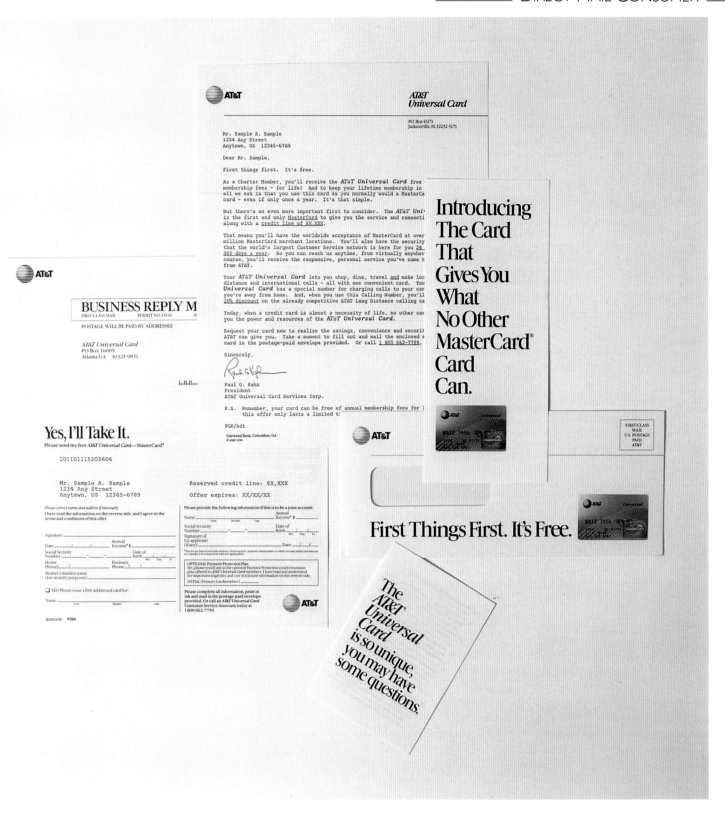

Award: Silver
Program: Direct Mail Campaign—First Things First and One Simple Connection

Client: AT&T Universal Card Services, Corp.
President & CEO: Paul G. Kahn
Executive Vice President: F. Alan Schultheis
Vice President, Advertising & Communications:
Barbara J. Bromberg
Vice President, Consumer Acquisition: Dorothy Schechter

Agency: Chapman Direct Advertising
Sr. Vice President/Account Director: Michael Sugzda
Sr. Vice President/Creative Director: Michael Hawkins
Creative Supervisor: Linda King
Copywriter: Mark DiMassimo
Vice President/Management Supervisor: Francesca Carter
Account Supervisor: Irene Fortgang
Account Supervisor: Louise Slater
Suppliers:
Printers: Lasky Company
Typesetting: Characters Typographic Service, Inc.
Lettershop: Data-Mail, Inc.

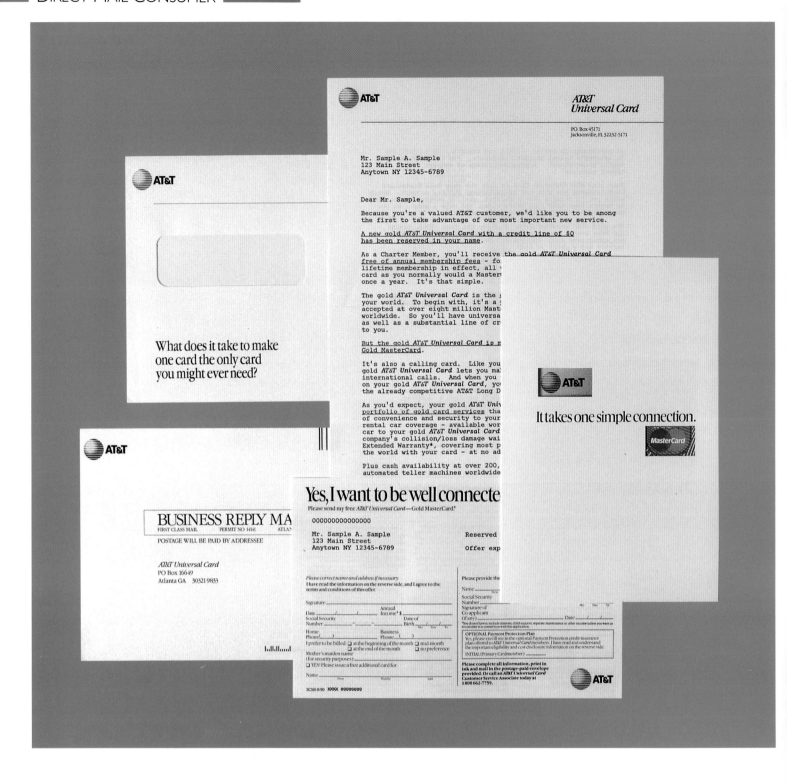

To launch the AT&T Universal Card combining a credit card and calling card, the decision was made to address the audiences of the standard and gold card independently, stressing the free offer to the former and the synergy of a credit/calling card to the latter. The result was spectacular by any measure, indexing at 1,000 against the industry average of 100 and exceeding projections by 230 percent.

Award: Bronze
Program: The Platinum Card
Client: American Express Europe Limited, *England*
Director: Ajay Sood
Marketing Director: Elisabeth Cohen
Marketing Manager: Alison Copus

Agency: Wunderman Worldwide Limited
Managing Director: Iain Shapley
Executive Creative Director: Tony Platt
Group Account Director: Lindsay McEwan
Account Supervisor: David Daly
Creative Group Head, Copywriter: Phil Brisk
Creative Group Head, Art Director: Janetta Lewin
Art Director: Stephen Aldridge
Copywriter: Rachael Yarham
Art Director: Paul Walton
Print Production Manager: Simon Grinsted
Art Buyer: Louise Kerssemakers

To maintain its premium position within the financial services market, the UK Platinum Card offered members the advice and assistance of a Personal Account Manager for an annual fee of $520. This appropriately elaborate six-part series introducing the service exceeded its target by 16 percent, while a further 5 percent of target have submitted positive white mail in addition to applications, a level not previously experienced in the UK.

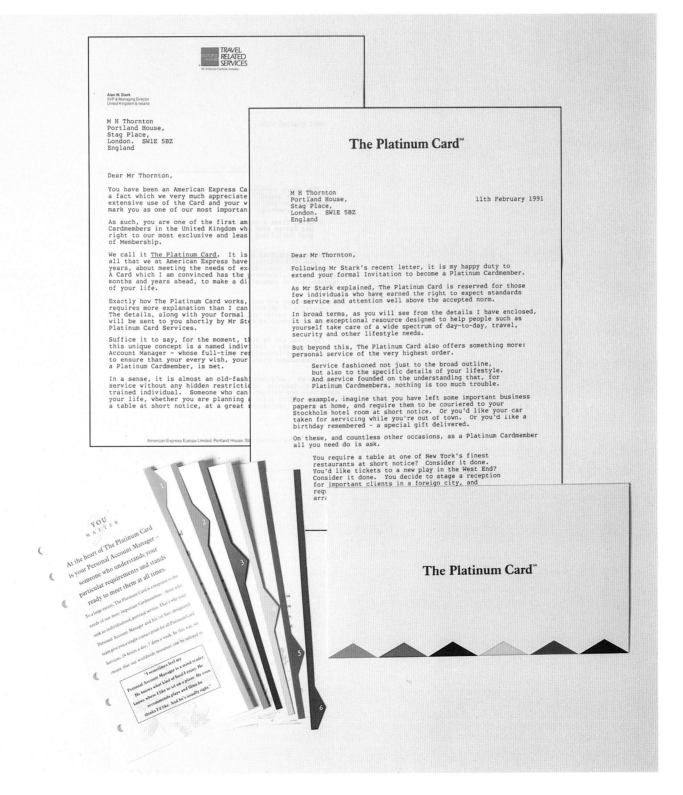

Award: Leader
Program: Card Man

Client: First Interstate Bank

Agency: Kern/Mathai
Creative Director: Jerry Mathai
Copywriter: Linda Latshaw
Art Director: Richard Escasany

Offering a gold credit card with little to distinguish it from multitudes of competitors, Interstate Bank decided to create a personality for their product. They therefore sent out this "warm and fuzzy" mailing to selected segments of their house file, with a cartoon credit card making its own introductions. The result was creditable indeed: an 8.3 percent response, beating the previous campaign by 112 percent.

Make room in your wallet for me, your First Interstate Gold Visa® card with a low 16.9% APR.

First Interstate Bank of California
1700 Surveyor Avenue
Simi Valley, CA 93097

Gary M. Lamont
Vice President

John Q. Sample
11601 Wilshire Blvd.
Los Angeles, CA 90025

Dear John Q. Sample:

Make room in your wallet for a very special credit card -- your First Interstate Gold Visa card with a $5,000 line of credit. It's special for several reasons:

* Low 16.9%* interest rate. This is one of the lowest fixed rates of any major bank in California, which means you can save on finance charges. And you can use the enclosed Balance Payoff Request to pay off your balances on higher-rate cards!

I'm free for a full year.

* You are pre-approved. Because you are a First Interstate customer, and we know you so well, we've eliminated the application process for you.

* No fee for the first full year. We've waived the annual fee for the first full year. It's our way of saying "thanks".

Your First Interstate Gold Visa card is special, too, because it enables you to receive many valuable services at no additional charge, such as $500,000 automatic travel accident insurance, car rental insurance, credit card protection, and extended warranty protection on retail purchases.*

Save money with my lower APR.

COMPARE THESE INTEREST RATES:	
First Interstate Bank of California	16.9%
Wells Fargo Bank	19.8%
Bank of America	19.8%
Security Pacific Bank	19.8%

This chart contains fixed Annual Percentage Rates, quoted as of November 1990 for gold cards exclusive of special promotions.

(over please)

First Interstate Bank

First Interstate Bank of California
1700 Surveyor Avenue
Simi Valley, CA 93097

Say "yes" and I'll bring you a low 16.9% APR!

Award: Leader
Program: Christmas Tree
Client: American Express, *Australia*
Carol Giuiseppi, Bill Wood, Jane Butler
Agency: Ogilvy & Mather Direct
Art Director: Dave Stapleton
Writer: Tracy Bailey
Account Manager: Kate Jedlin
Management Supervisor: Iain Good
Finished Artist: Scott Hignett
Production Supervisor: Jenny Horniman

American Express had identified a huge potential for growth in retail sales in Australia, but retail spending in the country had hit an all-time low. The company therefore sent out this festive holiday mailing to select Cardmembers, offering a free bottle of cognac and a box of premium chocolates if the recipient charged $500 or more to the Card during the promotion period. American Express soon found their own present under the tree: more than four times the number of responses forecast, resulting in sales of AUS $15 million!

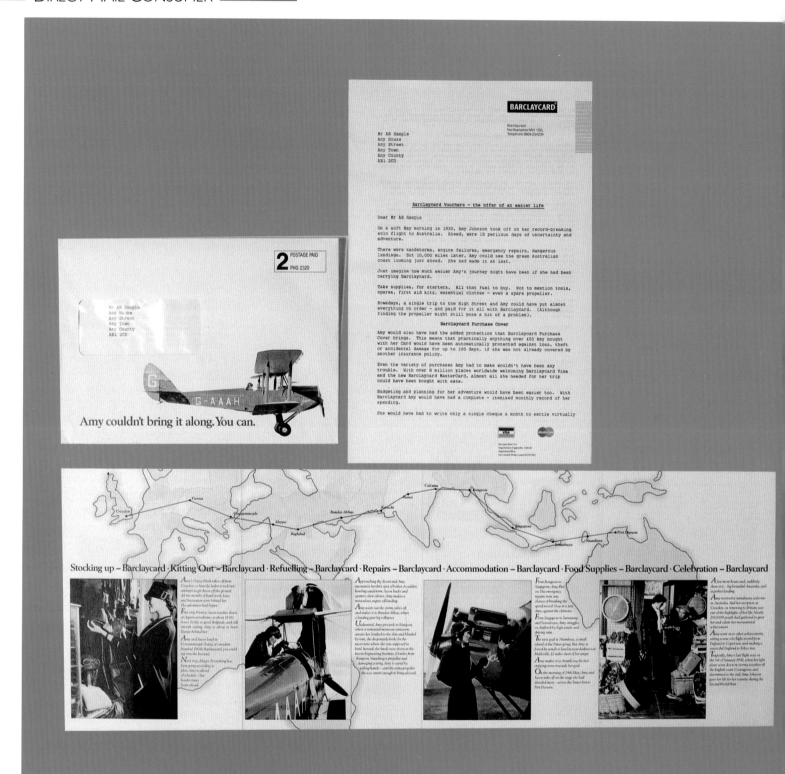

Award: Leader
Program: Amy Johnson
Client: Barclaycard, *England*
Mark Duckworth, Jacky Allen

Agency: Kobs & Draft London
Creative Director: Matthew Kahn
Art Director: Brian Ennals
Copywriter: Katie Breach
Client Services: Karen McCallie
Account Team: David Hodson, Leonie Wilfred
  Michael Stevenson

Dormant customers cost Barclaycard money yet represented potential for development into extended credit customers. To stimulate usage, this unusual mailing was sent out to cardholders who hadn't used their cards in six months, relating the many ways famed British aviatrix Amy Johnson could have used the card in her historic solo flight to Australia—and offering third party savings vouchers on purchases charged to the card. The response soared too: 25 percent redeemed their vouchers, charging more than $3.1 million to their reactivated cards.

Award: Silver
Program: *Money* Magazine Wrap

Client: Home Savings of America

Agency: Griffin Creative Group—
    Home Savings of America
Creative Director: Joan Levine
Copywriters: Blair Walker, John Klawitter
Art Director: Carlos Perez
Account Manager: Tom Woolman
Production Manager: Susan Crowther
Photographer: Jeff Li

The name of the game in selling apartment loans is getting referrals from real estate and mortgage brokers and bankers. To cultivate this valuable audience, Home Savings of America sent their prospects a complimentary subscription to *Money* Magazine—with special quarterly wraparounds communicating the company's strengths and its commitment to a long-term relationship with the prospect. This clever program elicited 500 responses, resulting in total documented sales of $6 million on a total program budget of just $80,000!

Award: Gold
Program: Youth Program 1990

Client: Barclays Bank Plc, *England*

Agency: Brann Direct Marketing
Account Director: Chris Lovell
Sr. Account Manager: Paula Daniel
Account Managers: Fiona MacMillan, Debbie Langley
Copywriters: Kate Cullum, Will Luckhurst
Art Directors: Phil Lambert, Belinda Armstrong
   Rona Hardy

To generate response from high school and college graduates wary of hard-sell promotions, Barclays Bank created a series of mailings and inserts using unusual shapes and formats, and featuring colorful graphics and copy relating to student lifestyles. The campaign pulled a response in excess of 20 percent, at a cost per response of just $1.30.

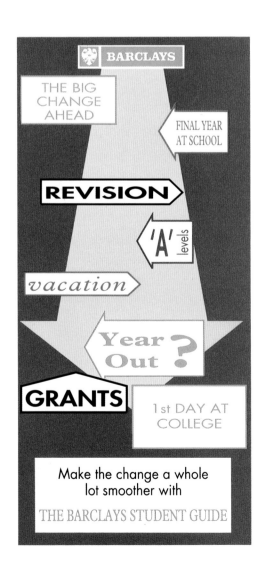

Chapter

2

Non-Financial Services

Walt Disney's Magic Kingdom Club

A Division of Buena Vista Pictures Distribution, Inc.

August 29, 1990

Mr. Deane Swanson
Regional Director H. R.
American Bank Stationery Co.
P.O. Box 105306
Atlanta, GA 30348

Dear Mr. Swanson,

Come along, sing a song, and join our company!

We know you're a busy, busy, <u>busy</u> person. Which is ex
why you should take some time out and have a little fun.

HOW? Disney makes it easy...
Now that your company has been chosen
to join our Magic Kingdom Club.

This exciting employee benefit program wil
your face, and to each one of your staff membe
fantastic Disney vacations at Club member savi
<u>you'll get all the credit</u> after they return fr
trips they've ever taken...one they couldn't h
you.

AND AT NO COST TO YOUR COMPAN

Membership in the Magic Kingdom Club is fr
your organization need only have 200 or more e
need to agree to the easy terms listed on the
application.

Once your application is approved, we'll
package containing:

(1) Personalized Member
(2) Membership Guides
(3) Price Guides

Simply distribute the Club materials to yo
issue a Membership Card to any employee who re

The Membership Card is good for two full y
your employees to special membership benefits
year-round reduced prices at Disneyland Park i
Disney World Resort in Florida and Tokyo Disne

And that's not all...

As Club members, you and your employees ha
other exciting options...things like fabulous
special prices and discounts at The Disney Sto

National Headquarters / P.O. Box 4489 / Anaheim, California 92803-4489 / 714-490-3200

Part of the Magic of The Walt Disney Company©

Walt Disney's Magic Kingdom Club.

The Employee Benefit Program
that brings smiles to
the faces of your employees.

©The Walt Disney Company

Award: Gold
Program: New Member Acquisition Program

Client: Walt Disney's Magic Kingdom Club

Agency: In-house
Project Manager: Lisa Hiatt
Strategic Direction: Richard Rosen
Creative Direction: Bill Brown; Nick Paccione
Copywriting: Bill Brown, Tracy Danish
Art Direction: Larry Ball
Production: Nick Paccione

This attention-getting dimensional mailing used a pair of Mickey Mouse ears to overcome the resistance of corporate Human Resource Directors to consider another employee benefit offer, dramatizing the unique fun of the Disney vacation experience and the ease with which the program could be implemented at their companies. There was nothing Mickey Mouse about the results: 583 responses, leading to total sales of $7.2 million and beating the previous campaign by 600 percent.

Award: Gold
Program: The Rational Alternative

Client: Communication Dynamics, *South Africa*

Agency: Grey Response Marketing (Pty.) Ltd.
Creative Director: Andrew Phillips
Reprographics: Beith Process
Ceramic Work: The Fireworks
Printer: Standard Press
Client Service: Sarah Monro
Copywriter: Janine Pike

This unique dimensional mailing offered a "rational alternative to lobotomy" to high profile prospects who might need help improving their image and communications skills—and included a head detailing all the areas of the brain relating to communications skills. With a mind-boggling 99 percent response rate and 80 percent conversion, the business generated in the first six months topped R280 000, increasing the client's business by 1000 percent.

FROM BRONNER SLOSBERG'S INCREDIBLE

LOBSTER GROVES

From secret Boston Lobster Groves to you. Traditional Holiday Lobster Seeds. Packed in the greetings of the season.

WHEW! WHO WANTS TO MESS AROUND GROWING FOUR DELICIOUS LOBSTERS WHEN YOU GUYS AT BRONNER SLOSBERG WILL DO IT ALL FOR ME.

Yes, we will! And here's how it works. As soon as you decide exactly when you want to enjoy your four delicious lobsters, just do two things. First, call 1-800-227-1116 and let us know. We may have some questions about the overnight delivery. Like, will there be someone home to accept the package? That sort of thing.

Once we get all the details settled, fill out the order form. Don't forget to enclose the lobster seeds. (After all, lobsters don't grow on trees!) And mail it right out to us. Remember, when you call, make sure you tell them you're retrieving Bronner Slosberg Lobsters.

YES, BY GOLLY, I'M READY TO ENJOY MY FOUR FREE HOLIDAY LOBSTERS!

Please fill out this order form and enclose your four lobster seeds. (Okay, okay...you can keep the colorful, funny seeds, if you want. Just make sure you send in the completed order form.) And, please, in addition to sending in this form, also call 1-800-227-1116 to set up the date you want your four fully grown, jumbo lobsters delivered. Remember to mention that the lobsters are from the Bronner Slosberg Groves.

NAME ....

ADDRESS ....

CITY .... STATE .... ZIP ....

PHONE (......) ....

DESIRED DELIVERY DATE ....
(Available Tuesday through Friday)

Dear Friend,

Since the beginning of beginnings, the very freshest, most delicious lobsters have always been grown from lobster seeds gathered during the festive days of December. For that is when the air is crispy cold and the New England earth rich with a touch of sweetness.

So it is that each December the fussy folks at Bronner Slosberg go forth to their secret groves and carefully pick and pack the choicest lobster seeds to send to their closest friends.

And, since only the very best of the lobster seeds are lovingly chosen and hand-picked, they are unconditionally guaranteed to grow the sweetest, most succulent and tasty lobsters under the sun.

In order to achieve the best growing results for your lobster seeds, simply plant them in any rich soil...making sure it is identical to soil found in the Bronner Slosberg Groves. If you are not sure the soil you have is correct, no problem. Just place your seeds carefully in the envelope provided, fill in the requested information and mail it off to the Lobster Groves of Bronner Slosberg. We will do the rest. The planting, the fertilizing, the watering, weeding and harvesting.

What better way for you to celebrate the Holidays than with the classic and traditional Bronner Slosberg lobster greeting!!

Just let us know when you want the four little beauties to arrive, and that's all there is to it.

And remember, the seeds you've just received come packed with the very warmest wishes and sincerest holiday greetings from the entire staff at Bronner Slosberg Associates.

Michael Bronner

Michael Bronner

Mike Slosberg

Mike Slosberg

Award: Gold
Program: Holiday Lobster Seed Package
Client: Bronner Slosberg Humphrey Inc.
Agency: Bronner Slosberg Humphrey Inc.
Executive Creative Director: Mike Slosberg
Art Director: Marsha Huber
Copywriter: Mike Slosberg
Production Manager: Gary Benson

How does an agency top its annual holiday gift of four lobsters for each client? With this humorous and attention-getting package of "lobster seeds," allowing a client to grow his own—or return the reply form for four lobsters pre-grown at Bronner Slosberg's fertile lobster groves. A whopping 85 percent returned the reply form!

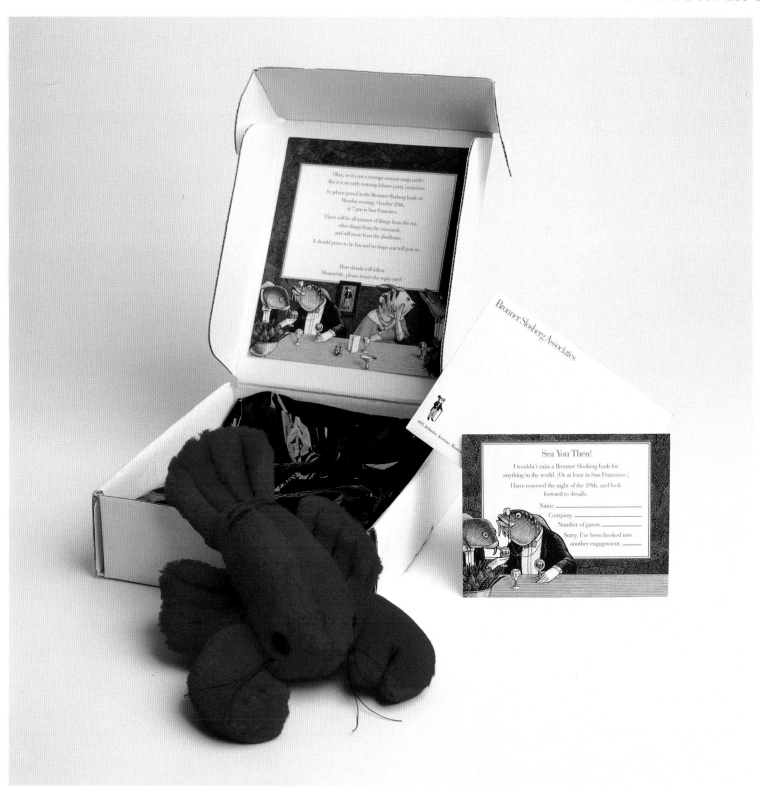

Award: Leader
Program: DMA Lobster Invitation

Client: Bronner Slosberg Humphrey Inc.

Agency: Bronner Slosberg Humphrey Inc.
Executive Creative Director: Mike Slosberg
Art Director: Marsha Huber
Copywriter: Michael H. Reingold, II
Illustrator: Linda Schiwall Gallo
Production Managers: Gary Benson, Katherine Holzman

With only a few evenings available during the DMA conference in San Francisco, agencies compete fiercely to attract clients to *their* party. To make Bronner Slosberg Humphrey's invitation stand out, they sent out this amusing two-part mailing series, the first of which included a stuffed lobster—the agency's mascot—plus a thermographed invitation noting that their party would feature "all manner of things from the sea, other things from the vineyards, and still more from the distilleries." This attracted all manner of clients, with a 50 percent response rate, beating their previous year's effort by 100 percent.

Award: Gold
Program: Launch Campaign
Client: Hotel Conrad, *Hong Kong*
Manager: Dario Regazzoni
P.R. Manager: Judy Arundel
Marketing Director: Joe Hickman

Agency: Ogilvy & Mather Direct
Creative Director: Ellen Meltzer
Writer: Diana Cheung
Art Director: Karen Wu
Client Service: Louise-Anne Louw

To introduce Hong Kong's new 5-star Conrad Hotel and induce corporations to open an account, this ambitious mailing series was sent out to decision makers, influencers, and bookers. Mailings to top executives and their wives included elegant invitations to a free bottle of wine with a meal at the Conrad, while secretaries received invitations to lunch and membership in a "frequent booker" program, incentivizing bookings with travel rewards and coupons redeemable at the Conrad. The response: a luxurious 36 percent.

Award: Silver
Program: Bird For Breakfast

Client: Ogilvy & Mather, *New Zealand*

Agency: Ogilvy & Mather Direct
Creative Director/Art Director: Tony Beard
Writer: Jerry Beale
Account Director: Alan Brodeur

To inform and excite existing clients about new strategies and techniques developed by Ogilvy & Mather Direct—and demonstrate the potential of direct marketing to prospective clients—the agency invited both groups to a breakfast featuring their Worldwide Creative Chairman, Drayton Bird. To deliver this invitation in a memorable way, this bright red and white box was sent out, containing a white linen napkin and a small feather, and offering "Eggs, Bacon & Bird." The response was an eye-opener as well, with 84 percent attending.

Award: Bronze
Program: Sign 'em up, Doc!

Client: Holiday Inns, Inc.

Agency: Carlson Frequency Marketing
Creative Director: George Rabasa
Associate Creative Director: Bob Hatlestad
Art Director: Kristen Anderson
Copywriter: Julie Carpenter
Account Manager: Roger Martin
Project Development Specialist: Kari Gulbrandsen
Senior Marketing Specialist: Layne Rosen
Traffic Coordinator: Christopher Seitz
Production Specialist: Val Sjolin
Program Administrator: Mary English

To encourage employees to sign up enrollees for Holiday Inn's Priority Club frequent stayer program, launch materials were sent bulk to each site for distribution by the General Manager. To cut through the clutter of the usual procedural communications, Looney Tunes characters were featured in this colorful promotion, offering cash rewards and incentives. The campaign pulled a 78.6 percent response rate, and the program generated 100,000 new members at a cost per sale of just $3.22.

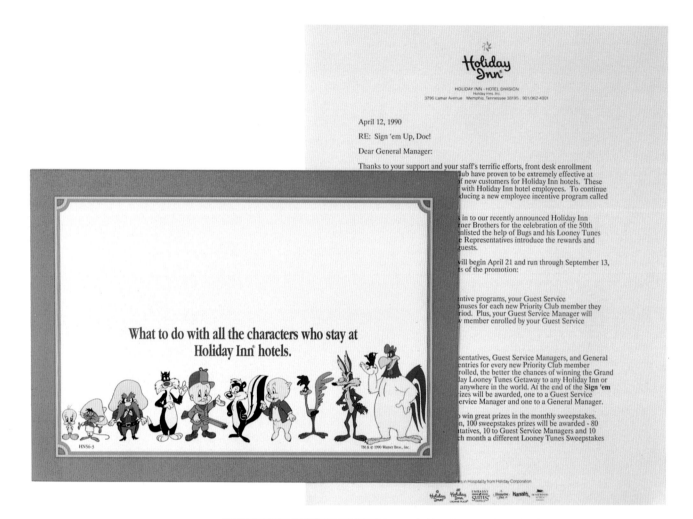

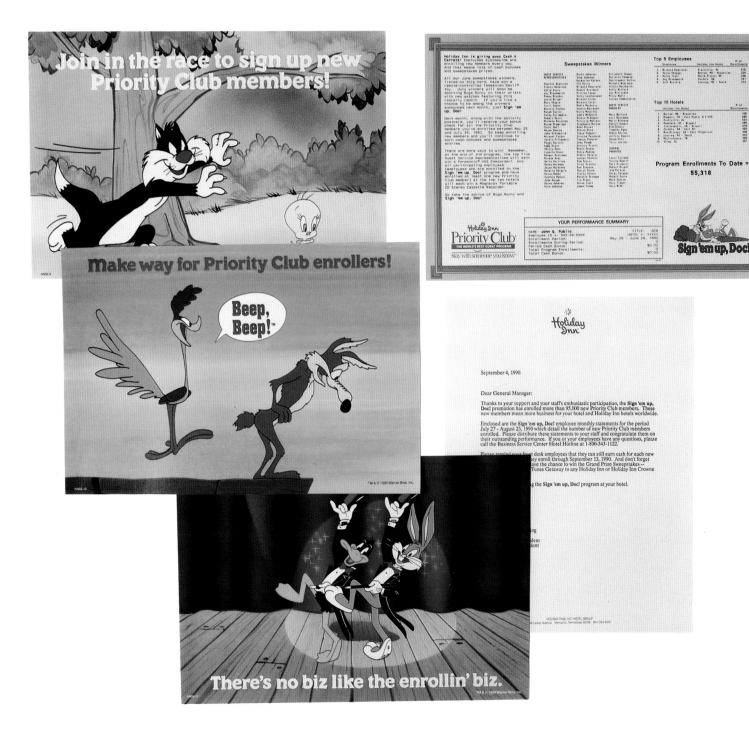

Award: Bronze
Program: Rubberstamp Mailer

Client: Merrell Remington Direct (formerly RPM Direct)

Agency: Merrell Remington Direct

Creative Director: A. Kent Merrell
Illustrations: Jack Martin
Copy: A. Kent Merrell
Art Director: Noel Hilden

To demonstrate their creativity and mastery of personalization to prospects, the direct response agency RPM Direct sent out a box containing a rubber stamp with the prospect's name on it, plus a letter showing how clumsy and obvious most personalized mailings are. The reader was invited to send for a free booklet on personalization, which was in turn profusely personalized in clever ways with the prospect's name. The response rate was 26 percent, with a 31 percent conversion, leading to total sales of $480,000 at an out-of-pocket cost of just $1,800.

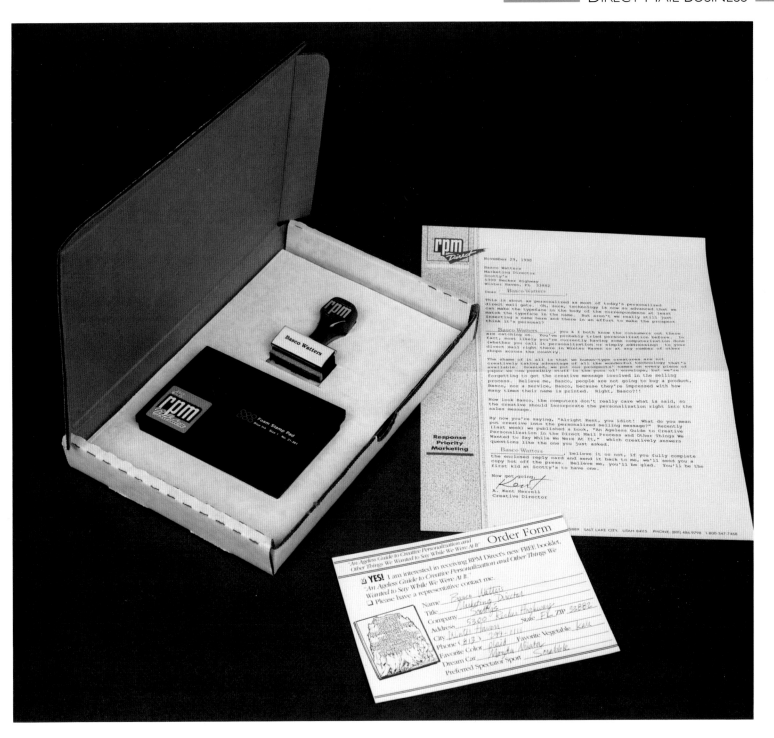

Award: Bronze
Program: "Club Acapulco"

Client: Acapulco Tourism Board, *Mexico*

Agency: Bowes, Dentsu & Partners
Senior Vice President/Creative Director: Peter Eaton
Art Director: Jeannine Hemmingsen
Copywriter: Richard Wachter
Production Manager: John Cluckie
Account Management: Bob Jensen

As a resort destination, Acapulco had lost a good portion of its top-of-mind awareness among consumers and travel agents. To create renewed interest, travel agents were offered free membership in Club Acapulco, a promotional program promising referrals as well as travel savings for agents and their clients. The response rate of this two-part mailing effort was 47 percent, at a cost per response of $24.28.

Dear Travel Agent:

Welcome to Club Acapulco™!

We're so pleased that you decided to join the most unique and exciting destination travel program ever.

As a member, you'll enjoy many exclusive personal and professional benefits. Benefits that will save you money every time you visit Acapulco—and benefits that will bring profitable new business to your door.

Your personal Club Acapulco Membership Card is enclosed. Use it to enjoy a 20% discount at many of Acapulco's finest hotels, restaurants, clubs, shops, tours and excursions.

Also enclosed are your Club Acapulco Window Decals. The decal tells your clients that when it comes to planning the very best trip to Acapulco, you're the one to see.

Inside, you'll also find details on your exclusive customer bonus gift; a great opportunity to order Club Acapulco Peso Cheques for 75,000 pesos to pass along to your Acapulco-bound clients. See the enclosed Membership Booklet.

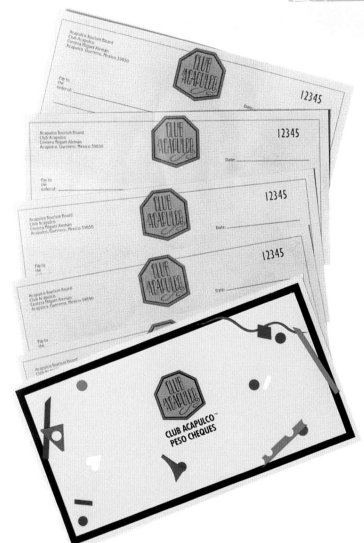

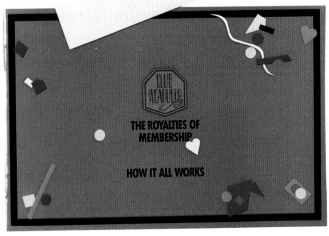

Award: Bronze
Program: Total Recall

Client: The Advertising Club of Greater Boston

Agency: Bronner Slosberg Humphrey Inc.
Executive Creative Director: Mike Slosberg
Copywriter: Michael H. Reingold, II
Art Directors: Marsha Huber, Gary Reynolds
Production Manager: Gary Benson

Seminar and workshop attendance had declined in the slow economy. To increase attendance at the Ad Club of Boston's annual Marketing Day, this clever self-mailer was sent out, promising on the outside an appearance by the star of "Total Recall"—who was revealed inside to be the keynote speaker, Perrier Beverages. The result was an 11 percent response, making the event a sellout for the first time ever.

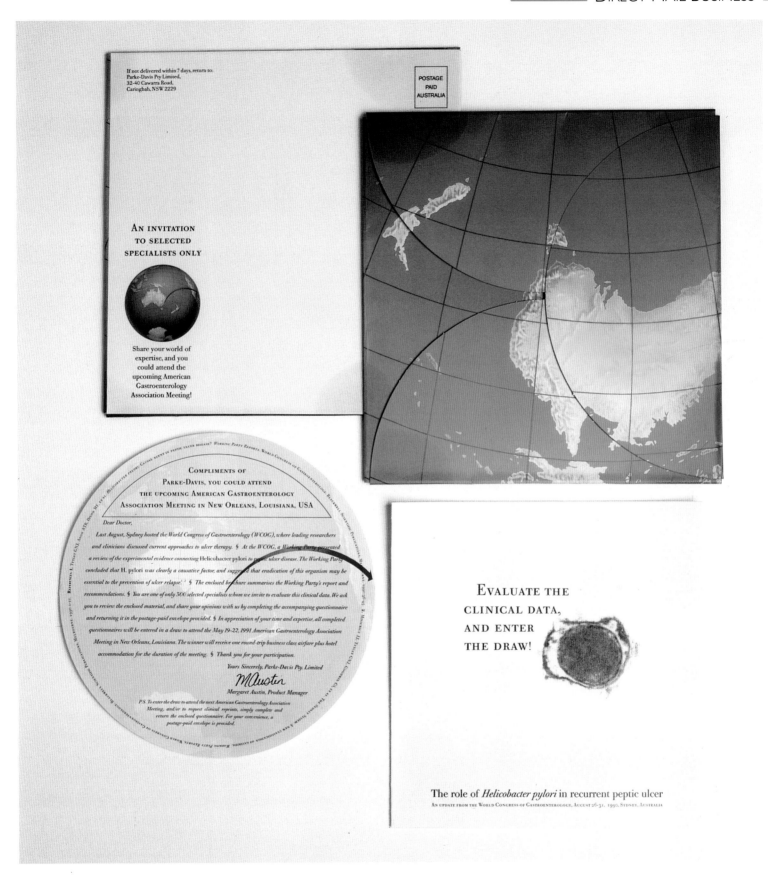

If not delivered within 7 days, return to:
Parke-Davis Pty Limited,
32-40 Cawarra Road,
Caringbah, NSW 2229

POSTAGE
PAID
AUSTRALIA

AN INVITATION
TO SELECTED
SPECIALISTS ONLY

Share your world of
expertise, and you
could attend the
upcoming American
Gastroenterology
Association Meeting!

COMPLIMENTS OF
PARKE-DAVIS, YOU COULD ATTEND
THE UPCOMING AMERICAN GASTROENTEROLOGY
ASSOCIATION MEETING IN NEW ORLEANS, LOUISIANA, USA

Dear Doctor,

Last August, Sydney hosted the World Congress of Gastroenterology (WCOG), where leading researchers and clinicians discussed current approaches to ulcer therapy. § At the WCOG, a Working Party presented a review of the experimental evidence connecting Helicobacter pylori to peptic ulcer disease. The Working Party concluded that H. pylori was clearly a causative factor, and suggested that eradication of this organism may be essential to the prevention of ulcer relapse. § The enclosed brochure summarises the Working Party's report and recommendations. § You are one of only 500 selected specialists whom we invite to evaluate this clinical data. We ask you to review the enclosed material, and share your opinions with us by completing the accompanying questionnaire and returning it in the postage-paid envelope provided. § In appreciation of your time and expertise, all completed questionnaires will be entered in a draw to attend the May 19-22, 1991 American Gastroenterology Association Meeting in New Orleans, Louisiana. The winner will receive one round-trip business class airfare plus hotel accommodation for the duration of the meeting. § Thank you for your participation.

Yours Sincerely, Parke-Davis Pty. Limited

Margaret Austin, Product Manager

P.S. To enter the draw to attend the next American Gastroenterology Association Meeting, and/or to request clinical reprints, simply complete and return the enclosed questionnaire. For your convenience, a postage-paid envelope is provided.

EVALUATE THE
CLINICAL DATA,
AND ENTER
THE DRAW!

The role of *Helicobacter pylori* in recurrent peptic ulcer
AN UPDATE FROM THE WORLD CONGRESS OF GASTROENTEROLOGY, AUGUST 26-31, 1990, SYDNEY, AUSTRALIA

Award: Leader
Program: Earth Mailer

Client: Parke-Davis Pty. Ltd., *Australia*

Agency: Sudler & Hennessey
Creative Director: Robert Lallamant
Associate Creative Director: Joseph Loewy
Copywriter: Diane Ohye
Product Manager: Margaret Austin

Denol ulcer medicine had a meager market share despite the fact that recent research had proven the medication's unique ability to kill the bacteria that causes ulcers. To highlight this research, this large square mailing was sent out to gastroenterologists, with a circular letter offering the chance to win a free trip to an upcoming medical convention in exchange for some opinions on the research. The results also went down well: a 50 percent response rate and 95 percent conversion.

Award: Leader

Program: Holiday Brochures

Client: Deutsche Lufthansa, *Germany*

Marketing Director: Axel Achten

Agency: Ogilvy & Mather Direkt
Creative Director: Sebastian Zuleger
Art Director: Gudrun Muschalla
Copywriters: Eckard Fleischer, Norbert Weiz
Management Supervisor: Peter Raesch
Account Executives: Gabriela Franck, Charlotte Sammet

Though Lufthansa is known for its high quality and reliability, the airline has to compete with special low fare promotions in the leisure market as well. Since tickets in Germany are sold almost entirely through travel agents, two mail packages were sent, asking them to order Holiday Fare brochures for their customers and holiday manuals for their businesses, while a third went to frequent flyers offering the brochures. Sales took off, with 74 percent of the agents responding to the promotion and holiday market share up 18.5 percent from a year before.

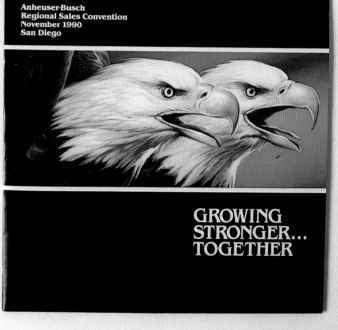

Award: Leader
Program: Eagle Pop-Up Mailing

Client: Anheuser-Busch
James Cash, Dave Calahan

Agency: DMCA Direct
Copywriter/Associate Creative Director: Kim Carpenter
Art Director: Ed Cosby
Illustrator: Don Keuker
Creative Director: Mike Goodwin
Account Supervisor: Rich Stone
Group Account Director: Marsha McConnell
Account Executive: Dave Marty

Every year, Anheuser-Busch had had a problem getting wholesalers to respond promptly to its regional meeting invitations, so planners could make the necessary preparations. This year, they sent out a piece so heavy and intrusive, it had to attract wholesalers' attention—and it did, with a vengeance (and a pop-up corporate mascot eagle). Response and attendance were virtually 100 percent.

Award: Leader
Program: Loyalty Program

Client: DHL International Ltd., *Hong Kong*
Marketing Manager: Herman Fung
Marketing Officer: Anita Lai

Agency: Ball Direct Marketing
Creative Director: Beth Craig
Associate Creative Director/Art Director: Ogar Wan
Chinese Copywriter: Betsy Ng
English Copywriter: Caroline Rose
Account Director: Lesley Watson
Account Executive: Jacqueline So

In Hong Kong, DHL International was the most expensive of the courier services and couldn't compete with special offers from other firms. To build loyalty among occasional users, this mailing was sent out to a house list of the people who actually packaged shipments and called for pick-ups: secretaries and receptionists. A frequent user program offering different levels of rewards, the effort has so far pulled 3,500 responses, for a swift 34 percent response rate.

AT&T 800 AT YOUR SERVICE.

Triple the power of your AT&T 800 Service without spending a dime.

AT&T

AT&T 800 AT YOUR SERVICE.

Want To Expand Your AT&T 800 Service For Free?

AT&T

AT&T 800 AT YOUR SERVICE

One Mississippi Two Mississippi Three Mississippi

Pull

AT&T

Award: Leader
Program: Triple the Power

Client: AT&T

Agency: Bronner Slosberg Humphrey Inc.
Executive Creative Director: Mike Slosberg
Group Creative Director: Betsy Oshlo
Associate Creative Director: Jane Stouffer
Art Director: John Gonnella
Copywriter: Joe McCambley
Account Management: Jean Alexander, Gretchen Gayton
    Janice Rudenauer, Katherine Konig
Production Manager: Dan Borden

Helping AT&T increase 800 usage and enhance retention was this AT&T 800 AT YOUR SERVICE series of self-mailers, sent to 800 customers. With bold, bright colors, simple but compelling graphics and promises, the "Triple the Power" and "Want to Expand for Free" self-mailers produced more than $5.5 million in sales, at a cost per response of just $1.14.

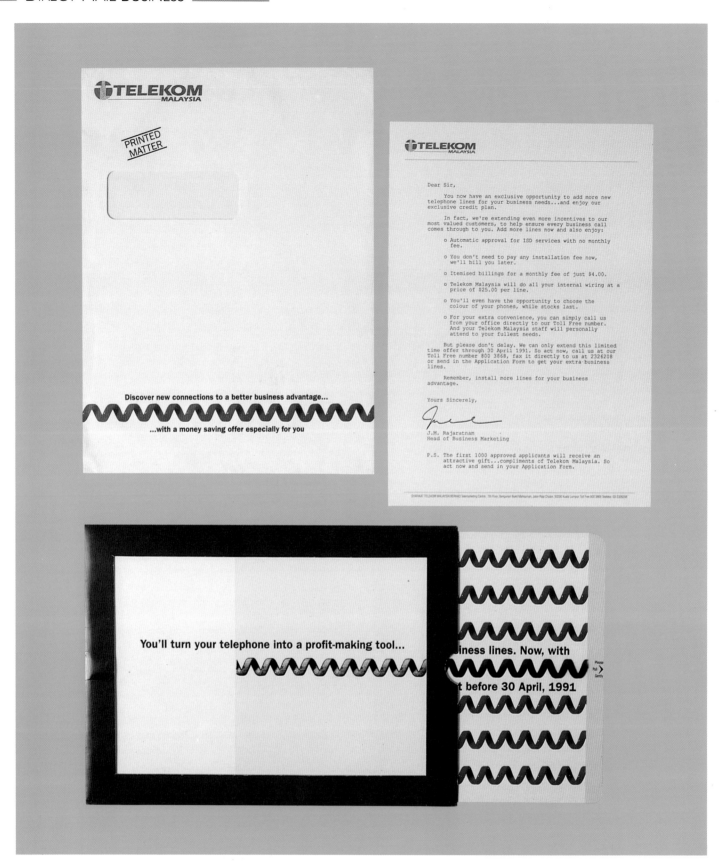

Award: Leader
Program: More Lines

Client: Telekom Malaysia, *Malaysia*
Product Manager: Fatimah Zakaria
Assistant Product Manager: Zulkifli Mansor

Agency: Ogilvy & Mather Direct
Creative Director: Kurt Crocker
Copy Supervisor: Christopher Yin
Copywriter: Chris Yap
Art Director: Tan Kien Eng
Account Service: Ann Teoh, Liza Low

While certain areas in Malaysia were over-subscribed for business phone lines, others were greatly undersubscribed, presenting the perfect opportunity for mailings targeted to small businesses in the underdeveloped areas. Conveying the advantages of installing more lines in a memorable way, this oversized package included an attention-getting slide display that, when pulled, turned one line into several. The mailing rang up a 19 percent response rate, with 74.4 percent converting, for total sales of more than $1 million at a total cost of just $13,010.

Award: Gold
Program: Market Launch Program

Client: Smartfoods/FritoLay

Agency: Mullen Advertising
Agency Representatives: Edward Boches, J. Tormey
Amy Werfel, Charles Hughes, Lisa Bernier
Laura Balboni, Claudia Krimsky, Harry Barrett
Printer: W.E. Andrews, Inc.
Lettershop: Hub Mail
List Service: Ed Burnett Consultants
List Broker: Marianne Gonzales

To stimulate demand for Smartfood popcorn, this humorous and unusual mailing series was sent to 18–35-year-old "opinion leaders" nationwide, with the third mailing delivering a product sample and eliciting feedback via a postpaid reply card.

Greetings from Bean Town!

We made it! Just had a frosty
at your favorite bar.
(Sam & Rebecca say
hi.) Actually
found my old
dorm room. It's
co-ed now. Tried
my key. it still
worked! Boy
were those two
surprised! Gotta
go. Time to go
find some tail.
Maybe a couple
of claws and some
drawn butter too.
See ya,
ken

(Place fingers
as shown)

P.S. sending
you a
souvenir.

P.O. Box 842, Marlborough, MA 01752

Sam Sample
Mullen Adve
36 Essex S
Wenham, M

Yo!

Spent today in Bean Town.
Went to Boston Common and
goosed a duck for you.
Wild party last night near
Bunker Hill -- still can't
see the whites of my eyes.
Glad I brought that video
camera! Ever hear of
a place called the
Combat Zone? Have
I got some stories
for you!

ken

P.S. Didya
get your
souvenir
yet?

Place left index
finger as shown.

P.O. Box 842, Marlborough, MA 01752

Sam Sample
Mullen Adve
36 Essex St
Wenham, MA

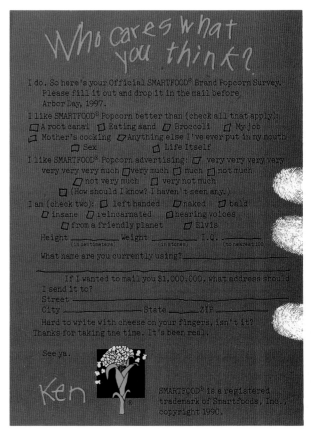

Who cares what you think?

I do. So here's your Official SMARTFOOD® Brand Popcorn Survey. Please fill it out and drop it in the mail before Arbor Day, 1997.

I like SMARTFOOD® Popcorn better than (check all that apply):
☐ A root canal ☐ Eating sand ☐ Broccoli ☐ My job
☐ Mother's cooking ☐ Anything else I've ever put in my mouth
☐ Sex ☐ Life Itself

I like SMARTFOOD® Popcorn advertising: ☐ very very very very very very very much ☐ very much ☐ much ☐ not much ☐ not very much ☐ very not much
☐ (How should I know? I haven't seen any.)

I am (check two): ☐ left handed ☐ naked ☐ bald
☐ insane ☐ reincarnated ☐ hearing voices
☐ from a friendly planet ☐ Elvis

Height _____ Weight _____ I.Q. _____
(in centimeters)   (in stones)   (to nearest 100)

What name are you currently using? _____
_____

If I wanted to mail you $1,000,000, what address should I send it to?
Street _____
City _____ State _____ ZIP _____

Hard to write with cheese on your fingers, isn't it?
Thanks for taking the time. It's been real.

See ya.

Ken

SMARTFOOD® is a registered trademark of Smartfoods, Inc., copyright 1990.

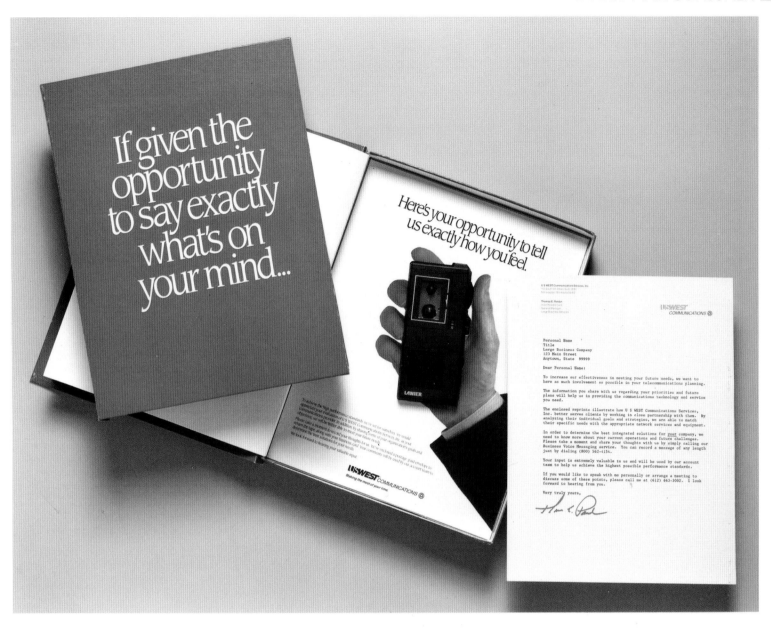

Award: Silver
Program: Executive Relationship Campaign

Client: US WEST Communications, Inc.
Advertising/Promotions Manager: Mike Grandchamp
Vice President: Clifford G. Rudolph

Agency: The Stenrich Group, Inc.
President: Steve Isaac
Creative Director: Joseph Krueger
Copywriter: Brigette White
Art Director: Dave Parrish
Account Supervisor: Barbara Thornhill
Account Executive: Melissa Harp
Production Manager: Jeff Davis

Production Mail Shop: Deridder, Inc.
Dan Nistico, Don Guentner

Printer: Mobility, Inc.
John McGrath

Agency: The Martin Agency
Management Supervisor: Stan Matus
Copywriter: Steve Bassett
Copywriter: Luke Sullivan
Art Director: Diane Cook-Tench

Increased competition threatened US WEST's pre-divestiture standing with its 465 key accounts. To show top decision-makers the value US WEST provided, this high-impact mailing was sent out to target CEO's, inviting the prospect to record his thoughts about his company's telecommunications needs on the working tape recorder included and return the tape CEO-to-CEO. The campaign played well, achieving a 4.95 percent response rate, a 30.43 percent conversion rate, total sales of $1.8 million—and beating projections by 275 percent.

Award: Silver
Program: Cameron House

Client: Craigendarroch Ltd., *Scotland*
Managing Director: Chris Gordon
Marketing Manager: Margaret Robertson

Agency: Watson, Ward, Albert, Varndell (WWAV) Limited
Art Director: Judy Po Chu Lam
Copywriter: Maria Phillips
Account Director: Rick Mills
Senior Account Manager: Joanne Barclay

Cameron House is an exclusive time ownership development on the banks of Scotland's Loch Lomond. To sell the high ticket time shares, the development needed to overcome the industry's poor reputation and position itself as an exclusive property very different from most. As a result, they rejected the usual prize drawings and free gift offers in favor of an elegant and dignified mailing offering a great value on a weekend visit to the property. The result was 110 sales, at a cost per response of $95, beating the control by 10 percent.

Award: Bronze
Program: Parenting Micro Directory

Client: AT&T

Agency: Bronner Slosberg Humphrey Inc.
Executive Creative Director: Mike Slosberg
VP, Group Creative Director: Betsy Oshlo
Art Director: Lisa Costanzo-Ryan
Mechanical Artist: Ann Thorpe
Copywriter: Eva Okada
Account Management: Jean Alexander, Gretchen Gayton
Katie Mercier, Susan Canaveri, Karen Keefe

To promote 800 number usage by consumers, it was decided to target an audience at a transitional time in their lives, when they are most in need of support and information. Thus this dimensional piece was sent to new parents lists and included in co-op packages delivered to LaMaze classes and postnatal wards; inside the box was a directory of 800 numbers of particular use to new parents, plus a child safety decal, a coloring sheet for kids, and more. The result was a healthy, happy response rate of 15 percent—and an increase in 800 network usage of 35 percent!

Shop The GYMBOREE® Kids' Catalog And Save 15%.

This one is physical!! Finally, a catalog for kids who run, climb, bend, crawl, touch, and explore. Clothes, toys, tapes, and videos to help children develop all their muscles…in body and mind. And as a special offer, receive 15% off your first order.

To take advantage of this offer, look up the Gymboree® Catalog under Toys in the 800 number section. Tell them you saw their offer in the AT&T Mini Directory, and save 15%. Offer expires December 31, 1990.

Consumer Hotlines   Dial 1 +

Special Offers

PRINCESS ≈ GRAM

☐ **YES!** I'd like to save $750 per person on an 11-day, 8-port Amazon cruise! I've instructed my travel agent to reserve a place for me by October 1, 1990, on the Pacific Princess® Amazon cruise departing October 23, 1990 (V4034). Please arrange for me to receive my cRand McNally World Atlas after my cruise.

☐ I've arranged through my travel agent to travel with a group on this cruise -- but I would still like to receive my complimentary Rand McNally World Atlas after my cruise.

The Mysterious Amazon
And Sunny Caribbean--
Save $1,500 Per Couple!

0000123456   S   90G27
Ms. Susie Sample
1234 Main Street
Anywhere, USA 12345

PACIFIC PRINCESS R.S.V.P. CERTIFICATE

▼ DETACH HERE AND PRESENT THIS CERTIFICATE TO YOUR TRAVEL AGENT. ▼

July 24, 1990

Dear Ms. Sample,

It's the world's second longest river, named for the fierce female warriors who attacked its first European explorer. Winding nearly 4,000 miles from the Andes to the Atlantic Ocean, it flows through dense rain for... jungle, past colorful plants and animals found nowhere else on earth.

It's... ous Amazon. And you're invited to spend 11 days cruising a thousand miles ...er -- meeting new adventures at every twist and bend -- for as low as $1,930 ...ncy, including airfare!

...As a member of Circolo del Comandante/The ...ptain's Circle℠, you can save $1,500 per couple!

...ic cruise, you can save $1,500 per couple ($750 per person) sailing from ...uerto Rico -- visiting 8 ports along the Amazon and in the Caribbean. ...990, you'll receive a beautiful, 65-page full-color Rand McNally World ...ts of Princess Cruises.

...savings, a Rand McNally World Atlas and a cruise adventure that ...memories!

...oard Pacific Princess in Manaus -- ...metropolis in the heart of the jungle.

...'ll welcome you aboard Pacific Princess, TV's original Love ...mosphere of this luxurious ship, with her 7 spacious decks, ...aterooms.

...ning of this cruise -- you'll spend your first night aboard ...g you plenty of time to explore this city of one million people ...tro Amazonas -- a magnificent opera house built by rubber barons

...vice, dense Amazon jungle forms an exotic, alluring backdrop for Princess' gracious ...vice, superb continental cuisine served with Italian flair, and today's best original on ...entertainment, including our newest and most exciting spectaculars, *Tin Pan Alley* and *That's ...roadway*.

You'll visit 3 fascinating Amazon villages.

First stop is Boca do Valerio, where you can travel to a local settlement that seems to have never heard of the modern age. The next day brings a double treat -- Alter do Chao and Santarem. Alter do Chao is located on the clear waters of the Tapajoz River, an Amazon tributary ... you'll marvel at finding a brilliant white sand beach right in the middle of the jungle! Santarem is an important trading center, where local fishermen still paddle their dugout canoes to trade with ocean-going ships.

From the heart of the jungle toward the sunny Caribbean.

After sailing through the mouth of the Amazon, you'll arrive at Devil's Island in French Guiana, a rocky islet that once housed France's notorious prison settlement. The flowered paths and gentle Caribbean breezes provide a stark contrast to the preserved sheds and watchtowers of the prison.

Your next stop is British Barbados, equally as famous for its pink and white beaches as it is for its gold-colored rum. Martinique, the "Island of Flowers," is the birthplace of Napoleon's Josephine ... it's delightfully French and difficult to leave. St. Thomas, in the U.S. Virgin Islands, makes a perfect final port of call -- its duty-free shopping is the best in the Caribbean, and the many historical attractions, such as Bluebeard's Castle, bring its fascinating history alive.

(Over, please ...

≈.
PRINCESS CRUISES®

Award: Leader
Program: Gram Campaign

Client: Princess Cruises
Director of Direct Marketing: Dexter Donham
Manager of Direct Mail: Michele Willis
Direct Marketing Coordinator: Julie Wagner
Database Coordinator: Shelia Cronin

Agency: Lintas: Marketing Communications
Sr. VP, Account Director: Eileen Fraser
VP, Account: Kathy Church
Sr. Account Executive: Pam Haynie
Systems Manager: Les Wamsley
VP, Creative Director: Elaine Claussen
Writer: Sue Logar
Art Director: Terry Sharbach
Production: Wendy Gulock
Project Coordinator: Maria Chapdelaine

To promote customer loyalty—and fill last-minute vacancies—Princess Cruises mailed this series of "CruiseGrams," which could be copywritten, laser printed, and mailed in just 10 days. The targeted mailings were sent to an audience selected according to criteria like destinations previously sailed, their history with Princess and its competitors, their last expressed destination intention, and more. So far, the campaign has generated $17 million in sales at an average cost per piece ranging from 52¢ to 80¢, for a return on investment of 8.5 to 1.

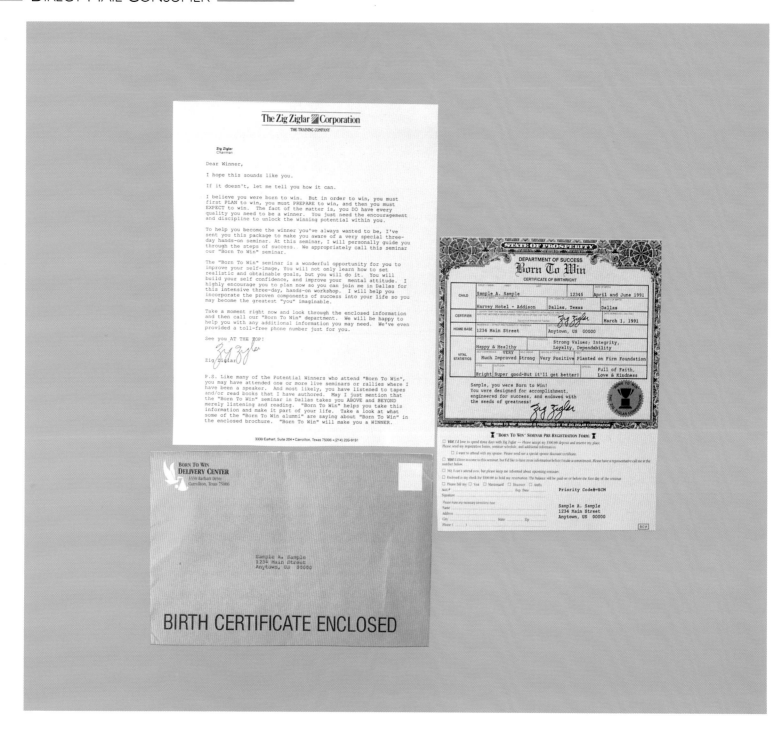

Award: Leader
Program: Born to Win

Client: The Zig Ziglar Corporation

Agency: Merrell Remington Direct (formerly RPM Direct)

Creative Director: A. Kent Merrell
Art Directors: Noel Hilden, Jack Martin
Copywriters: Kent Merrell, Noel Hilden

Printing: Texas Direct

To boost attendance at the "Born to Win" self-improvement seminar, this intriguing mailing was sent out to lists of previous Zig Ziglar customers. With an envelope proclaiming, "Birth Certificate Inside," the package included a personalized birth certificate facsimile, with the reader's name, date and place of birth, and "vital statistics" listing such positive attributes as "happy & healthy." There was plenty to be happy about in the results: a 4 percent response with a 7 percent conversion, beating the previous control by a healthy 400 percent.

Award: Leader
Program: Frontline

Client: A/S Dansk Shell, *Denmark*

Agency: ACTION I/S

To promote gas and home heating oil sales and create customer loyalty, Shell offered each customer entering a service station or sales center a Cash-Card providing rebates on purchases—provided the customer filled out and returned a questionnaire enabling Shell to build its database and customize future offers to meet individual customer needs. The resulting sales beat the previous year's by up to 18 percent, exceeding the anticipated response by 26 percent.

17 OCT 1991

Prof P.R. Mudge
16 Charlane Ave
Indooroopilly QLD 4068

Dear Prof Mudge,

Thankyou for your order from the 1991/92 Qantas Frequent
Flyer Catalogue.

We have representatives around the world working on the
Frequent Flyer programme, and we expect fulfilment of your
order within 6-8 weeks.

As stated in the Catalogue, Qantas will endeavor to provide
the same items worldwide. However, if a particular item is
unavailable in your country, a replacement of equal quality
with similar features will be arranged for you.

If you have any further questions regarding your order,
please contact our Customer Service Department between
9am-5pm Australian EST, Monday to Friday. Our international
toll-free numbers are listed below:

Japan	0031-61-6089
Hong Kong	800-6199
Singapore	800-6140
United Kingdom	0-800-89-5642
New Zealand	0-800-44-1069
United	
Canada	

Should you find
facsimile numbe
to the attentio
quote your Freq
details.

Yours Sincerely,

JENNY GREEN
Customer Service
Your Reference

Qantas Frequent Flyer Box 489 GPO

QANTAS FREQUENT FLYER REWARDS 1990

Award: Gold
Program: Qantas Frequent Flyer
Client: Qantas Airways , *Australia*

Malcolm Pryor
Agency: Pinpoint Pty. Ltd.
Kim Harding, Belinda Piggott

To stand out from other frequent flyer programs—and eliminate planeloads of nonpaying
passengers—Qantas offered customers more
merchandise than travel rewards. The payoff?
A 52 percent response rate, beating the previous
campaign by 38 percent and netting sales of
$1.4 billion.

LEVEL 9   500,000 KM

*If you would like to drop out
for a few days on a South Sea Island paradise
you'll find what you're looking for in Fiji
whether it's enjoying your favourite water sport
or relaxing at a superb resort. Qantas has been
operating services to Fiji for over 30 years
and can take you there from Australia
and the USA several times each
week in 747 comfort.*

250,000 KM

**LEVEL 8: 250,000 KILOMETRES
OR 39 SECTORS**

L8-19 – WILDLIFE SAFARI, AFRICA
'The African Experience' is an exclusive 16
day photographic safari for two through
Zimbabwe and Kenya with Wildlife Safari,
Africa's premier safari company. It starts and
finishes in Harare and includes time there and
in Africa's big game sanctuaries. A sample of
highlights include an overnight 'in the
treetops' at Mountain Lodge with
all night game-viewing from your room
overlooking a floodlit waterhole;
the world-famed flamingo sanctuary at Lake
Nakuru; three days in the Masai Mara Game
Reserve. You'll safari in style with luxury
accommodation and private facilities each
night, ground transfers by custom-built
'safari cruiser', all meals whilst on safari
and the best guides in the business.
You'll also enjoy a comprehensive tour of
Nairobi plus a special farewell dinner
at the famed Carnivore restaurant.

**L8-20 – ORPHEUS ISLAND,
BARRIER REEF**
24 kilometres off the coast about halfway
between Cairns and Townsville, Orpheus
Island is a sophisticated Great Barrier Reef
resort on the otherwise uninhabited 3400 acre
National Park. A maximum 50 guests enjoy a
freshwater pool and spa, tennis court, deep-sea
fishing, snorkelling, windsurfing and coral-
viewing, swimming at seven deserted beaches
you reach by powered dinghy. No day trippers
are allowed and there's no provision for
children under 12. This holiday is for two for
six nights, and includes all meals and return
seaplane transfer from Townsville.

L8-19

L8-20

52

Award: Gold-Diamond
Program: Crying
Client: Ryder Truck Rental

Agency: Ogilvy & Mather Direct
Creative Supervisor: Bob Cesiro
Associate Creative Supervisor: Shelley Lanman
Art Supervisor: Janet Penello
Copywriter: David Evans
Broadcast Manager: Helen Carney
Business Affairs Manager: Gail Grubman

Account Director: Becke Karl
Account Supervisor: Eric Raff
Assistant Account Executive: Michelle Morris
Assistant Account Executive: Kristin Paulus
Production Manager: Barbara Aly Amer
Associate Media Director: Marion Somerstein
Associate Broadcaster Director: Robin Friedman

To sell its used trucks at a premium price in an increasingly depressed market, Ryder Truck Rental leveraged its reputation for superior truck maintenance with these humorous spots, depicting the Ryder mechanics sobbing as their well-cared-for vehicles find new owners. The results were nothing to cry about: more than 35,000 responses at a cost of $18 per response, beating the previous campaign by 173 percent.

STEVE: See what I mean? They look after these trucks like they were their own.
MECHANIC #3: They've got their whole lives ahead of them.
STEVE: You're going to be okay. Do you believe these guys?

STEVE: Ryder sells more kinds of used trucks than anyone. Trucks, vans, tractors, trailers. Even specialized equipment. Just call and they'll tell you where to get them. They'll even—
MECHANIC #1: Not the book!
STEVE: Eh, I have to do this. They'll even give you free advice before you look. It's in here: "How to Buy a Used Truck." You gotta get this. It's the inside story. What to look for, and avoid. Whether you're buying now or just kicking some tires.

MECHANIC #1: (VO) Steve!
STEVE: It's okay, relax.
MECHANIC #1: Don't give 'em the number, please.

STEVE: Just call for the free book: "How to Buy a Used Truck." Even if you're not buying now, you'll be an expert. But you gotta call.

MUSIC UP—SAPPY, SENTIMENTAL VIOLINS
MECHANIC #1: (*Tearful*) There goes my baby.
STEVE LANDESBERG: Here we go again. I knew it. Every time Ryder sells a used truck this happens.

MECHANIC #2: (*Sobs*)
STEVE: There, there. You didn't know Ryder sells used trucks? They do. They sell 'em. (*to Mechanic #2*) Excuse me.
The same quality trucks they rent and lease to businesses, they also sell to businesses. Makes these guys fall apart.
MECHANIC #2: (*Sobbing*) We've been caring for them since they were new.

STEVE: Course, with a Ryder used truck you know what you're getting into. See this tag, "Road Ready." It means this truck has been maintained at the highest standards since it was new. Ryder has the records to prove it. And a limited warranty to back it. Impressive stuff.
MUSIC UP
STEVE: How ya doin'?
MECHANIC #4: (*downcast*) Great.

STEVE: These guys put their hearts into these trucks. They even fix things before they go wrong.
MECHANIC #4: (*VO*) (*Sniffs*) Brakes. Steering. Engine.
STEVE: You'll love your Road Ready truck as much as they do.
MECHANIC #2: Oh please, I don't want to see you go!
STEVE: Only you get to keep yours. So call for the Ryder Road Ready Center nearest you. And ask about financing.

MECHANIC #4: (*Sobbing*) Please take good care of her.
STEVE: Don't worry. You'll get more trucks. Sorry I'm out of tissues. It's a new jacket. Get off me...

I'm not kidding.
MUSIC UP AND OUT.

Award: Gold
Program: Membership Acquisition
Client: Reial Automobil Club de Catalunya, *Spain*

Marketing Manager: Jordi Losantos
Assistant Managing Director: Joan Pla
Head of Advertising Department: Gabriel Borras

Agency: Ogilvy & Mather Direct Barcelona
Creative Director: Juan Carlos Menal
Art Director: Xavier Parcerisas
Account Director: Jaume Martínez
Account Supervisor: Pilar García Miranda
Media Planner: Juana Mary Ribó
Producer: Xavier Vidiella

Research indicated that previous mailings had lacked the emotional quality as well as the immediacy required to get drivers to join the Reial Automobil Club de Catalunya. The solution, generating new members at less than half the cost of previous efforts, was this virtually wordless TV spot focusing on the club's key benefit of emergency assistance. Sales exceeded $1.1 million, at a cost of $52.66 per order.

A couple drives through a hilly landscape.

The car suffers an unexpected breakdown.

He has seen a house in the distance, from where he will try and make a phone call.

He calms down his wife, asking her to hold off for a few minutes.

He runs toward the house.

They look up to the sky.

There hovers the RACC helicopter-ambulance.

The woman seems more at ease.

The situation is truly dramatic, for the wife is pregnant and starts labor pains.

The husband gets nervous.

Suddenly he recalls he is a member of RACC and takes out his membership card.

He begs the tenant to let him make an urgent phone call.

He dials RACC's number and explains his ordeal.

A RACC van appears to look after the mechanical repair required.

900 31 32 33. This service is available free to all RACC members 24 hours a day. Change of scenario: The nurse at the hospital appears with the newborn in her arms.

900 31 32 33. Call now 900 31 32 33 to become a new member.
The looks of the young father show that there has been a happy ending.

900 31 32 33. Whatever happens, we will fix it. The technician returns the car keys to their owner. RACC has efficiently looked after the breakdown and the transport.

Award: Bronze
Program: Conga Line

Client: Ryder Truck Rental
VP, Quality and Rental: Jerry Riordan
Director, Rental & Field Marketing: Bill Hudson
Sr. Marketing Specialist: Chip Smith

Agency: Ogilvy & Mather Direct
Creative Supervisor: Bob Cesiro
Associate Creative Supervisor: Shelly Lanman
Art Supervisor: John Palisay
Copywriter: Ellen Sobotik
Art Director: Cynthia Derosier

Broadcast Manager: Helen Carney
Business Affairs Manager: Gail Grubman
Account Director: Becke Karl
Account Supervisor: Rob Rothschild
Account Supervisor: Debby Chow
Assistant Account Executive: Kristin Paulus
Associate Media Director: Marion Somerstein
Associate Broadcast Director: Robin Friedman

SFX: CONGA MUSIC THROUGHOUT
STEVE: How ya doin'?

I love this town. Let me tell you, this is my fifth housewarming party this week.
I think the whole world is moving here.
Nice plant.
It's a great place to live. But with all these people moving in, and nobody moving out...

STEVE (VO): Let me tell you, it's no party at Ryder. They got enough trucks to make their own Conga line.

So, if you're moving, you're in luck.
'Cause right now Ryder's got this great deal when you rent. It's really gonna pay you to get out of town!
Not only will Ryder save you money...

...they'll save your sanity.
They've got this free book "Movers Advantage" that makes moving easy. It's a gold mine. You can call to get it...
...even if you're not moving now.

But, hey, with Ryder's great deal, if I were you I'd stay on the phone, reserve a truck and get outta town.
'Cause you'll save a ton of money and then you can throw your own party.
Invite me.
I'll bring a plant.
WOMAN: Hey, Steve...

STEVE: (VO) Get cash back from Ryder on moves to selected destinations. Call now.
(MUSIC OUT)

78

To minimize the cost of repositioning its fleet as young movers relocate around the country, Ryder Truck Rental devised this promotion offering limited rebates on rentals to select destinations. The campaign produced a conversion rate of 40 percent and total sales of more than $8 million, at a cost per response of $14.63.

One month
before you move

Basic planning

Take an inventory. Your object here is to get a clear tally of what you own and then divide your possessions into three groups:

1. Things you're going to move into your new home.
2. Things you're going to put into storage.
3. Things you're going to sell or give away.

By using the enclosed item-by-item inventory list, you'll have an accurate record of what you're going to be moving.

Note that we've included the cubic foot requirements of each item (for anything not listed, multiply length times width times height).

Living Room, Dining Room, Den	Cubic Feet	Quantity	Total Cubic Feet
Bookcase	12		
Breakfast Table	10		
Buffet	25		
Buffet With Hutch Top	30		
Chair, Arm	10		
Chair, Occasional	14		
Chair, Overstuffed Recliner	20		
Chair, Rocker	12		
China Cabinet	20		
Corner Cabinet	14		
Couch, Sofa	30		
Desk	20		
Drapes	3		
Extension Table	14		
Floor Lamp	3		
Hide-A-Bed	35		
Mirror	3		
Rugs or Pads	8		
Table Chair	4		
Tables, Coffee or End	4		
Table Lamp	2		
Table Radio or Phonograph	2		
Television, Combination	18		
Television, Portable	8		
Television, Console	12		
Small Box	1.5		
Medium Box	3		
Large Box	4.5		
Dish-Pack	6		
Wardrobe Box	13		
Total			

Kitchen, Bedroom, Children's Room	Cubic Feet	Quantity	Total Cubic Feet
Bathinette	4		
Bed, King	75		
Bed, Queen	55		
Bed, Double	45		
Bed, Single	30		
Bed, Youth	20		
Bureau, Dresser or Chest	20		
Cedar Chest	10		
Chair, Straight	4		
Clothes Hamper	3		
Crib	8		
Dishwasher	15		
Double Dresser	25		
Dresser Chair or Bench	4		
Dryer, Clothes	20		
Freezer	45		
High Chair	3		
Ironing Board	2		
Night Table	4		
Playpen	6		
Range	25		
Refrigerator	40		
Roaster (Rotisserie)	3		
Sewing Machine (Portable)	3		
Sewing Machine (Upright)	8		
Toy Chest	4		
Utility Cart	3		
Vacuum Cleaner	3		
Wardrobe Closet (Armoire)	36		
Washing Machine	20		

Kitchen, Bedroom, Children's Room Continued	Cubic Feet	Quantity	Total Cubic Feet
Small Box	1.5		
Medium Box	3		
Large Box	4.5		
Dish-Pack	6		
Wardrobe Box	13		
Total			

Garage, Patio, Toys & Tools	Cubic Feet	Quantity	Total Cubic Feet
Barbecue	5		
Garden Cart	3		
Chaise Lounge	10		
Garden Hose & Tools	8		
Lawn Chair	3		
Lawn Mower	5		
Lawn Swing	20		
Picnic Bench	5		
Picnic Table	20		
Stepladder	5		
Swing Set	20		
Wheelbarrow	6		
Bicycle	6		
Card Table	1		
Clothes Basket	1		
Cot, Folding	2		
Fan	1		
Filing Cabinet	8		
Foot Locker	5		

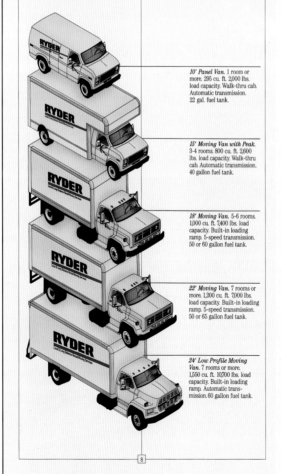

10' Panel Van. 1 room or more. 295 cu. ft. 2,000 lbs. load capacity. Walk-thru cab. Automatic transmission. 22 gal. fuel tank.

15' Moving Van with Peak. 3-4 rooms. 800 cu. ft. 2,600 lbs. load capacity. Walk-thru cab. Automatic transmission. 40 gallon fuel tank.

18' Moving Van. 5-6 rooms. 1,000 cu. ft. 7,400 lbs. load capacity. Built-in loading ramp. 5-speed transmission. 50 or 60 gallon fuel tank.

22' Moving Van. 7 rooms or more. 1,200 cu. ft. 7,000 lbs. load capacity. Built-in loading ramp. 5-speed transmission. 50 or 65 gallon fuel tank.

24' Low Profile Moving Van. 7 rooms or more. 1,550 cu. ft. 10,700 lbs. load capacity. Built-in loading ramp. Automatic transmission. 60 gallon fuel tank.

Get your boxes and supplies. Packing boxes are crucial to your move. But, unfortunately, all boxes aren't created equal. For instance, the boxes that are sometimes available from supermarkets and other stores tend to crush easily and hence won't protect your possessions. What's more, their odd sizes make loading a truck difficult.

Because of this, we recommend that you call your Ryder dealer now, ask about the packing boxes in stock, and order your supply. We can offer you small, medium and large boxes, dish-pack boxes and wardrobe boxes.

To help you estimate how many different-sized boxes you're going to need, we've included a very easy-to-use Box Guide. Your Ryder dealer can help you with any questions that arise while computing your estimate.

Keep in mind that boxes should be underpacked and cushioned. Newspapers make good padding, so stock up on them.

Recommended Box Guide

Bedrooms in House	5	4	3	2	1	Studio Apt.
Small Box	30	25	20	15	10	7
Medium Box	20	15	12	8	5	3
Large Box	12	10	8	6	5	3
Dish-Pack Box	4	4	3	2	1	1
Wardrobe Box	8	8	6	4	2	2
Total	74	62	49	35	23	16

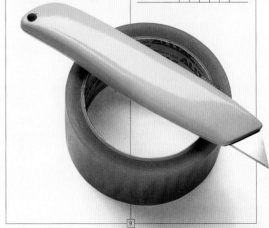

One month before you move

Bear in mind that some groups have toll-free 800 numbers: you may want to change your address over the phone. As you work your way down the list, check off the ones you've notified.
1. Magazines and periodicals.
2. Credit cards and charge accounts.
3. Clubs and organizations.
4. Insurance companies.
5. Finance companies.
6. Car loan company.
7. Investment companies.
8. Stockbroker.

Collect your important records. You should gather together all personal and family records, requesting copies whenever necessary. Don't forget your medical records (and X-rays), dental records (and X-rays), veterinarian records (and pet immunization papers), school records, legal documents and titles, banking records, financial

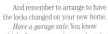

records, tax returns, stock and bond certificates, birth certificates, passports and insurance documents.

It may be best to lock these papers in a secure briefcase and keep them with you during the move.

Your future home may need advance preparations. If you want work done on your new home before you move in, now is the time to schedule it.

Contact painters, gardeners, carpet installers and shampooers, house cleaners, carpenters, plumbers, roofers, window washers—whichever services you need.

And remember to arrange to have the locks changed on your new home.

Have a garage sale. You know which of your possessions you're going to be moving.

But what about the things you don't want to move?

One option is to donate some things to charity. Many charitable organizations will even pick up the goods at your home.

A garage sale, though, may be the best way to sell what you don't want. And, of course, to make some extra money in the bargain. Keep these tips in mind:
1. Ask your local authorities what, if any, restrictions apply to garage sales.
2. Consider a joint sale with your neighbors. The more merchandise, the greater the appeal.
3. Advertise. Tell friends, neighbors and co-workers. Run a classified ad.
4. Clean everything you're going to sell, and do any appropriate minor repairs.
5. Mark every item with a price sticker. It's best to keep prices in multiples of five—5¢, 10¢, 25¢, $1.
6. Accumulate coins and small bills so you can make change.
7. On the day of the sale, arrange everything attractively. Hang clothing on a rack (a clothesline stretched across the garage is good). If you're selling anything electric, provide an outlet for testing.
8. Be prepared to bargain.
9. Enjoy yourself.

Your children should be given special considerations. Moving has become a common aspect of family life. But while adults are usually able to take a move in easy stride, children can be deeply affected in unexpected ways.

It is important, therefore, to give your children special attention during this period of transition. Here are some suggestions:
1. Give them time to adjust to the idea of moving by talking about it now.
2. Answer all their questions, giving them as many details as their age and level of maturity warrant.

3. Encourage them to participate in moving chores.
4. Tell them about the new schools they'll be attending.
5. And, if appropriate, let them know that their old friends will be welcome for a visit.
6. Above all, let them know that you're looking forward to the move. Your positive attitude will carry the day.

New schools and old schools. You may want to—or, if you're moving during the school year, you may have to—enroll your children in their new schools before you actually move.

It's best to check with their present schools and follow official advice.

Remember that some schools require *you* to furnish transcripts of school records. To be on the safe side, be sure to

get a copy. (They may also request medical records.)

You may also want to call ahead and ask officials at the new schools if your children can prepare for their transfer in any special ways.

Membership fees. Certain fee-charging clubs and organizations allow you to sell the unused portion of your membership, or they may offer you a partial refund.

Ask.

Two weeks before you move

Taking charge

Two weeks before you move, you should begin to pack.

How to pack like a pro. To pack quickly, efficiently and safely, follow our item-by-item directions.

While you're packing, keep the following points in mind:

1. Use the enclosed stickers to label your boxes by room: master bedroom, kitchen, etc.
2. Label appropriate boxes "fragile."
3. Where needed, use mothballs and other pest-control products.
4. Clean your home as you pack.

Air conditioners. It's best to consult the user's manual or your appliance dealer for special moving instructions.

Appliances (small). Pack small appliances in factory boxes whenever possible. Cushion with wadded newspaper. Do not use shredded newspaper: it can get into the machines.

Appliances (major). Leave these for last, and follow our instructions in "Two Days Before You Move."

Beds. When you disassemble the beds, mark the pieces so they're easy to put back together. Lash bed rails together with rope or masking tape. Protect mattresses by leaving sheets on them —or, better still, wrap them in Ryder's special mattress covers.

Bicycles (tricycles and baby carriages). Loosen, lower and tilt two-wheeler handlebars at right angles. Cover chains and pedals so they don't snag or soil other items.

Books. Always use small cartons. Keep them below 30 pounds. Pack books flat, alternate the bindings, and cushion with wadded newspaper.

Bureaus. Fill the drawers with small, fragile items (clocks, picture frames) wrapped in plenty of loose clothing. Cover the piece with a pad or blanket and tie securely with rope. Don't tape the drawers down—tape can ruin the finish.

Chairs. Wrap the legs with newspaper or bubble wrap. Wrap finished arms. Leave the slipcovers on upholstered chairs and cover them with Ryder's furniture pads.

Clothing. Everything that hangs in a closet—suits, dresses, coats—will do best in Ryder's wardrobe boxes. Leave small garments in bureau drawers.

Curtain Rod Hardware. Put the hardware in a plastic bag and tie it to the rod.

Dishes. Treat everything like fine china. Wrap each piece separately in bubble wrap or newspaper (if you use newspaper, put each piece in a plastic bag first—it will save you dishwashing time later). Do not stack anything flat. Pack dishes, saucers and platters

on edge. Nestle cups and bowls. Cushion with dish towels, pot holders and paper.

Glassware. Wrap every piece separately in a lot of bubble wrap or newspaper. Use a lot of newspaper for cushioning.

Kitchenware. Pots, pans, colanders, etc., can be stacked with a piece of newspaper between each piece. Cushion with newspaper.

Lamps. Pack lamp shades in individual boxes. Use bubble wrap—newspaper can stain. Bases should be wrapped and packed in separate boxes (or in bureau drawers, freezers or washing machines).

Mirrors (and frames). Small mirrors can be wrapped in newspaper and packed in boxes. But large mirrors should be wrapped heavily in newspaper and then covered with cardboard. Tape the package together securely. Plan to stand them on edge along the sides of the truck. Never pack flat.

Outdoor furniture. Disassemble any pieces that are screwed or bolted together. Place the hardware in plastic bags, tape to a furniture piece, and then tie the pieces together.

Paintings (and artwork). Treat them like large mirrors and load them the same way.

(MUSIC THROUGHOUT)
ANNCR: (VO) This is no
ordinary phone book.

It's the AT&T Toll-Free 800
Directory. Packed with
thousands of toll-free numbers

nationwide.

The only place you can 800
your way across the USA

and now you can get it free.

FIRST MAN: I feel like a
lobster.

FIRST WOMAN: Funny, you
don't look like a lobster.
Besides, we're in Arizona.
(SFX: COYOTE HOWLING)

FIRST MAN: Check the 800
Directory. I'll bet there's a place
in Maine that ships overnight.

SECOND MAN: I'm in L.A. but
I found the best deal on this
camera in New York

through the 800 Directory.

SECOND WOMAN: Hey, let's
go sailing on our honeymoon.

ANNCR: (VO) The AT&T
Toll-Free 800 Directory. It'll take
you places and get you things

beyond your imagination.

And for a limited time it's free.
(SFX: SWIRLING WATER)

Call 1-800-237-6666 EXT. 61.
There's a five dollar shipping
and handling charge.
LOBSTER: Arizona?

ANNCR: (VO) AT&T. The right
choice.

Award: Leader
Program: 800 Your Way Across the U.S.A.

Client: AT&T

Agency: Bronner Slosberg Humphrey Inc.
Executive Creative Director: Mike Slosberg
Group Creative Director: Betsy Oshlo
Producer: Arthur English
Art Director: Lisa Costanzo-Ryan
Copywriter: Eva Okada
Account Management: Jean Alexander, Gretchen Gayton
  Susan Canaveri

The A&T 800 Directory is a very different sort
of phone book—all the numbers are free, but
one had to pay a $5 shipping and handling charge
to get the book. Using the humor of claymation
to demonstrate how easy it is to "800 your way
across the U.S.A.," this spot was the most successful 800 commercial AT&T has ever produced,
generating more than 37,000 responses at a cost
of just $8.50 per response despite the steep s&h
charge.

Award: Silver
Program: DSB Travel Planner

Client: DSB (Danish Railways), *Denmark*

Marketing Manager: Bent Bentsen
Product Manager: Carsten Engstroem
Product Manager: Erik Noerskov

Agency: Ogilvy & Mather Direct
Art Direction: Else Prior
Copy: Kim Hvarre
Production: Morten Urhammer
Programming: "Soap Development" & Kim Hvarre
Account Supervisor: Susser Feit

To get business travelers to use the new Intercity 3 high speed train instead of planes and cars, a floppy disk was sent out to prospects, positioning the Intercity 3 as a high quality, high tech mode of transportation—and offering an easy-to-use travel planner with an interactive reservation form right on the diskette. The results exceeded projections by 100 percent, with a 62 percent response rate and a 9.6 percent conversion rate, amounting to sales of $554,000.

Nat og dag -
i al slags vejr

DSBs moderne tog punkterer ikke eller løber tør for benzin. De lader sig heller ikke standse af storm eller tåge. De bliver på skinnerne - også når vejene er spejlblanke.

Derfor kan De altid regne med DSB i Deres planlægning af rejsen. Hvilket er vitalt, hver gang der står væsentlige aftaler på dagens kalenderblad.

De møder frisk og udhvilet. Uanset om De har valgt at rejse i bløde sæder om dagen eller i

dunede dyner om natten. Med indtryk fra en bekvem tur gennem landsdelene.

Danmark er dejligst
fra toget

Danmark indbyder på mange måder til at rejse med tog. Korte afstande lige meget, hvilken vej vi vender blikket. Og altid en charmerende natur til lise for øje og sjæl.

De geografiske forhold har da også haft en afgørende indflydelse på Danmarks infrastruktur. Ja, faktisk finder man

næsten ikke andre lande, hvor tognettet er så fintmasket som i Danmark. Vi har nemlig tradition for at rejse godt med tog - mere end 140 år. En tradition, som stadig fortsætter takket være DSB, der hvert år bringer 140 mio. mennesker sikkert frem til deres bestemmelsessteder.

299 Jefferson Road
Room 1D24
Parsippany, NJ 07054

"Cold Cash"
Customer Rebate
Advertising Materials
Enclosed

Letter Type:	VOICE - ADVERTISING
Subject:	COLD CASH PROMOTION
Date:	DECEMBER 19, 1990
Letter Number:	AV-033-90
Related Letters:	AV-032A-90
To:	AT&T AUTHORIZED VOICE DEALERS
From:	PEGGY BARHAM
	DISTRICT MANAGER, SALES SUPPORT
Contact:	REGIONAL ACCOUNT MANAGERS, TERRITORY MANAGERS OR HQ STAFF. FOR PROMOTION QUESTIONS CALL DENISE SABEH ON (201) 952-1685. FOR ADVERTISING QUESTIONS CALL CAROL APPEZZATO ON (201) 952-1673.

PURPOSE: TO DELIVER ADVERTISING MATERIALS FOR THE AT&T AUTHORIZED VOICE DEALER "COLD CASH" END-USER PROMOTION

TEXT: You recently received a Cold Cash Promotion announcement letter along with a copy of the official program rules. As promised, for the first time we are pleased to deliver advertising materials to support your selling efforts during this promotion (Jan. 2, 1991 - March 31, 1991).

You are being provided with advertising materials for a "two step" campaign. Run the print ad and mail the "Cold Shoulder" postcard in January, and mail the "You Have Until March 31st" postcard in February (you can also run the print ad a second or third time). Since this promotion is only three months long, advertising it in two steps gives you several advantages - it sustains and reinforces customer awareness and conveys a sense of urgency. "Reminding" prospects that the rebate is available for a limited time can provide the extra motivation they need to take action - and to maximize your sales.

When you need additional advertising materials to promote this End-user promotion call Carol Appezzato.

AT&T PROPRIETARY
USE PURSUANT TO COMPANY INSTRUCTIONS
AV-033-90, PAGE 1 OF 1

Award: Leader
Program: Cold Cash Rebate

Client: AT&T/General Business Systems
Advertising Manager: Judy Paulus

Agency: Ogilvy & Mather Direct
Sr. VP, Group Director: Cathy Tweedy
Sr. VP, Creative Group Head: Tina Cohoe
VP, Associate Creative Supervisor: Maria Lucca
Associate Creative Supervisor: Hal Silverman
Copywriter: Adrienne Collier
VP, Account Director: Beth Lanigan
VP, Account Supervisor: Maria Olson
Account Executive: Liz Westermann
Assistant Account Executive: Sharon Stockwell
Production Coordinator: Rich Campanella
Traffic Coordinator: Ed Safdieh

AT&T had a problem: more than 50 percent of small business owners didn't even consider them when buying a new phone system. The solution was to arm the company's most aggressive sales channel—AT&T authorized dealers—with camera-ready materials to advertise a time-limited promotion, including a last chance postcard highlighting the March 31 deadline and advising prospects to avoid feeling foolish on April 1. That postcard alone generated more than a quarter of all responses, with the overall promotion producing sales of more than $2.5 million on a budget of just under $17,000.

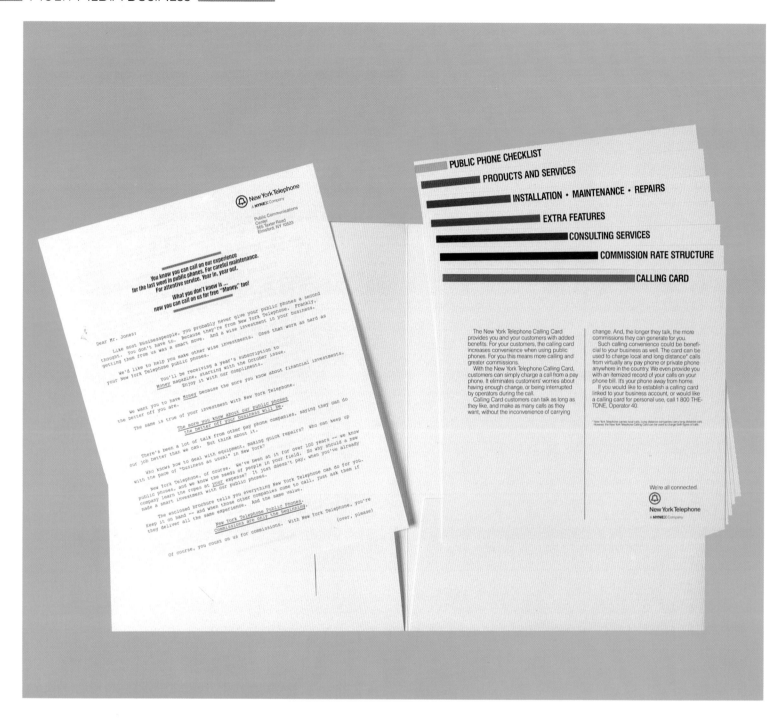

Award: Leader
Program: Public Phone Retention Program

Client: New York Telephone
Jerry Cadigan, Jaimie DePeau, Mary Bennett
Robert Bellhouse, Jim Parla, Maureen McDonald

Agency: Grey Direct Marketing Group, Inc.
Gary Andrews, Margaret Myhan, Paula Mason,
Jane Ackerman, Annemarie Haggerty, David Drohan,
Karen Henkin, Stephen Sullivan, Agnes Lau,
Peter Travis, Liz Poole

Since budgetary concerns had reduced the size of New York Telephone's sales force, direct mail was used to retain business proprietors with 10 or more of the company's public phones on their premises. The kick-off mailing, delivered by Airborne Express, featured an attention-getting box detailing New York Telephone's public phone services and promising a free subscription to *Money* magazine. During the next year, four issues of the magazine arrived with "outserts" selling the service and soliciting feedback. So far, the program has achieved a 100 percent retention rate.

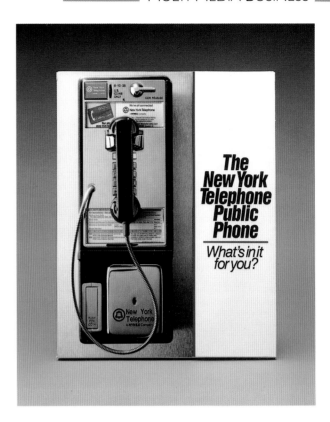

Award: Gold
Program: "Isn't He Worth It?"

Client: Heinz Pet Products
General Manager: Ed Johnson
Product Manager: Chris Connolly

Agency: Leo Burnett U.S.A.
Executive Vice President: Tom Ross
Account Director: Jeff Herscovitz
Account Supervisor: Rishad Tobaccowala
Creative Director: Jeff Millman
Copywriter: Kent Middleton
Art Director: Mike Malatak
Production: Bob Mertes
Photographer: John Welzenbach

When seven new competitors entered the ultra-gourmet cat food category, Amore's share plummeted. To halt further share erosion and promote customer loyalty, this "Isn't He Worth It?" campaign focused on the intimate relationships between cats and their owners and sidestepped the product-specific claims of competitive brands. The results were something to purr about: responses to a cat owner's questionnaire as well as coupons redeemed exceeded expectations by 202 percent, to beat the previous control by 23 percent.

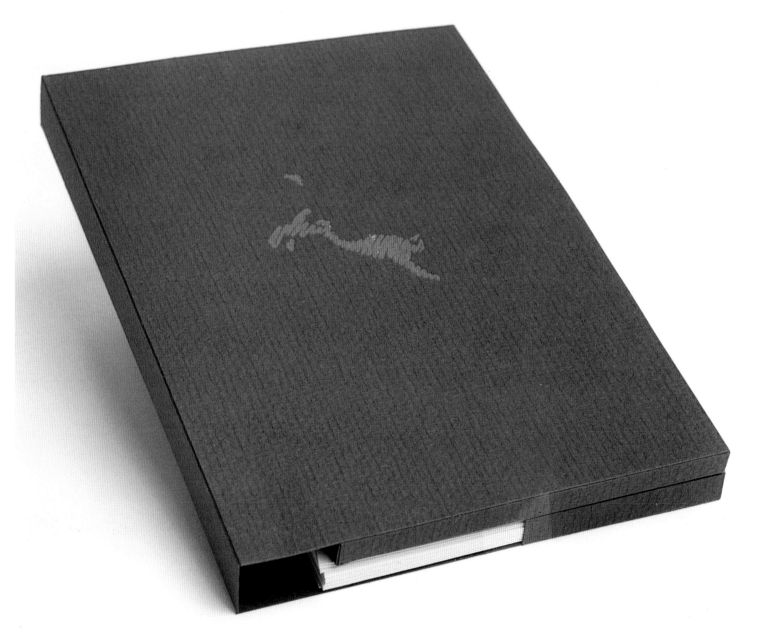

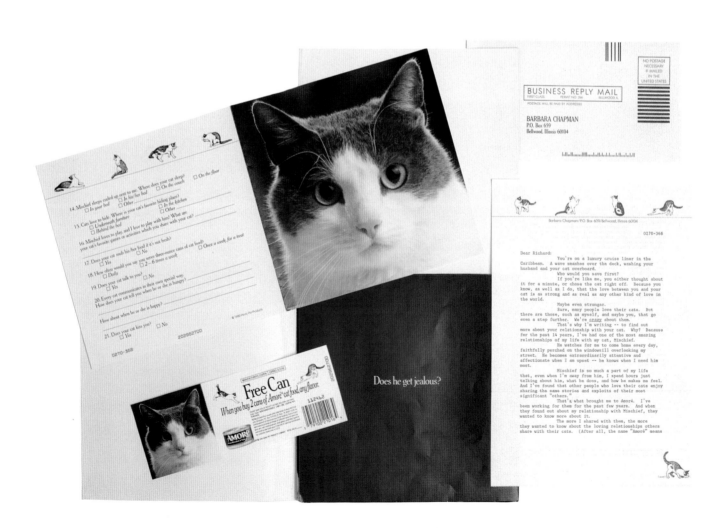

Award: Silver
Program: Cutting Edge

Client: Chicago Blackhawks Hockey Team, Inc.
William W. Wirtz, Peter R. Wirtz, James M. Fitzgerald

Agency: A. Eicoff & Company
Writer: Judy Rohner
Producer: Nancy Gohla
Creative Director: Larry Vienna
Director of Client Services: Rick Sangerman
Account Supervisor: Bill McCabe
Media Buyer: Rick Shreuder
Executive Creative Director: Sandy Stern

Rather than continue handing out team catalogs at
the stadium, the Chicago Blackhawks converted
their hotline from a free call to a 900 number. At
a cost of $2.25 per call, callers could leave their
name and address to receive a team catalog, key-
chain, and bumper sticker. This enabled the
Blackhawks to build a database of qualified prospects—and the revenue from the calls help offset
the marketing costs. So far, the TV commercial
has drawn more than 15,000 callers and resulted
in catalog sales of more than $175,000.

Award: Bronze
Program: Meaty Bone Challenge

Client: Heinz Pet Products
President: Bill Johnson
Gen. Manager: Mike Milone
Marketing Manager: Joe Sirgy
Production Managers: David Rhode, Carolyn Fobar
Assistant Production Manager: Holly Craver

Agency: Leo Burnett U.S.A.
Executive Vice President: Tom Ross
Vice President/Art Director: Jeff Herscovitz
Vice President/Creative Director: Jeff Millman
Vice President/Media Director: Bob Kirkpatrick
Sr. Vice President/Art Director: Tom Collinger
Vice President/Art Director: Ashleigh Groce
Account Supervisors: Jeff Hiller, Rishad Tobaccowala
Media Supervisor: Laura Desmond
Account Executives: Taylor Bridgeport, Susan Kann
Assistant Account Executive: Chris Nicklo
Group Supervisor: Bob Mertes
Print Services Manager Direct: Nancy Bird

Meaty Bone dog biscuits had had a hard time challenging category leader Milk Bone, which held a price advantage, despite the fact that Meaty Bone cleaned dogs' teeth as well and dogs preferred it two to one over its entrenched competitor. Thus TV and print were used to solicit requests for the "Meaty Bone Taste Challenge Kit," a mailing which included free samples, a 50¢ coupon—plus a template showing where to place the competing bones *and* the taster's front paws. The results made more than a few tails wag, besting the previous effort by 8 percent.

How to perform the Meaty Bone Taste Challenge. Just like the professionals.

It's even been on TV. The commercial where the dog calls us for his very own Meaty Bone® Challenge Kit. Then he proves that dogs prefer Meaty Bone 2 to 1 over Milk-Bone® dog biscuits. Dogs love Meaty Bone's delicious meaty coating. You'll love the fact that Meaty Bone is a teeth cleaner like Milk-Bone® Now, let your best friend prove it to himself. And to you.

The necessary materials. Inside this kit you'll find a sample box of Meaty Bone dog biscuits. All you need now is some Milk-Bone® biscuits from your cupboard. Ideally, you

Us: Them: should perform this taste test once a day, for three days. Ready to start? Good.

Let the Taste Challenge begin. For complete details on how to perform the Meaty Bone Taste Challenge, simply turn over this page, follow the instructions (they're a breeze), and have possibly the most fun you and your dog have had together since puppyhood.

Don't peek. It might be a good idea not to let the old pup hang around while you're setting things up. We're not suggesting you actually blindfold your dog, but you know how crafty dogs can be.

So... whaddya think? We'd really like to know what you and your dog think of Meaty Bone dog biscuits. So please complete the enclosed response card, and just drop it in your nearest mailbox. And, by the way, you might want to fill out the card for him. (Sometimes dogs don't always have the neatest penmanship, y'know.) Thanks to both of you for taking the Meaty Bone Taste Challenge.

Note: Original Milk-Bone® is a registered trademark of Nabisco Brands, Inc. © 1990 Heinz Pet Products.

So whaddya think?

Dog's name: _____
Address: _____
City: _____ State: _____ Zip: _____
My owner's name: _____
My usual brand of dog biscuits: _____
What happened? Well, I picked (circle one):

1st Day: **Meaty Bone® Milk-Bone®**

2nd Day: **Meaty Bone Milk-Bone**

3rd Day: **Meaty Bone Milk-Bone**

Please tell us! Do you or your owner have any comme about Meaty Bone and the Taste Challenge? _____
_____
_____
_____
_____
_____

Please have your owner drop this in the mailbox.

Meaty Bone Challenge
1830 Lunt Ave.
Elk Grove Village, IL 60007

IT'S HERE!
YOUR VERY OWN
MEATY BONE TASTE
CHALLENGE KIT!

BULK RATE
U.S. POSTAGE PAID
PERMIT NO. 111
NORTH
SUBURBAN, IL

JOHN Q. ANYONE
1234 ANYWHERE
ANYWHERE, IL. 12345

Award: Bronze
Program: TCI Photopak

Client: TCI Central, Inc.

Agency: Merrell Remington Direct (formerly RPM Direct)
Creative Director: A. Kent Merrell
Art Director: Noel Hilden
Copy: Noel Hilden, Mary Keifer

Printing: Blaine Hudson Printing

To promote its cable TV services and premium movie channels—as well as the cause of conservation in the area—TCI Central mailed out a PhotoPak Mailer with photos of the local scenery and pledged to donate $5 to local conservation projects for each order received. The mailer pulled a 6 percent response, beating the previous campaign by 33 percent.

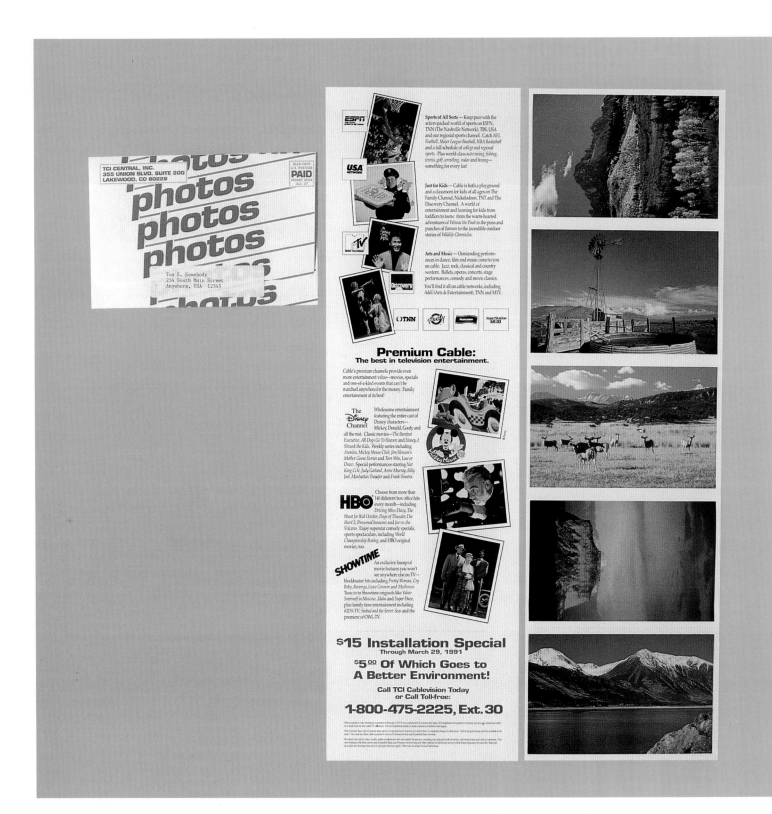

A SPECIAL (
FOR PEOPLE
GOT NO CL

$20 MID-WEEK LIFT

You don't have to attend an eco
understand the value of the Mount S
lege pass. In fact, to best appreciate o
pass, you're better off having no clas
For a taped ski report, call (802)
information, call (802) 464-8501.

Mount Snow.
When It Comes To Big Mountain Skiing, No One Else Is Close.

*Offer good Monday through Friday, non-holiday with a current college ID. © Mount Snow Ltd. 1990

FOR $20,
WE'LL LET YOU
HANG OUT
IN THE QUAD.

$20 MID-WEEK LIFT TICKET.*

Why hang out between the student union and the library, when
you can be letting it all hang out at Mount Snow, Vermont on any one
of our 84 trails.
To hang-out even longer, join SnowBreak '91, Jan. 7-11 and 14-18
—a week of parties, games, parties, parties and skiing!
For a taped ski report, call (802) 464-2151. For more information, call (802) 464-8501.

Mount Snow.
When It Comes To Big Mountain Skiing, No One Else Is Close.

*Offer good Monday through Friday, non-holiday with a current college ID. © Mount Snow Ltd. 1990

E US $20,
WE'LL GIVE
THE RUNS.

MID-WEEK LIFT TICKET.*

v, Vermont is giving all you college stu-
ur money. In fact, we're giving you all
ing from our six new Sunbrook inter-
he North Face expert terrain. And all for

ki report, call (802) 464-2151. For more
(802) 464-8501.

Mount Snow.
When It Comes To Big Mountain Skiing, No One Else Is Close.

*Offer good Monday through Friday, non-holiday with a current college ID. © Mount Snow Ltd. 1990

$20 Mid-week Lift Ticket*

Mount Sn
just elimin
one of the
obstacles in
skiing— the
Simply prese
current colleg
and we'll give
day on the slope
just $20.
Now at least th
skiing won't wipe y

Mount St
Mount Snow, Vermont 05356

*Offer good Monday through Friday, no
For ski report, call (802) 464-2151.

SO WHAT, DO YOU WANT FOR $20?

Alpine skiing is a recreational activity that continually
challenges the human spirit. Natural and man-made
obstacles are part of the challenge of man against the
mountain and the elements. But, collisions with these
obstacles can cause serious injury or death.

THE PRICE OF A SKI TICKET BEARS NO RELATION TO THE CHALLENGES AND DANGERS ASSOCIATED WITH ALPINE SKIING.

Award: Bronze
Program: College Multi-Media Campaign

Client: Mount Snow Resort

Agency: Orsatti & Parrish
Creative Director: Frank Parrish
Art Director: Robert Levers
Copywriters: Martin Stadtmueller, David Abend
Management Supervisor: NancyJane Goldston
Account Manager: Elaine McCarthy

To boost traffic during the week, the Mount Snow
ski resort targeted this irreverent multi-media
campaign to college students living within a 90-
minute radius of the site. With flexible schedules,
disposable income, *and* a sense of humor, the students responded in droves to "a special offer for
people who got no class"—a $20 mid-week lift
ticket. In fact, lift ticket sales increased 770 percent, generating $950,000 plus an additional $2.1
million in incremental revenues.

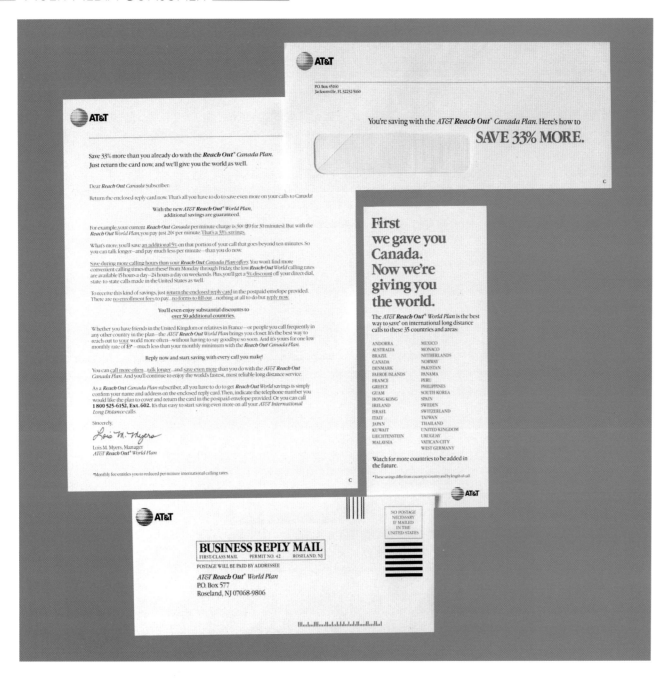

Award: Bronze
Program: Launch Program

Client: AT&T Reach Out World Plan
Division Manager: Jackie Woodall
District Manager: Mark Burgess
Product Marketing Manager: Dennis McLynn
Staff Supervisor: Lois Myers

Agency: Chapman Direct Advertising
Vice President/Creative Supervisor: Alfred O'Neill
Vice President/Creative Supervisor: Gary Bucca
Creative Supervisor: Linda King
Creative Supervisor: Mark DiMassimo
Art Director: Brenda Baskin
Art Director: Lucia Barrientos
Art Director: Roberta Jarrett
Art Director: Sonya Cashner
Copywriter: Chris Seid
Copywriter: Garth Winfield
Copywriter: Steve Hogan
Senior Vice President/Production Director: Len Ross
Producer: Helen Nelson
Assistant Producer: Shawn Lacey
Music Producer: Craig Hazen
Vice President/Management Supervisor: Gloria McKenna
VP/Account Supervisor: Margaret Yates
Account Executive: Shelley Brauner
Account Executive: Annette St. John
Account Executive: Nancy Aaronson

The Reach Out® World Plan was launched to bolster AT&T's consumer international long distance market share by offering savings on calls to friends and family abroad. To target the ethnic groups who produce a disproportionate share of international long distance revenue, this ambitious campaign used variations in media and languages. The response exceeded expectations by 78 percent, at a cost less than half that anticipated.

Only with the new *AT&T Reach Out World Plan.*

The sound of a loved one's voice. The laugh of a good friend. Now you can hear them again and again—and save.

Introducing the *AT&T Reach Out World Plan.* It's a new way to call family and friends in over 40 countries, while lowering your monthly AT&T international phone bill by 20%.*

Only *Reach Out World* give you so much of the world in one plan with one low $3 monthly fee. And the savings begin with low per-minute costs—you can call Canada for 20¢, Europe for 62¢, and the Pacific for 83¢.

With this plan you can call almost anytime—15 or more hours a day during the week. And 24 hours a day on the weekends.

The more you talk, the more you save. Because *Reach Out World* lets you enjoy an additional 5% discount on that portion of your call after the tenth minute. There's even a discount on state-to-state long distance calls made from your home.

And all your international calls will have the clear connections and superior customer service you've come to expect from AT&T.

Now there's more reason than ever to say hello again and again. Call today to sign up for the *AT&T Reach Out World Plan.*

Call 1 800 222-1776, Ext. 628.

AT&T
The right choice.

*Based on an avg. 10-minute residential call compared to AT&T International Long Distance direct-dialed rates.
© 1990 AT&T

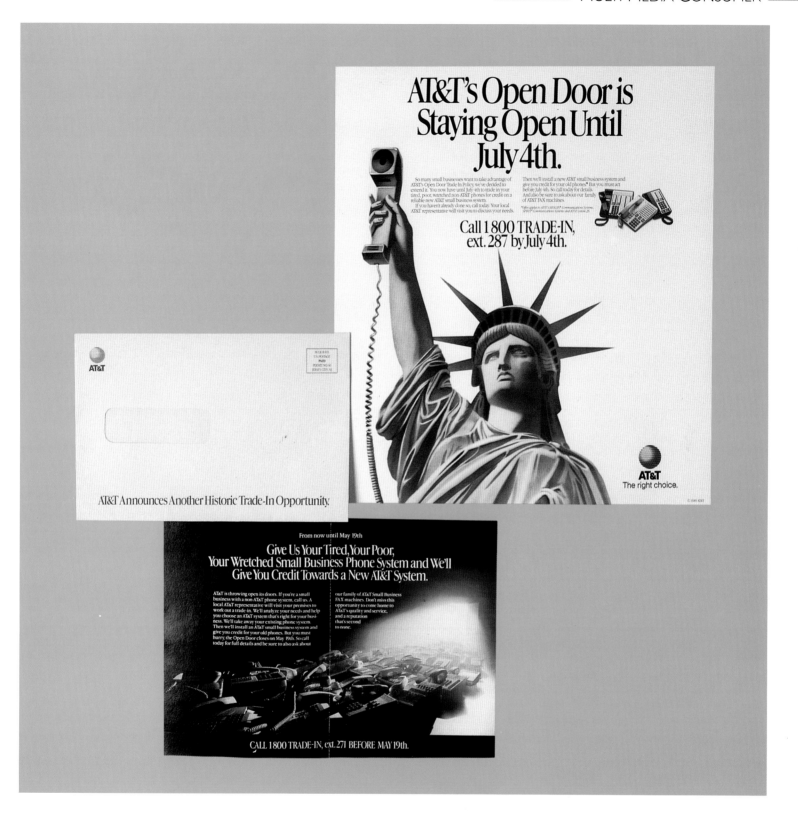

Award: Leader
Program: Trade-In Event

Client: AT&T/General Business Systems
Ira Cohen

Agency: Ogilvy & Mather Direct
Creative: Tina Cohoe, Maria Lucca, Richard Muehlberg
  Hal Silverman, Niall Kelly, Michael Rosenbaum
  Sheryl White, Christine O'Hanlon, Scott Pinkney
  Brenda Lampert, Steve Keltz, Adrienne Collier
  Heather Higgins
Account: Becke Karl, Tea Romano, Meaghan O'Connell
  Tracey Owens, Stacia Goddard, Kathy Orr
  Diane Colon, Paul Gitter, Maria Olson
  Liz Westermann
Media: Marion Somerstein

AT&T needed to move their premium small business phone systems without resorting to fire-sale tactics. The answer was this multi-media campaign inviting small businesses to "give us your tired, your poor, your wretched phones" in exchange for a trade-in allowance toward the purchase of a new system from AT&T. The campaign's return on investment was an astonishing 27 to 1, with highly targeted mail follow-up yielding a return of 6.6 to 1.

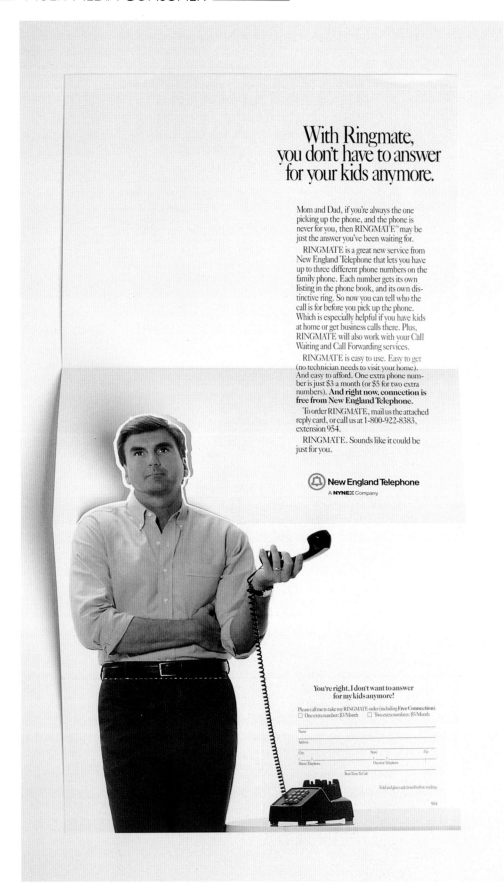

With Ringmate, you don't have to answer for your kids anymore.

Mom and Dad, if you're always the one picking up the phone, and the phone is never for you, then RINGMATE™ may be just the answer you've been waiting for.

RINGMATE is a great new service from New England Telephone that lets you have up to three different phone numbers on the family phone. Each number gets its own listing in the phone book, and its own distinctive ring. So now you can tell who the call is for before you pick up the phone. Which is especially helpful if you have kids at home or get business calls there. Plus, RINGMATE will also work with your Call Waiting and Call Forwarding services.

RINGMATE is easy to use. Easy to get (no technician needs to visit your home). And easy to afford. One extra phone number is just $3 a month (or $5 for two extra numbers). **And right now, connection is free from New England Telephone.**

To order RINGMATE, mail us the attached reply card, or call us at 1-800-922-8383, extension 954.

RINGMATE. Sounds like it could be just for you.

New England Telephone
A **NYNEX** Company

You're right, I don't want to answer for my kids anymore!

Please call me to take my RINGMATE order (including Free Connection).
☐ One extra number: $3/Month   ☐ Two extra numbers: $5/Month

Name
Address
City   State   Zip
Home Telephone   Daytime Telephone
Best Time To Call
Fold and place card closed before mailing.
954

Award: Leader
Program: Residential Ringmate—RI/MA

Client: New England Telephone

Agency: Cabot Direct
Account Executives: Cynthia Purmort, Wendy Kane
Account Supervisors: Peter Sutters, Arthur Sweetser
Copywriters: Marty Donahue, Kirt Snyder
Art Directors: Brad Pruett, Len Rallo
Production Manager: Sheryl Phillips
Creative Director: Marvin Fried

Printer: United Lithograph
Lettershop: W. A. Wilde
List: Donnelley Marketing

New England Telephone's new Ringmate Service offered distinctive ringing patterns for up to three separate numbers, with three directory listings, on one line. Realizing their primary audience was families with teenage children, the company targeted direct print, radio, and mail at the parents, promising, "you don't have to answer for your kids anymore," and radio and TV at the kids, promising, "you can have your own phone number, listing, and personalized ring." The distinctive ring of the cash register was the result, with a 21 percent response rate and 98 percent conversion.

NEW ENGLAND TELEPHONE
1991 RESIDENCE ADVERTISING
"RINGMATE"

SFX: (GUITAR RIFF)
ANNCR: "When you're a kid

it's great having your own stuff. Well now you can have your own phone number with RINGMATE.

It's new from New England Telephone, and it's wild.

For three bucks a month

you get your own number,

your name in the phone book

SFX: (PHONE RING)
and your very own ring, so you know the call's for you.

RINGMATE Service from New England Telephone. Now in most areas with a one-time connection fee.

SUPER: New England Telephone. A NYNEX Company.
SINGER: WE'RE THE ONE FOR YOU NEW ENGLAND. NEW ENGLAND TELEPHONE. PART OF THE NYNEX FAMILY.

Award: Leader
Program: Pro Wats California

Client: AT&T

Agency: Ogilvy & Mather Direct
Sr. VP, Creative Group Head: Michael Cancellieri
VP, Copy Supervisor: Susan Francesco
VP, Sr. Art Director: Ronni Reider
Production Coordinator: Al Nelson
Assistant Art Director: Denise Shuba
VP, Production Services: Rhonda Saltzman
Sr. VP, Group Director: Cathy Tweedy
VP, Account Dirctor: Becke Karl
VP, Account Supervisor: Mario Olson
Account Executive: Linda Califano
Assistant Account Executive: Kristin Honchen

In the extremely competitive California market, AT&T needed something powerful to protect their share of in-state long distance calls. When the tariff was approved reducing the cost of their PRO WATS plan, therefore, the company marshalled this multi-media campaign directed at owners of growing businesses, trumpeting golden opportunities to save in the Golden State. The result was golden as well: a 3 percent response rate with 74 percent conversion, translating into sales of more than $13.6 million.

Award: Leader
Program: New York Launch

Client: NYNEX Service Company
Director, Product Development: Dr. Ellen Powley
Staff Director: Brian Cahill
Staff Manager: Nancy Torres

Agency: Chapman Direct Advertising
Sr. VP Director of Client Services: Rosemary O'Brien
Vice President, Production: Leonard Ross
Production Manager: Dorothy Barnett
Media Manager: Debra Haut
Account Supervisor: Robert Grammatica
Assistant Account Executive: Efren Vaca
Vice President, Creative Director: Robert Earl
Creative Supervisor: Bill Uscatu
Art Director: Louis Principato
Art Director: Sean O'Neill

Vendor Resources: Art Fliss Studios, Omni
    Quality House of Graphics, Seaboard Litho
    S. Shoob and Company, Studio Design, TPD

To introduce the INFO-LOOK interactive video-tex service, NYNEX sent out this dramatic two-part mailing to lists of home PC owners, offering free starter kits with communications software. Claiming that tonight, "some of the best network programming won't be on your TV," the first self-mailer emphasized the wide range of information services available and offered a special deal on a modem for users without one. The response rate was 4.6 percent, with qualified leads from direct mail proven to be 92 percent less expensive than other media used, delivering 31 percent more triers vs. preestablished benchmarks.

Award: Gold
Program: Wishing for Westin

Client: Herring/Newman

Agency: Herring/Newman
Account Supervisor: Jill Eenigenburg
Creative Directors: Gini Lawson, Phil Herring
Art Directors: Chris Bulloch, Judy Stuckey, Darby Roach
Jamie Stone
Copywriters: Phil Herring, Gini Lawson, Dennis Globus
Jeff Spagnola

To get invited to Westin Hotel's forthcoming agency review, Seattle's Herring/Newman devised this ingenious six-day campaign, which was hand delivered to their prospects at Westin. After a day-one letter introducing the agency and the campaign to follow, each subsequent day's delivery featured one of the agency's unique benefits, including a Gold Echo Award; a basket with goods representing current clients; a local bus ticket to their offices; a towel stolen from Westin Hotels (representing creative that breaks rules!); and a suitcase with travel stickers from around the world, representing the agency's depth of travel experience. The result? Herring/Newman got to pitch—and they landed the account!

HERRING·NEWMAN
direct response advertising

August 24, 1990

Dear Mr. Coleman

We couldn't help noticing in a recent advertising trade magazine that you're parting company with MPI. While we're never particularly happy about a competitor's misfortune, it nonetheless presents us with an opportunity to tell you who we are, what we do, and why we do it.

Herring•Newman, which was founded in 1982, had billings of $21 million with a staff of 45. While this may or may not strike you as meaningful, it made an impression on Inc. Magazine who listed us as one of America's fastest growing companies.

We're not quite in the Fortune 500 yet. But some of our clients are -- including Apple Computer, Nike, and Hewlett-Packard.

As you'll see from the enclosed document "A few words about Herring•Newman," the rest of our client list ain't too shabby either. But what should be of particular interest to you is our staff's depth of experience in hotel marketing on accounts such as Four Seasons Hotels and Resorts, Mariott Corporation, Sheraton and Holiday Inn.

One of the reasons we (as a relatively unknown agency in the upper left-hand corner of the map) are able to get such prominent business is because we offer something virtually no other direct response agency can: startling creative work supported by innovative direct response strategies. It's the kind of thinking that helped us win a Gold Mailbox Award for the world's most inventive and successful use of direct mail, presented by the Direct Marketing Association.

Another factor you may find appealing is our location. We're in Pioneer Square, just a stone's throw away from your office. That means we can more easily service your account and avoid the billable costs associated with travel.

101 Yesler Way • Seattle, Washington 98104 • (206) 343-9654

HERRING·NEWMAN
direct response advertising

In addition to the above mentioned document, we've included a folio box which will provide you with a glimpse at the kind of work we do.

Lastly, we will be sending you five packages next week. Our goals is to communicate a little bit more about ourselves each day. If during this time you find yourself overcome with the desire to call us, please feel free to rip the phone off the hook and do so. But if you'd like to wait out the entire five days, we'll give you a call at the end of the day on Friday to arrange a time when we can get together.

From all of us at Herring•Newman, thanks for taking the time to read this. And enjoy next week's onslaught.

Sincerely,

Chris Altwegg   Shelley Baker   Bly Berken   Bruce Bulloch
Chris Bulloch   Mary Lou Calo   Jan Calvert   Janice Cannon-Kyte
Yueh-O Chang   Larry Cook   Catha Cowgill   Martha Craig
Anne Crawford   Mark Davis   Dustin Dickenson   Samantha Durst
Jill Eenigenburg   Julie Engel   Laile Fairbairn   Kristie Frey
Dennis Globus   Lorin Guenette   Donna Herak   Phil Herring
Deb Hobson   Jeff Idler   Pat Klopich   Gini Lawson   Jill Nelson
Dermot Noonan   Pamela Plowman   Karen Ridings   Teresa Riefflin-Ellis
Darby Roach   Jim Schuknecht   Fred Schwartz   Claire Celeste Simecek
Sandra Simonson   Nerissa Smeeth   Mary Ward-Smith   Jeff Spagnola
Kim St. Ours   Jody Stroh   Judy Stuckey   Pat Stuckey   Teresa Robertson

HERRING·NEWMAN
direct response advertising

**Very few agencies
get the point.**

That plastic pointy object you're holding isn't what you think it is. It's not a sadistic party gag akin to the whoopie cushion. Or a place to stick memos.

It's an Echo Award. And every year we seem to run off with a disproportionate share of them. Okay, what's the big deal about an Echo, you ask?

Well, simply put, it's the only award that's given solely to agencies whose work is creative *and* successful. So to win one, you've got to have all your creative ducks in a row, then produce that... well, works.

Easier said than done, judging by how few agencies win Echoes each year.

What all this is leading up to is that we'd like to engrave your name on the Echo Award that's enclosed. Of course, in order to do that, we'd need to be handling your direct response business. But let's not quibble over minor details.

We think we're the right agency for you not because we win lots of awards. But because of the *reason* we win awards. We do innovative work that pulls like gangbusters.

And after all, isn't that the point?

P.S. Seeing as Echos are so hard to come by, we'd like to have this one back. So if you don't mind, please hang on to it, and we'll have it picked up in the next week or so.

101 Yesler Way • Seattle, Washington 98104 • (206) 343-9654

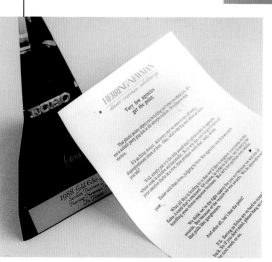

HERRING·NEWMAN
direct response advertising

Our basket case.

We're not in the habit of sending baskets filled with eclectic junk to prospective clients. However, in your case we made an exception.

Each item in the basket represents one of our clients. And given the size and reputation of the advertisers we work with, it's not too hard to figure out what represents whom.

We think its important that you know who works with us because nothing defines an agency better than its clients. Not that we're in the Fortune 500, of course, but some of our clients are that big:

Apple Computer
(Cupertino, California)
Nike
(Beaverton, Oregon)
Airborne Express
(Seattle, Washington)
Hewlett-Packard Test & Measurement
(Mountain View, California, plus 12 other cities worldwide)
McCaw Cellular One
(Minneapolis, Pittsburgh, Denver, Portland, Seattle)

And although we're not travel agents, our travel and tourism clients are all over the map:

Australia Tourist Commission
(Sydney, Australia/Los Angeles, California)
Alaska Tourism Marketing Council
(Anchorage, Alaska)
Quantas Airways
(Sydney, Australia/San Francisco, California)

Of course, we've done pretty well in our own backyard, too.

101 Yesler Way • Seattle, Washington 98104 • (206) 343-9654

HERRING·NEWMAN
direct response advertising

First Interstate Bank of Washington
(Seattle, Washington)
United Way of King County
(Seattle, Washington)
Liberty Orchards Aplets & Cotlets
(Cashmere, Washington)

So, how does this basket of stuff define Herring/Newman?

It tells you that we're diverse. We've created successful work for every client on this list.

It tells you that we're comfortable with the demands of national clients and international campaigns.

And finally, we hope it proves that we're capable of handling an account as large, as diverse, and as prestigious as Westin.

If you agree give us a call. We'd love to add you to our basket.

101 Yesler Way • Seattle, Washington 98104 • (206) 343-9654

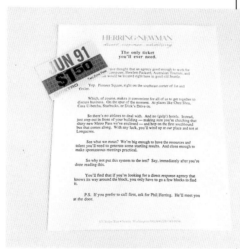

HERRING·NEWMAN
direct response advertising

The only ticket you'll ever need.

Who would have thought that an agency good enough to work for the likes of Apple Computer, Hewlett-Packard, Australian Tourism, and Airborne Express would be located right here in good old Seattle.

Yep. Pioneer Square, right on the southeast corner of 1st and Yesler.

Which, of course, makes it convenient for all of us to get together to discuss business. On the spur of the moment. At places like Chez Shea, Casa U-betcha, Starbucks, or Dick's Drive-in.

So there's no airline to deal with. And no (gulp!) hotels. Instead, just step out in front of your building -- making sure you're clutching that shiny new Metro Pass we've enclosed -- and hop on the first southbound bus that comes along. With any luck, you'll wind up at *our* place and not at Longacres.

See what we mean? We're big enough to have the resources and talent you'll need to generate some startling results. And close enough to make spontaneous meetings practical.

So why not put this system to the test? Say, immediately after you're done reading this.

You'll find that if you're looking for a direct response agency that knows its way around the block, you only have to go a few blocks to find it.

P.S. If you prefer to call first, ask for Phil Herring. He'll meet you at the door.

101 Yesler Way • Seattle, Washington 98104 • (206) 343-9654

HERRING·NEWMAN
direct response advertising

Uh, here's your towel.

Kleptomania isn't usually at the top of the list of attributes to look for in an agency. But in this case, we hope it illustrates a point.

We break rules.

You see, most direct response advertising is based on a long list of rules and techniques. They make our business seem so simple almost anyone can do it. Just follow the rules, throw in a few trendy techniques for good measure, and *Voila!* You've got a campaign.

It may look like everyone else's. It may sound like everyone else's. But by golly you've followed the rules, and that should ensure success, right?

Well, not exactly. That's because most of these traditional rules and techniques were developed 20 or more years ago...for somebody else's product, in somebody else's marketplace. And what worked in the 60's won't necessarily work in the 90's. (Remember the Nehru jacket?)

Never ones to blithely choose the easy way, we believe it's better to begin with *your* product, *you* target audience, and *your* marketplace. We take all this info, digest it, examine it, and make assumptions about it. Then we feed it back to you as a strategy.

The strategy may be somewhat surprising, often opinionated, but it always reflects a strong point of view.

Which lets us look at your product from a fresh perspective. Kick around new ideas for programs. Produce breakthrough creative which takes you as far from the dreaded "junk" word as you care to go.

And lets us get results that are, shall we say, better than traditional.

101 Yesler Way • Seattle, Washington 98104 • (206) 343-9654

HERRING·NEWMAN
direct response advertising

Sure, this approach has caused a few people to label us as rabble-rousers. But it has also proven itself in the marketplace. Just ask Apple Computer. The Australia Tourist Commission. Or Hewlett-Packard.

They'll tell you that our brand of direct response advertising isn't about following rules.

It's about selling products.

We'd like to help you do that. And we promise, after this one time, we'll stick to breaking our own rules.

Instead of yours.

P.S. If you don't want the towel, we'll take it back. We can add it to Phil's collection.

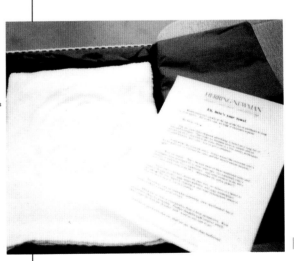

HERRING·NEWMAN
direct response advertising

Going our way?

We've told you about our location, our client list, our philosophy, and the fact that we've won several dozen awards. But there are just a few more things we'd like to mention.

Four Seasons Hotels
Holiday Inn
Marriott Hotels
Ritz Carlton Hotel
Sheraton Hotels
Alaska Airlines
American Airlines, SABRE Division
Qantas Airways
UTA French Airlines
Exploration Cruise Lines
Columbia Glacier Cruises
Holland American Westours
Johansen Royal Tours
Princess Tours
Princess Cruises
Royal Highway Tours
Seattle Harbor Tours
Society Expeditions
Stena Line
Sundance Tours
Yukon River Cruises
Spruce Goose/Queen Mary
Alaska Visitors Association
Alaska Tourism Marketing Council
Australian Tourist Commission
Greek National Tourist Organization
Netherlands National Tourist Office
Mutual Travel

This represents the collective experience, past and present, of our staff. It is perhaps the longest list of travel accounts you'll find at any direct response agency in the U.S.

101 Yesler Way • Seattle, Washington 98104 • (206) 343-9654

HERRING·NEWMAN
direct response advertising

It sure would be a shame to let all that travel experience go to waste. So let's travel somewhere together.

Like, say, to lunch?

As promised, Phil will be calling you this afternoon to select a time and a restaurant.

In the meantime, we hope you've enjoyed our campaign as much as we've enjoyed preparing it.

Sincerely,

All of us at Herring/Newman

101 Yesler Way • Seattle, Washington 98104 • (206) 343-9654

Award: Leader
Program: Corporate Literature

Client: Drake Beam Morin, Inc.

Agency: In-house
Group Vice President/Marketing Services:
Marilynn Williamson

A career management firm specializing in out-placement services, Drake Beam Morin sought a collateral piece that would distinguish the company from its competitors, educate customers on the features and benefits of services offered, and exude an image of competence and caring. Using gold accents and muted colors, plus intimate photos and customer testimonials, the brochures were responsible for a 50 percent conversion rate, with total sales of $67 million.

Chapter

3

Non-Profit
Fundraising

Award: Silver
Program: 1991 DMAW MAXI Awards

Client: Direct Marketing Association of Washington

Agency: Hodgins Design, Inc.
Barbara Hodgins, Paul Swetz

Creative Marketing Management: Marti Campbell
Warren Publishing: Gary Madderom

Illustrations: Tony Fitch, Design House
Invitation Printing: Marilee Gibson, Lithotech
Envelopes: Robert Muma, Allen Envelope
Admarking: Julian Kasten, Capital Mailing Services, Inc.
Production: Paul Swetz, Hodgins Design, Inc.
   Cathy Brandenburg, Brandenburg Production
   Management

To stimulate attendance at the Direct Marketing Association of Washington's MAXI Awards Presentation and Gala at the French Embassy, this French-themed mailing was sent out around Valentine's day. The response? The event sold out for the first time since the MAXI's were introduced twelve years before, with registrations increasing by 62 percent from the previous year.

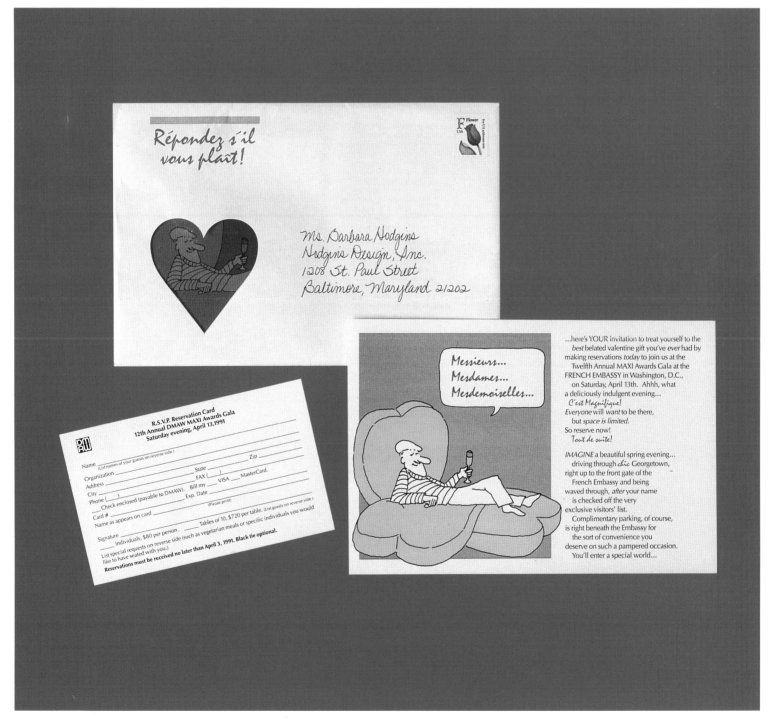

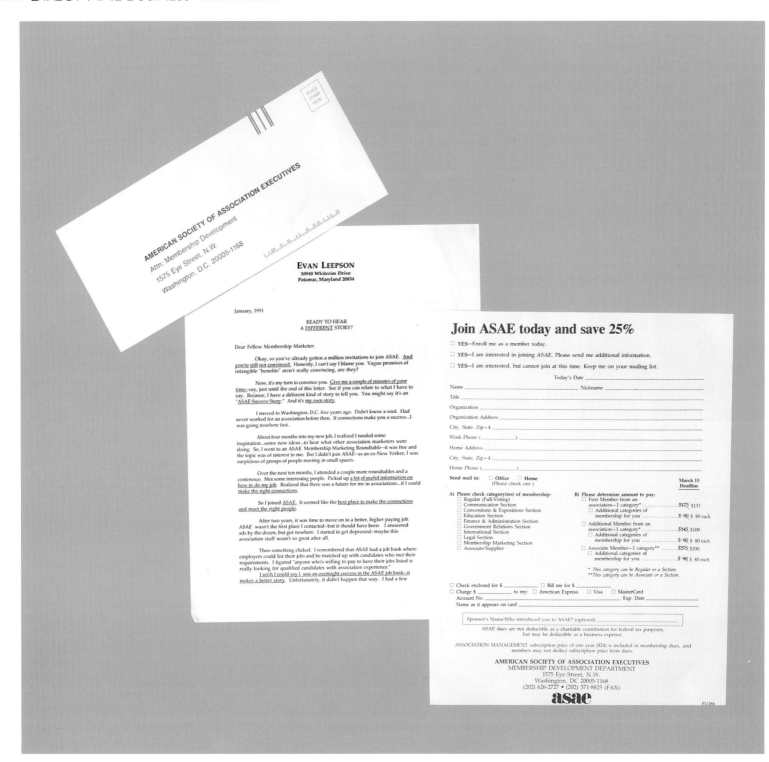

Award: Leader
Program: A Different Story

Client: American Society of Association Executives
Section Manager: Sandi Reese
American College of Radiology & ASAE Member:
Evan Leepson

Agency: Creative Communications
Copywriter: Jill Zaklow

The American Society of Association Executives had never had success recruiting members through the mail. Recognizing that the primary reason to join was the opportunity to network and enhance one's career, the society sent out this mailing, featuring a first-person account of how a member had overcome his own skepticism and discovered the rewards of membership. Even skeptics were silenced by the results, which beat previous efforts by 105 percent.

Award: Leader
Program: 65 Roses Sports Club

Client: Massachusetts Cystic Fibrosis Foundation
Program Director: Molly McQuade

Agency: Irma S. Mann, Strategic Marketing, Inc.
Creative Director: Gary Leopold
Art Director: Sandra Marsh
Copywriter: Brian Feuerman
Photographers: Rick Hornick, Sandy Rivlin
Account Executive: Jim Rosenberg

To raise contributions from small businesses in the Boston area, the Massachusetts Cystic Fibrosis Foundation developed this ingenious 65 Roses Sports Club program. They sent out a mailing with four-color team logos, offering a package of four hard-to-get tickets at five area pro sports events, including special pregame dinners and opportunities to meet the players. The result: everybody won, with total sales of more than $130,000 at a cost per response of just $8.73.

65 ROSES SPORTS CLUB

220 N. Main Street, Suite 104
Natick, MA 01760

Mr. Samuel A. Sample
President
HUB MAIL ADVERTISING
75 University Avenue
Westwood, MA 02090-2306

65 ROSES SPORTS CLUB

Don Baylor
National Chairman

Rick Miller
Honorary Chairman

Chris Ford
Celtics Chairman

Gord Kluzak
Bruins Chairman

October 8, 1990

Dear Sports Fan:

Do you like the Celtics, the Red Sox and the Bruins?

Would you like the opportunity to go to practices and games, have dinner with the players, have your picture taken with them, and be invited to all kinds of special events?

You can, when you join the 65 Roses Sports Club. It's a sports club made up of athletes and sports fans who are dedicated to winning the battle against Cystic Fibrosis, the number one genetic killer of children -- a disease which claims the life of a child every eight hours.

Our club name originates from the way a child first tried to pronounce "Cystic Fibrosis", calling it "65 Roses". And for nearly four decades, the funds we've raised have helped thousands of children with CF live longer and fuller lives.

We're excited with the recent discovery of the gene responsible for Cystic Fibrosis -- it opens many doors to achieving long term control and brings us closer than ever to finding a cure. But much more needs to be done. Your support guarantees continued research efforts, and gives kids with CF a sporting chance against the odds. And that's what joining the 65 Roses Sports Club is all about.

220 N. Main Street, Suite 104, Natick, MA 01760 / 1-800-966-0444 / 508-655-6000

Award: Gold
Program: Brossa Neta
Client: Ayuntamiento de Barcelona (City Hall), *Spain*

Councilor: Josep Mª Serra Martí
Coordinator: Luis Fontanals
Technical Advisor: Rosa Forcada

Agency: Ogilvy & Mather Direct Barcelona
Account Supervisor: Mònica Alonso
Account Executive: Cristina Ros
Creative Director: Ferran Cullel
Art Director: Xavi Parcerisas
Copywriter: Emma Riverola
Art Director: Marcos Gonzalez-Cuevas

Brossa neta
Llença-la bé

NO RECICLABLE

Hi ha brossa que no pot ser altra cosa que això. Com ara la matèria orgànica que fermenta: vegetals, pa i totes aquelles deixalles d'aliments que acostumen a llençar a les escombraries i que són utilitzables com a adob. Tampoc són reciclables les restes de terra, cendres, porcellanes, cel.lofanes, xeringues i fluorescents. Ni totes aquelles deixalles que estiguin molt brutes, com les llaunes i els envasos plens d'oli. Totes aquestes restes que van a parar al cubell de les escombraries no poden ser reciclades. Han deixat de ser útils.

RECICLABLE

Però hi ha brossa que encara té moltes coses a fer. El paper, el metall, el vidre, el plàstic i la roba poden tornar a ser útils. Només els hi cal una mica d'ajuda. Ara, amb una recollida selectiva d'aquestes matèries i amb un procés posterior de reciclatge es podran tornar a recuperar. Estalviarem molts diners i evitarem que es continuïn degradant les nostres reserves naturals i energètiques. **Defensi el medi ambient des de casa seva.** Perquè això sigui possible, és imprescindible la seva col.laboració. Només cal que llenci tota aquesta **brossa neta** als nous contenidors blaus. Així, es podrà tornar a fer servir per fabricar productes nous.

Res a fer

Nous de trinca

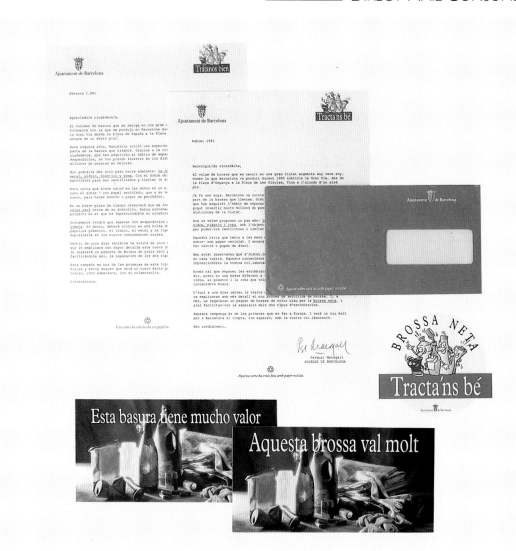

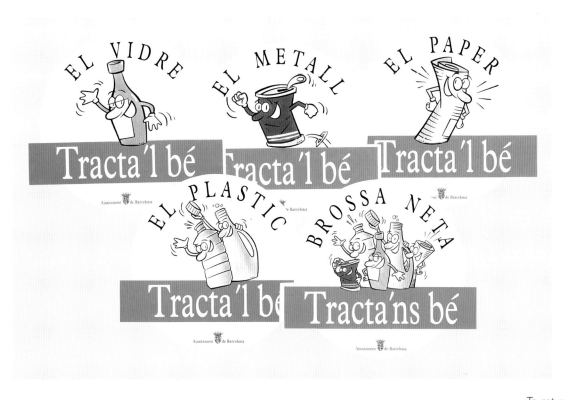

To get residents of Barcelona to sort their refuse for recycling, a two-part mailing series was devised, with the second mailing hand delivered to residents by Red Cross youth volunteers. The result was spectacular, with 65 percent of all households separating their refuse.

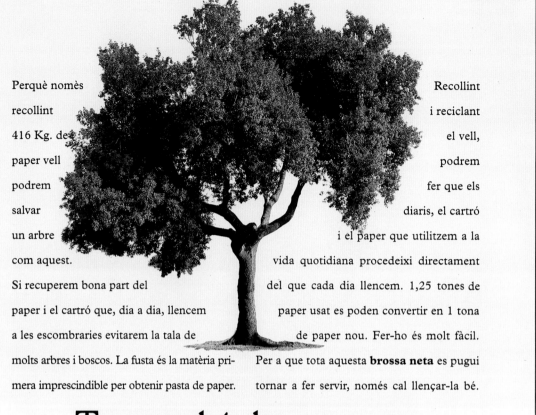

Perquè només recollint 416 Kg. de paper vell podrem salvar un arbre com aquest.

Si recuperem bona part del paper i el cartró que, dia a dia, llencem a les escombraries evitarem la tala de molts arbres i boscos. La fusta és la matèria primera imprescindible per obtenir pasta de paper.

Recollint i reciclant el vell, podrem fer que els diaris, el cartró i el paper que utilitzem a la vida quotidiana procedeixi directament del que cada dia llencem. 1,25 tones de paper usat es poden convertir en 1 tona de paper nou. Fer-ho és molt fàcil. Per a que tota aquesta **brossa neta** es pugui tornar a fer servir, només cal llençar-la bé.

Tractant bé el paper usat, salvarem molts arbres com aquest

JULIOL								AGOST						
DILLUNS	DIMARTS	DIMECRES	DIJOUS	DIVENDRES	DISSABTE	DIUMENGE		DILLUNS	DIMARTS	DIMECRES	DIJOUS	DIVENDRES	DISSABTE	DIUMENGE
1	2	3	4	5	6	7					1	2	3	4
8	9	10	11	12	13	14		5	6	7	8	9	10	11
15	16	17	18	19	20	21		12	13	14	15	16	17	18
22	23	24	25	26	27	28		19	20	21	22	23	24	25
29	30	31						26	27	28	29	30	31	

Brossa neta. Llença-la bé.

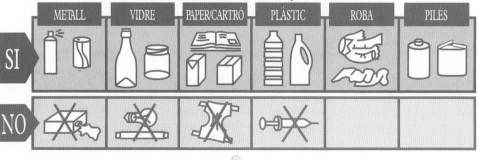

Perquè amb totes les llaunes d'aliments i de begudes, els sprays i la ferralla que normalment llencem a les escombraries encara es poden fer moltes coses. Entre d'altres baranes com aquestes, o nous fanals per a la ciutat i, fins i tot, nous envasos com els que llencem cada dia. Perquè tot aquest metall, si està net -sense restes d'oli o de greix- és reciclable cent per cent. Si el recuperem podrem aconseguir un important estalvi de matèries primeres de les quals som deficitaris. Fer-ho és molt fàcil. Per a que tota aquesta **brossa neta** es pugui tornar a fer servir, només cal llençar-la bé.

Tractant bé el metall usat, ...questes

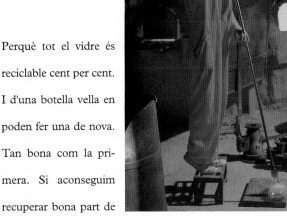

Perquè tot el vidre és reciclable cent per cent. I d'una botella vella en poden fer una de nova. Tan bona com la primera. Si aconseguim recuperar bona part de tot el vidre que, dia a dia, llencem a les escombraries aconseguirem reduir, en bona part, el consum d'energia necessària per fer-ne de nou. Així, podrem millorar el medi ambient i estalviar-nos molts diners. Fer-ho és molt fàcil. Per a que tota aquesta **brossa neta** es pugui tornar a fer servir, només cal llençar-la bé.

Tractant bé el vidre que llencem, el podrem fer servir de nou

Awards: Silver
Program: "DREAMS" Appeal

Client: The Zoological Society of San Diego
Associate Development Directors: Virginia Renehan
  Karen Lloyd-Amos

Agency: Epsilon
Creative Director: Wendy Katz
Account Manager: Janet Lee
Account Manager: Michele Pays
Production Associate: Darlene VanRavenswaay
Designer: Ove Nordenhok, Nordenhok Design

And They Lived Happily Ever After ...

GORILLA TROPIC
Opening March, 1991

The San Diego Zoo needed to raise $200,000 more to complete its long awaited African rain forest habitat, so they sent out this unusual package to members and previous donors. Bearing the theme of making dreams come true, the mailing included a letter with a first person narrative about the inception of the project plus something really special—an adorable actual color photo of the gorillas who would inhabit the new section, with a handwritten thank-you note from the zoo's president clipped on. There was plenty to be grateful for, too, like a 5.4 percent response rate, an average gift of more than $700, and total donations just under $347,000.

The Royal Star & Garter Home
for Disabled Sailors, Soldiers & Airmen
Richmond, Surrey TW10 6RR Tel: 081-940 3314
Patron: Her Majesty The Queen

January 1991

Dear Supporter,

I am writing to you today to tell you about a very special occasion for The Royal Star and Garter Home.

Seventy five years ago, on January 14th 1916, the Home admitted its very first residents, those wounded in the great battles of the First World War.

75 YEARS
of raising support

PAST

Ever since the Home opened in 1916, the residents have been fighting the on-going battle to win more funds and encourage support for their remarkable Home.

Some of the fund-raising ideas in those early days were quite remarkable. There was even a tree-climbing competition for the nurses one year!

The Home's annual Garden Fete and Exhibition of Handicrafts traditionally attracted a crowd of thousands, and it was not uncommon for the Exhibition to be opened by the Royal family or a distinguished celebrity such as Group Captain Douglas Bader.

It was at these events that the residents sold the products they made in the workshop during Occupational Therapy. These included wicker baskets, fishing flies and rugs, with the profits going directly to their 'Home'.

PRESENT

Just as our brave residents have pulled together and fought for our freedom and independence, so their valiant fund-raising efforts on behalf of the Home continue today.

In recent years, resident Charlie Hankins, who lost both his legs in North Africa during World War Two, has travelled the length and breadth of Britain in his vintage hand-propelled invalid carriage, raising many thousands of pounds in sponsorship to help The Royal Star and Garter Home.

But no matter how much residents like Charlie raise to help the Home, it will never be enough to meet the cost of caring, which increases with every passing year.

Nor can it completely meet the cost of refurbishing ageing equipment and improving facilities to make the residents' day-to-day lives more comfortable.

That is why your kind support is so vital for the future of the Home and its residents - especially in this 75th Anniversary Year.

Because you can help make sure the Royal Star and Garter Home is always here to care - just how much we can achieve, depends on your generosity.

Charlie Hankins on his way from Lands End to John O'Groats.

JOIN FALKLANDS VETERAN SIMON WESTON

and celebrate the
75th Birthday

OF THE 'HOME ON THE HILL'

Mrs H Grainger
The Villa
Kinsham
Nr Tewkesbury
Glos GL20 8HS

Mailsort
POSTAGE PAID
PHQ2254

Kindly sponsored by the Racing Pigeon 'Old Comrades' Show.

75 years of loving care

at the 'Home on the Hill'

Award: Silver
Program: 75th Anniversary

Client: Royal Star and Garter Home, *England*

Agency: Chapter One Direct Plc.
Account Manager: Sheila Ritchie
Creative Director: John Rawson
Art Director: Jane Gill
Copywriter: Samantha Cockerton & Simon Robinson
Production Manager: Doug Wilson
Fundraising Manager, RSGH: Ian Lashbrooke

A charity residential home caring for injured ex-servicemen, the Royal Star and Garter faced the problem of soliciting yet more donations from its regular supporters on the home's 75th anniversary. The solution was to send out a moving audio cassette starring a beloved hero of the Falklands War, who recently had toured the home and spoken with actual residents. The result? Donations of $561,000, for a return on investment of 1,750 percent.

Award: Silver
Program: Dog Registration Campaign

Client: RSPCA, *England*

Agency: Brann Direct Marketing
Copywriter: Paul Kitcatt
Art Directors: Judith Chandler, Paul Karpinski

SEVEN DAYS TO LIVE

Please Open

This was the second time the Royal Society for the Prevention of Cruelty to Animals had asked supporters to write to their MP's demanding a dog registration law from an obdurate government led by Mrs. Thatcher. They therefore sent out this mailing, including a forceful letter detailing the sorry fate awaiting stray dogs, a publisher's note from an MP—and a shocking brochure cover that couldn't be ignored. The results can't either: more than 18,000 supporters wrote their MP's, and the RSPCA got within 3 votes of defeating Mrs. Thatcher—the closest margin she ever faced!

WHAT kind of man takes a puppy and punches it, kicks it, and then finishes it off with a hammer?

What kind of man does the same thing again a week later, to the other three puppies in the litter?

RSPCA Inspector Pat Wilson can tell you. He's met such a man.

Mr D. of Bath didn't like the mess his puppies made. One night last April, they annoyed him so much that he started to beat one of them. He didn't stop when it cried and yelped; he didn't stop until it went limp. Then he fetched his hammer and smashed the puppy's skull with a couple of blows.

A week later his girlfriend walked out on him. He phoned her at her sister's and threatened to kill the rest of the puppies if she didn't come back. She refused; so he fetched his hammer again. On the kitchen step, one by one, he beat the puppies' brains out.

Inspector Wilson caught Mr D., and wouldn't believe his lies about what had happened to the puppies. He obtained a confession, then he stood beside Mr D. as he dug the shattered bodies of the puppies from their garden grave.

The Inspector later said: "During the 10 years that I have been an RSPCA Inspector, I have had to deal with virtually every form of cruelty. But none of the cases I have dealt with compare with this."

Mr D. was sentenced to four months in prison, and banned for life from keeping a cat or dog.

 RSPCA

CONVICTED for bludgeoning four puppies to death with a hammer

You should see some of the animals we have to deal with

 RSPCA

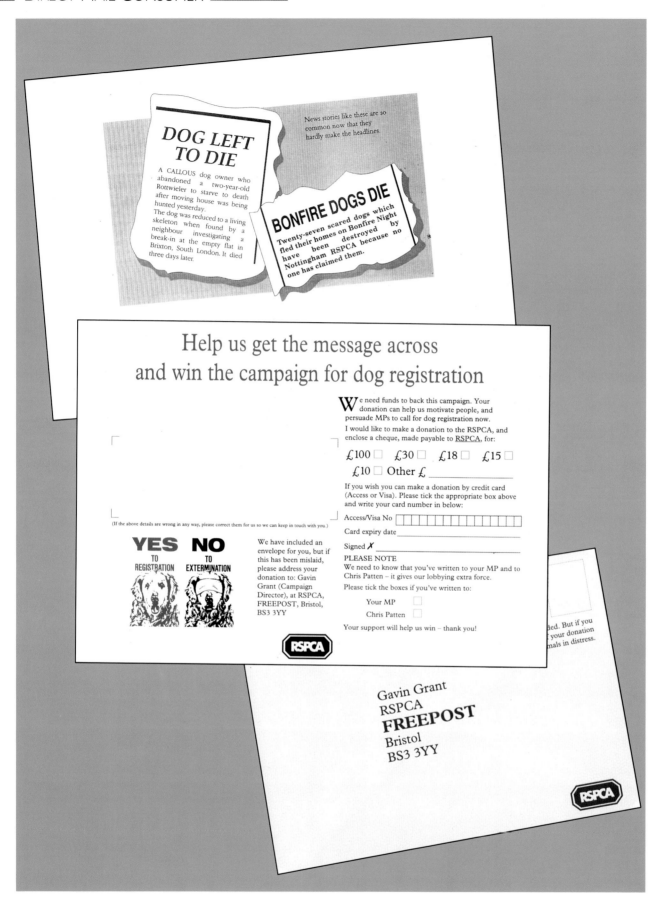

News stories like these are so common now that they hardly make the headlines.

DOG LEFT TO DIE

A CALLOUS dog owner who abandoned a two-year-old Rottwieler to starve to death after moving house was being hunted yesterday.

The dog was reduced to a living skeleton when found by a neighbour investigating a break-in at the empty flat in Brixton, South London. It died three days later.

BONFIRE DOGS DIE

Twenty-seven scared dogs which fled their homes on Bonfire Night have been destroyed by Nottingham RSPCA because no one has claimed them.

Help us get the message across and win the campaign for dog registration

We need funds to back this campaign. Your donation can help us motivate people, and persuade MPs to call for dog registration now.

I would like to make a donation to the RSPCA, and enclose a cheque, made payable to RSPCA, for:

£100 ☐   £30 ☐   £18 ☐   £15 ☐

£10 ☐   Other £ _____

If you wish you can make a donation by credit card (Access or Visa). Please tick the appropriate box above and write your card number in below:

Access/Visa No ☐☐☐☐☐☐☐☐☐☐☐☐☐☐☐☐

Card expiry date _____

Signed ✗ _____

PLEASE NOTE
We need to know that you've written to your MP and to Chris Patten – it gives our lobbying extra force.

Please tick the boxes if you've written to:

Your MP ☐

Chris Patten ☐

Your support will help us win – thank you!

(If the above details are wrong in any way, please correct them for us so we can keep in touch with you.)

YES TO REGISTRATION   **NO** TO EXTERMINATION

We have included an envelope for you, but if this has been mislaid, please address your donation to: Gavin Grant (Campaign Director), at RSPCA, FREEPOST, Bristol, BS3 3YY

RSPCA

...ded. But if you ...your donation ...mals in distress.

Gavin Grant
RSPCA
FREEPOST
Bristol
BS3 3YY

RSPCA

Award: Bronze
Program: Convictions Mailing

Client: RSPCA, *England*

Agency: Brann Direct Marketing
Copywriter: Paul Kitcatt
Art Director: Judith Chandler

In a year when all charity donations fell by a third, the Royal Society for the Prevention of Cruelty to Animals needed a powerful appeal to stand apart from other animal welfare charities. Realizing their problem was people, not animals, the Society sent out this mailing citing the kind of animals they had to deal with—the animal abusers. The package pulled a remarkable 15 percent, raising more than $330,000.

Award: Leader
Program: August Appeal

Client: World Vision
Project Director: Nancy Kyle

Agency: Russ Reid Company
Copywriter: Doug Brendel
Art Directors: Dona Cohan, Theresa Crooks
Creative Director: Bruce Ortman
Project Director: Amy Hunter

How do you request an additional contribution from sponsors who were already giving a monthly amount to care for a child? World Vision did it by sending out this inexpensive ShapeMaker tracing toy, which the sponsor was asked to sign and return for the child; the additional contribution was positioned as another way to express love and concern. The results were very gratifying, with a 35.6 percent response rate yielding total contributions of more than $870,000 and beating the previous year's response rate by 291 percent.

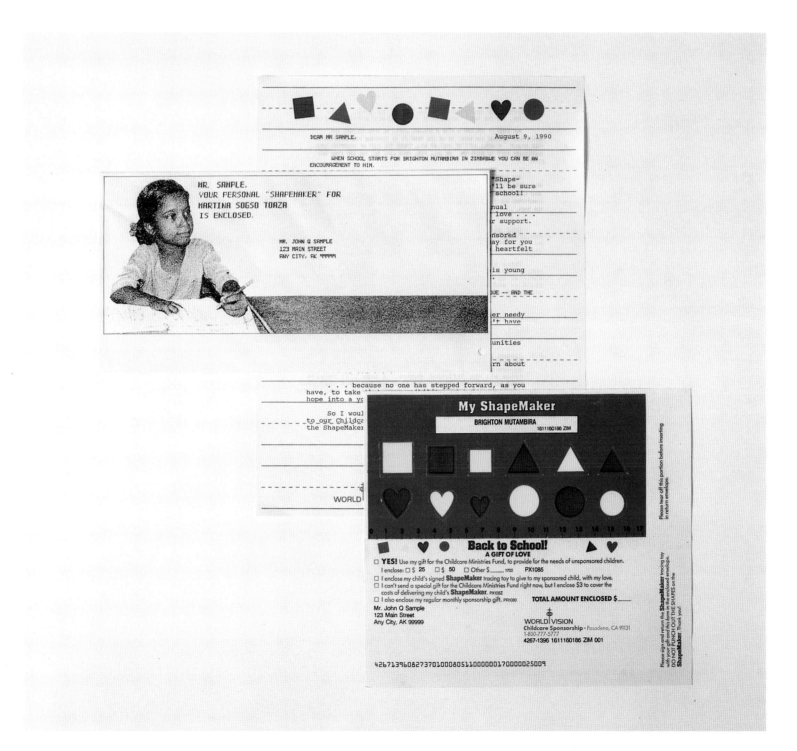

Award: Leader
Program: Doggie Pack

Client: National Canine Defence League, *England*
Fundraising Manager: Clarissa Baldwin

Agency: Chapter One Direct Plc.
Account Director: Mary Wilson
Creative Director: John Rawson
Art Director: Shaun Crawford
Copywriter: Helen Charlton
Production Manager: Doug Wilson

The one-to-one impact of direct mail powered this appeal for England's National Canine Defence League, thanks to the inclusion of a letter offering an emotional first-person account of a dog rescue and a handwritten, annotated photocopy of press clippings. The mailing pulled more than 8,000 responses, with an average donation of $35, achieving a return on investment of 1,000 percent.

THE PERFECT MOMENT
TO JOIN THE ICA

Calla Lily, 1984 © The Estate of Robert Mapplethorpe

Tulips, 1984 © The Estate of Robert Mapplethorpe

Self Portrait, 1980 © The Estate of Robert Mapplethorpe

Self Portrait, 1980 © The Estate of Robert Mapplethorpe

Award: Leader
Program: ICA: The Perfect Moment

Client: The Institute of Contemporary Art
Client Contact: Arthur Cohen

Agency: Ingalls, Quinn & Johnson
Agency Contact: Martha Bush
Account Executive: Nadia Belash
Copy: Evan Stone
Art: Candace Kuss

For their annual membership solicitation, Boston's Institute of Contemporary Art decided to exploit the upcoming show which had inspired such controversy, *Robert Mapplethorpe: The Perfect Moment.* Showing that a self-mailer can be strikingly attractive, the museum sent out this barrelfold piece announcing the show, showing samples of the work, and suggesting the benefits of joining the ICA. The response is something to admire as well: more than 11 percent, beating the previous campaign by 300 percent.

Every day, living animals are treated worse than apples

An apple's flesh suffers bruising and damage easily.
So it is handled very tenderly on its way from the farm to the shop.
But how gently are <u>live animals</u> handled?

Photo courtesy of Peter Nicholls, Today Newspaper.

It must stop now

Award: Leader
Program: Live Transportation

Client: RSPCA, *England*

Agency: Brann Direct Marketing
Copywriters: Paul Kitcatt, Kristian Sumners
Art Directors: Judith Chandler, Natalie Ash Daniels
Account Handler: Stephen Pidgeon

Britain's Royal Society for the Prevention of Cruelty to Animals had a problem depicting the suffering caused by live transportation: few still photos were available. Thus the Society sent out this two-part mailing, relying on the image of the apple to suggest that fruit is transported with more care than animals—and using stills from a video to dramatize the horror. The response was a gratifying 10.6 and 13.2 percent for the two mailings, raising total contributions of more than $850,000.

some spec...
Shetla...

coast.
know w.
gatheri

Thou...
razorbill...
of noise a...
them, the a...
or more.

To these ...
of each year i...
all year round.

A tragedy of...

For many years ... erned at the
growing problems a...

We have proteste... ...ave been polluted by the
dumping of raw sewage... continued discharge of lead,
zinc, copper, mercury ... ...oxins such as DDT and PCBs.

Throughout the world grave fears have been expressed at
the exploitation of some fish stocks - and the disastrous
effects this may have for our magnificent seabird colonies.

Now our birds are dying.

We must act before it is too late - and avert a disaster
of truly tragic proportions.

After years of poor breeding
success, numbers of arctic terns
breeding in Shetland have
already fallen by 75%.

Kittiwakes, arctic skuas and
puffins are also suffering.
While further south, our British
Isles population of roseate
terns face almost certain
extinction, (perhaps by the year
2000) if urgent action isn't
taken soon. These beautiful and
graceful birds have now suffered
a fall from 2,500 breeding pairs in 1970, to just 470 pairs
in 1988.

Help prevent the disaster.

So what can we do?

Sadly, no one knows for sure exactly what has caused such

...n the numbers of these breeding seabirds.
...thousands of their young have died
...on.

...prevent the disaster.

...t of a co-ordinated campaign of action we are
...g the government to
...greater steps to protect
these birds and fulfil its
obligations under EC
directives.

We are fighting to have
the feeding sites as well
as the nesting sites of
our endangered seabirds
declared as conservation
areas.

We are funding research
vital to the success of
future recovery
strategies.

We are pressing for a complete ban on sandeel
fishing in Shetland to give stocks their last
chance of recovery.

On top of all of this, we are funding our own research
projects at home and abroad to determine why these birds are
suffering such an appalling fall in their numbers. We are
also seeking to buy more nature reserves to help ensure the
future safety of their vital breeding sites within these
shores.

The costs are considerable, but we cannot turn away from
these urgent works - too many lives depend upon our success.

Once again, your generous support is essential.

I know many of you have given in the past, and you
have my most grateful thanks. But
if you can find a way to give
again, please do.

£30,000 a year is urgently
needed to fund research into
the Shetland seabird disaster
so that we can be sure of the
cause, and how best to take
action.

£25,000 a year will enable us
to expand our efforts to
persuade government to fulfil
its obligations under EC law,
and will help us continue the

Award: Leader
Program: Marine Appeal

Client: Royal Society for the Protection of Birds, *England*

Agency: Watson, Ward, Albert,
Varndell (WWAV) Limited
Art Director: Gordon McKee
Copywriter: Ivan Palmer
Account Director: Allan Freeman

To boost contributions in its latest quarterly appeal, the Royal Society for the Protection of Birds focused on a particular appeal—the plight of Shetland seabirds—by including a a Shetland officer's short firsthand account "clipped" to the main letter. In addition, incentives were offered to raise the amount of the average donation—an RSPB credit card holder for donations above £25 and an RSPB pen for donations above £100. The promotion flew, pulling 7 percent and beating the previous campaign by 77 percent, with donations averaging £17.

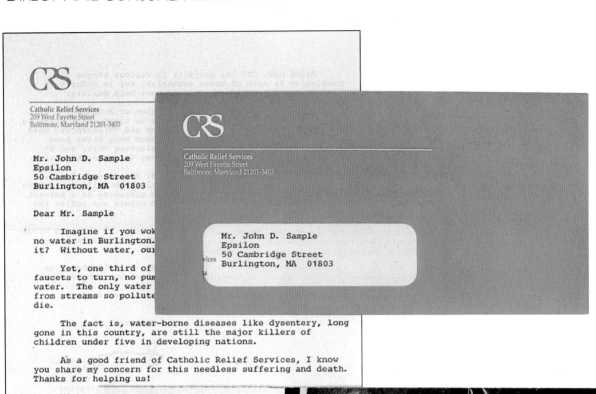

CRS

Catholic Relief Services
209 West Fayette Street
Baltimore, Maryland 21201-3403

Mr. John D. Sample
Epsilon
50 Cambridge Street
Burlington, MA 01803

Dear Mr. Sample

    Imagine if you wok
no water in Burlington.
it? Without water, our

    Yet, one third of
faucets to turn, no pum
water. The only water
from streams so pollute
die.

    The fact is, water-borne diseases like dysentery, long
gone in this country, are still the major killers of
children under five in developing nations.

    As a good friend of Catholic Relief Services, I know
you share my concern for this needless suffering and death.
Thanks for helping us!

    Without
development
gravity-flov
faucet syste

    Many ne
pipeline. Y
water of li:
world.

    In the
Longer Life
families anc
and the Phi:

CRS

Catholic Relief Services
209 West Fayette Street
Baltimore, Maryland 21201-3403

Mr. John D. Sample
Epsilon
50 Cambridge Street
Burlington, MA 01803

Without It, there is no LIFE

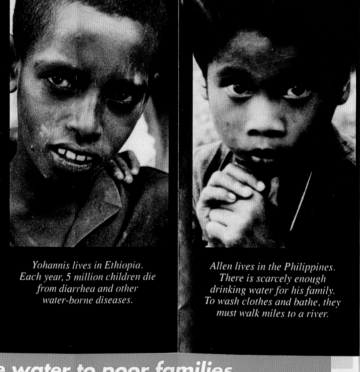

*Yohannis lives in Ethiopia.
Each year, 5 million children die
from diarrhea and other
water-borne diseases.*

*Allen lives in the Philippines.
There is scarcely enough
drinking water for his family.
To wash clothes and bathe, they
must walk miles to a river.*

e water to poor families

Award: Leader
Program: Water of Life

Client: Catholic Relief Services

Agency: Epsilon
Account Manager: Cathy DiFranco
Creative Director: Dick Murdock
Copywriter: Bette Boughton
Art: Tom Tringale
Production: Eileen Macrae

While Catholic Relief Services is primarily known for disaster relief programs, their water projects are just as critical. To raise money for the latter, the organization sent out a letter to previous donors personalized with the recipient's name, address, prior giving, and town—and including a brochure which personalized the problem by showing four children in four towns whose water the CRS had improved. The result was a 7 percent response, yielding more than $600,000 in donations at a cost per response of just 11¢!

Award: Leader
Program: Here's What You Won't Get from Ducks Unlimited.

Client: Ducks Unlimited, Inc.

Agency: In-house
Concept Creation: John Cummuta
Copywriting: John Cummuta
Graphic Design and Art Direction: Michael DiFrisco

To stand out from other conservation and sportsman organizations jumping on the "green" bandwagon, Ducks Unlimited—America's leading wetlands conservation organization—sent out this mailing stressing its seriousness of purpose. Promising "what you *won't* get from Ducks Unlimited…" and listing such typical premiums as a shooter's cap and tote bag, the mailing emphasized how much your membership dollar *would* get, including 80¢ devoted solely to wildlife habitat preservation. The promotion garnered more than $170,000 in sales, with the lifetime value of new members projected to be upwards of $1 million.

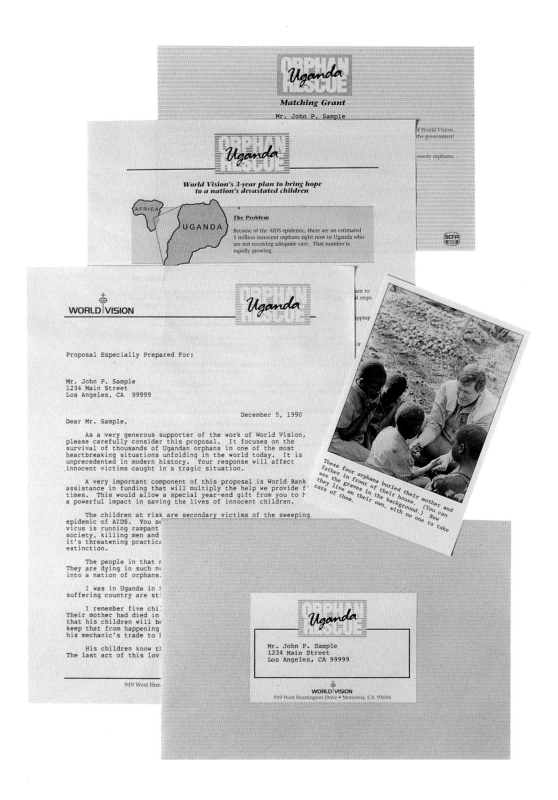

Award: Leader
Program: Orphan Rescue Mission

Client: World Vision
Project Director: Peter Torry

Agency: Russ Reid Company
Copywriter: David Withers
Art Directors: Michelle Parnell-Counts
    Theresa Crooks
Creative Director: Bruce Ortman
Project Director: Amy Hunter

World Vision is a Christian international relief and development agency. They needed desperately to raise funds to help children orphaned by the AIDS epidemic in Uganda but questioned whether their conservative donor base would respond to an appeal based on this controversial subject. The solution was to target only major donors with this businesslike proposal format, including a tempered but moving letter detailing firsthand descriptions of the situation. The response was a dramatic 13.9 percent, yielding donations of more than $680,000 at an average contribution of $730, beating previous average total contributions by 434 percent.

Award: Bronze
Program: Corporate Christmas Card Mailing
Client: UNICEF-UK, *England*
Fundraising Manager: Della Weight

Agency: Chapter One Direct Plc.
Account Director: Pauline Trevallion
Creative Director: John Rawson
Art Director: Caron Brisley
Copywriter: Daren Kay
Production Manager: Doug Wilson

The UK Committee of the United Nations Children's Fund relies on voluntary donations and the profits from its card catalogs to fund its work. The main challenge confronting the organization as it promoted its Christmas cards to corporations was to combine a pragmatic commercial message—these are good quality cards at a good price—with a charitable message about its work for children. The result of this mailing was a response rate of 34 percent, producing total sales of $340,000 at an average sale of $200, for a return on investment of 1,400 percent.

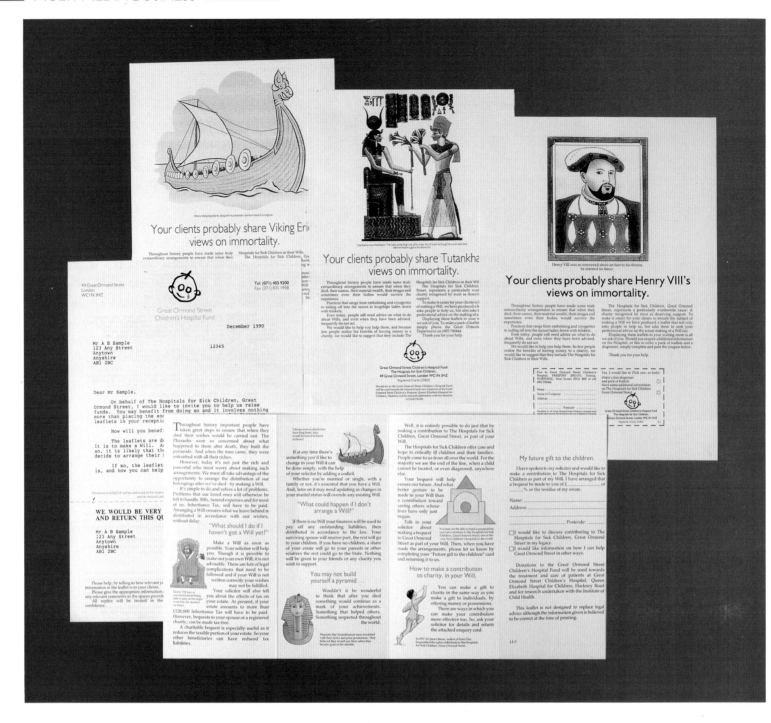

Award: Leader
Program: Legacy Campaign

Client: The Hospitals for Sick Children, *England*

Agency: Amherst Direct Marketing Ltd.
Account Director: Angela Walledge
Account Manager: Colleen Johnson
Creative Director: Jim Brackin
Art Director: Louise Thomas
Copywriter: Chris Stanley

To increase donations to the Great Ormond Street Children's Hospital charity, this print and mail campaign was targeted to lawyers and accountants, who were requested to display take-ones in their waiting rooms encouraging clients to make out legacies to the hospital. To date, the response rate has been more than 5 percent, with more than £54,000 in legacy pledges received.

Award: Silver
Program: Strike Back

Client: The Massachusetts Department of Environmental Protection

Agency: Orsatti & Parrish
Creative Director: Frank Parrish
Copywriter: Burr Johnson
Art Director: Lysle Wickersham
Photographer: Mike Ryan
Account Executive: Elaine Goetz

To encourage fearful employees to blow the whistle on their polluting employers, these hard-hitting transit posters equated the pollution portrayed with the moral turpitude of the polluters. The result has been a considerable increase in calls to the Fight Back hotline, which now average 30–40 a day instead of the 8–10 a week before the campaign broke.

Give us what you pay for this each week, and we'll help a teenager stay sober.

The next time you head to Old Town after work, consider this: The cost of one beer a week could buy a teenager 6 hours of substance abuse counseling. This year, please give a day's salary to the United Way. You won't believe how much it can do.

So Much Depends On You.

Pick up one less cup a day to help a homeless person put one down forever.

If you gave the United Way the fifty cents you pay for coffee each morning, we could give a homeless person food and shelter for eight days. Imagine that. You get a little less jittery. And the homeless get something amazing: a home. Won't you please contribute a day's salary to the United Way? It can do so much.

So Much Depends On You.

Award: Silver
Program: 1990 Chapman Direct United Way Campaign

Client: United Way

Agency: Chapman Direct Advertising
Creative Supervisor: Scott Stagg
Art Director: Abbe Eckstein
Sr. VP, Director of Client Services: Rosemary O'Brien
Account Executive: Mary Taffuri

Computer Systems Specialist: Cynthia Carpenter
Linotronic Output: Microcomputer Publishing Center, Inc.

To increase participation in the United Way among Chapman Direct employees, a multi-media program was assembled, including paycheck wraps, voice-mail reminders—and these striking dimensional posters dramatizing the low cost and great rewards of a contribution. The result was an increase of 234 percent over the previous year's campaign, with Chapman achieving the highest participation rate within the advertising community for 1990–1991.

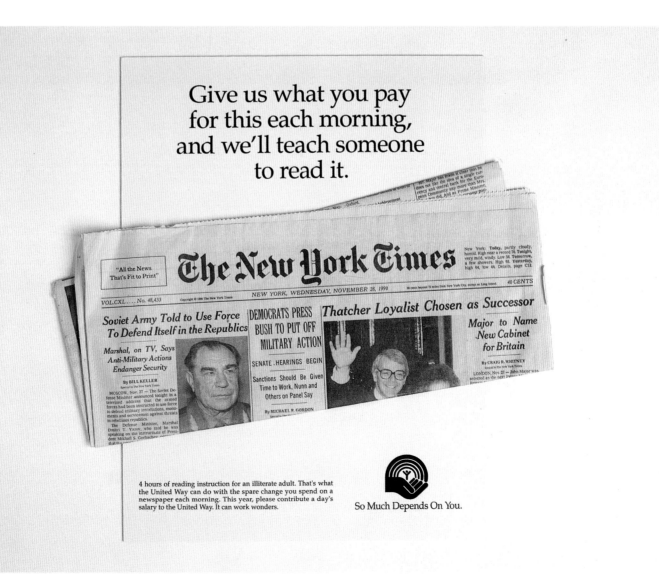

Give us what you pay for this each morning, and we'll teach someone to read it.

4 hours of reading instruction for an illiterate adult. That's what the United Way can do with the spare change you spend on a newspaper each morning. This year, please contribute a day's salary to the United Way. It can work wonders.

So Much Depends On You.

Chapter

4

Publishing Products & Services

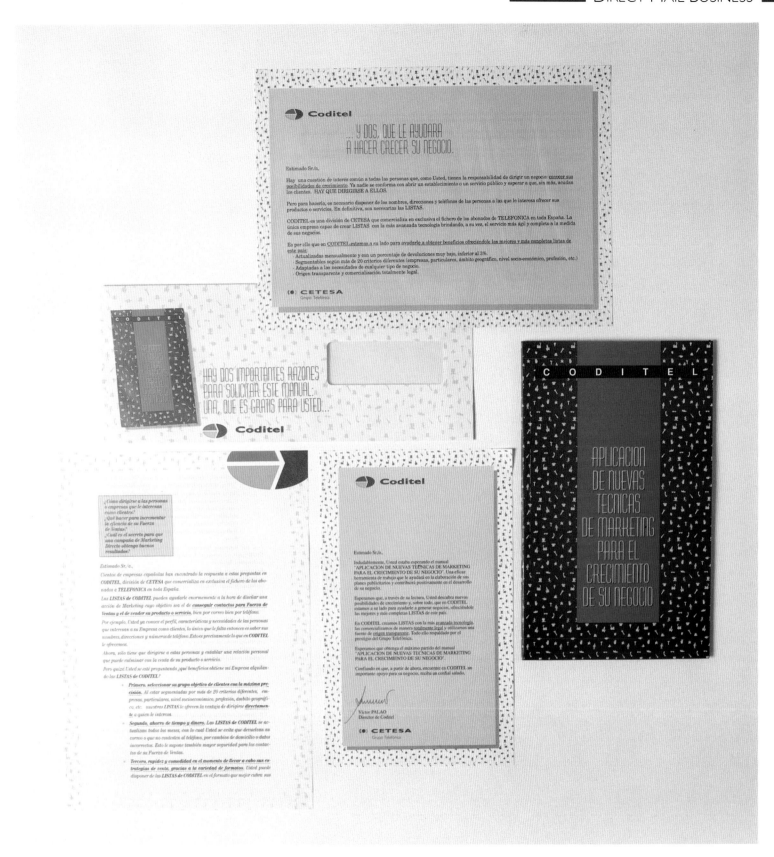

Award: Bronze
Program: Direct Marketing Manual

Client: CETESA-CODITEL, *Spain*
Amador Gonzalez Oblos, Victor Palau

Agency: Ogilvy & Mather Direct , Madrid
José Manuel Oyarzun

The problem facing list broker Coditel was its target audience's lack of understanding of the benefits and services a list broker can offer. The solution was to offer a free Direct Marketing Manual explaining in detail how a company could apply direct marketing techniques to improve their business, including, of course, selecting the appropriate databases from Coditel. The result was a 12 percent response rate, with a 58 percent conversion, producing more than $663,000 in sales.

Award: Silver
Program: Sweepstakes Promotion

Client: Gamepro Magazine
Publisher: Patrick Ferrel

Agency: Jordan-Savage Direct
President: Peter Savage
Executive VP, Creative Director: Dwight Ingram
Copywriter: Steven Cappellano
Art Director: Max Sewell
VP, Account Services: Sue Hadley
Production Manager: Felice Weinberg

Moore Direct Response:
Sweeps Prizes and Administration: Bill Cullen
    Linda Huntoon, Walter Karl

How do you reach a target audience as young as 10, get them to buy your offer—and pay for it? *Gamepro* Magazine did it with this lively sweepstakes promotion, which used graphics and involvement devices right out of the readers' favorite video games. The result beat the control by 75 percent, with a 9.43 percent response rate and a cost per response of just $4.10.

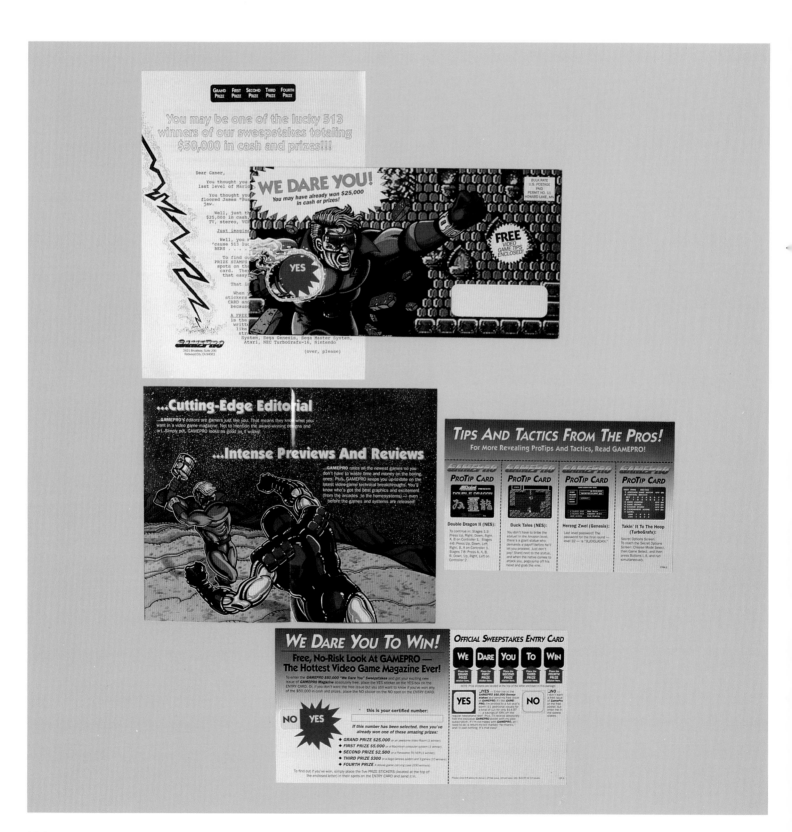

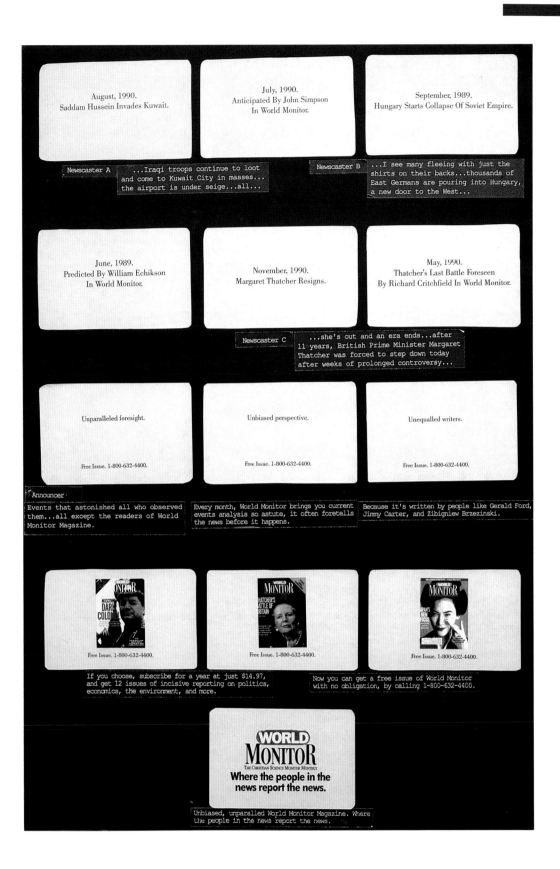

August, 1990.
Saddam Hussein Invades Kuwait.

July, 1990.
Anticipated By John Simpson
In World Monitor.

September, 1989.
Hungary Starts Collapse Of Soviet Empire.

Newscaster A ...Iraqi troops continue to loot and come to Kuwait City in masses... the airport is under seige...all...

Newscaster B ...I see many fleeing with just the shirts on their backs...thousands of East Germans are pouring into Hungary, a new door to the West...

June, 1989.
Predicted By William Echikson
In World Monitor.

November, 1990.
Margaret Thatcher Resigns.

May, 1990.
Thatcher's Last Battle Foreseen
By Richard Critchfield In World Monitor.

Newscaster C ...she's out and an era ends...after 11 years, British Prime Minister Margaret Thatcher was forced to step down today after weeks of prolonged controversy...

Unparalleled foresight.

Free Issue. 1-800-632-4400.

Unbiased perspective.

Free Issue. 1-800-632-4400.

Unequalled writers.

Free Issue. 1-800-632-4400.

Announcer
Events that astonished all who observed them...all except the readers of World Monitor Magazine.

Every month, World Monitor brings you current events analysis so astute, it often foretells the news before it happens.

Because it's written by people like Gerald Ford, Jimmy Carter, and Zibigniew Brzezinski.

Free Issue. 1-800-632-4400.

Free Issue. 1-800-632-4400.

Free Issue. 1-800-632-4400.

If you choose, subscribe for a year at just $14.97, and get 12 issues of incisive reporting on politics, economics, the environment, and more.

Now you can get a free issue of World Monitor with no obligation, by calling 1-800-632-4400.

WORLD MONITOR
THE CHRISTIAN SCIENCE MONITOR MONTHLY
Where the people in the news report the news.

Unbiased, unparalled World Monitor Magazine. Where the people in the news report the news.

Award: Silver
Program: Iraq

Client: World Monitor Magazine

Agency: Orsatti & Parrish
Creative Director: Frank Parrish
Copywriter: Burr Johnson
Art Director: Lysle Wickersham
Broadcast Producer: Paul Shannon
Management Supervisor: NancyJane Goldston
Account Executive: Elaine Goetz

Less than two years old, *World Monitor* Magazine had very little awareness among its well-informed target audience, in large part due to an offer-driven campaign. The solution, which exceeded response objectives by 130 percent and reduced cost per acquisition from $39 to $23.60, was to run a topical spot positioning the magazine as a news source so astute it foretold world events before they happened—including Saddam Hussein invading Kuwait.

Award: Bronze
Program: The Doctors Book of Home Remedies

Client: Rodale Press Books
President, Book Division: Pat Corpora
Group Marketing Manager: Brian Carnahan
Creative Director: Lynn Gavett
Associate Mail Order Marketing Manager: Linda Paist
Sr. Account Manager Client Services: Grace Paulnack
Editor-In-Chief: Bill Gottlieb

Agency: Shain/Colavito/Pensabene Direct, Inc.
President: Joseph Shain
VP, Broadcast Supervisor: Rosemary Jesward
Account Executive: Aileen Stickley

Production Company:
Writer/Director: Alan Bernhard
Producer: Joanne Silverman

Dispelling the idea that one-shot book offers can't succeed on television, this spot featured the Editor-In-Chief of Rodale Press Books reading samples from the Doctors Book of Home Remedies to establish credibility and promote interest. Running five months on spot stations and the major cable networks, the spot pulled more than 490,000 responses at a cost per response of under $7, generating more than $12 million in sales.

GOTTLIEB: How can you stop a throbbing toothache? Massage your hand with ice. How do you cure poison ivy? Try oatmeal.

GOTTLIEB: How do I know these cures really work? Because my staff and I spent months interviewing doctors and health professionals to bring you this incredible book, The Doctors Book of Home Remedies.

GOTTLIEB: I'm Bill Gottlieb, Editor in Chief, and after writing about health for over 14 years, I can assure you there has never been a more complete and practical encyclopedia of home healing techniques than The Doctors Book of Home Remedies.

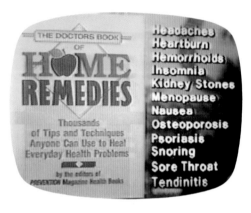

GOTTLIEB: Over 670 pages, 2,300 remedies, covering over 130 different health problems.

ANNCR: Call now for the Doctors Book of Home Remedies. Try it absolutely free for 21 days. If you choose to keep it, we'll bill you in 3 easy installments of only $8.98.

GOTTLIEB: And as a free gift, you'll also get this Meals That Heal Cookbook.

ANNCR: Remember, you can try The Doctors Book of Home Remedies free for 21 days. And the Meals That Heal Cookbook is yours to keep. Call 1-800-468-4600. That's 1-800-468-4600.

Award: Bronze
Program: Prodigy Campaign

Client: Dow Jones News/Retrieval
Senior Advertising Coordinator: Annie Kressaty

Agency: Look Creative Group; a department of Prodigy
    Services Company
Account Executive: Laura Brady
Artist: Jocelyn Fredrics
Copywriter: Debbie Dubin
Producer: Peter Abbate
Copy Manager: Karen Belove
Producer Manager: Robert Bossert
Creative Manager: Tim Walston
Account Executive Manager: Heidi Schwartz
Creative Director, Look Creative Group: Jennifer Carney
Director, Direct Response Marketing: Lynn Brannigan

To promote its online computer services, Dow
Jones News/Retrieval chose to advertise online,
on the Prodigy service. The problem was conveying the benefits of a complex service within the
confines of five computer screens, plus nine
open-up windows. Using colorful icons and a
menu system already familiar to Prodigy members, the advertising has proven remarkably
successful, producing 100 percent more leads and
orders than the client had experienced before,
for a total of more than 7,500 responses at a cost
per response of just $1.67.

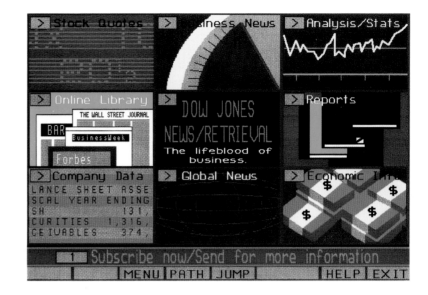

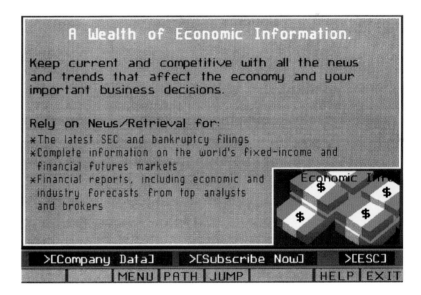

Award: Leader
Program: Take-A-Ride

Client: Home Box Office, Inc.

Agency: Kobs & Draft Advertising
Account Service: Chris Madden
Creative Supervisor/Copywriter: Steve Pimsler
Art Direction: Ted Eyes
Animation: Lamb & Company, Doros

Pay TV growth was flat, and the share of new cable TV homes ordering pay TV services was declining. To meet profit goals and maintain their consumer franchise, HBO and Cinemax pay cable services ran this spot promising all the thrills and excitement of a roller coaster when the respondent ordered the services with cable TV. Possibly the first computer-animated direct response spot, it broke new ground in results as well, pulling 112,000 orders at a cost per response of $14.70, exceeding goals by 13 percent.

Award: Gold
Program: "Book Clubs Can Be Hell" Print Campaign

Client: Quality Paperback Book Club

Agency: Ogilvy & Mather Direct
Creative Group Head: Tina Cohoe
Copy Supervisor: Niall Kelly
Art Supervisor: Michael Rosenbaum
Copywriter: Heather Higgins
Art Director: Steve Keltz
Account Supervisor: Carolyn McGee
Account Executive: Amy Rosenkrantz

Employing Matt Groening's decidedly non-traditional cartoons, this ad series for the decidedly non-traditional Quality Paperback Book Club reached out to a fresh audience of book-club "non-joiners"—and lifted response by as much as 21 percent, where an 8 percent lift is considered a winner.

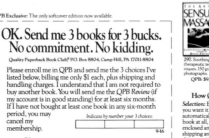

Award: Silver
Program: He May Already Be A Winner
Client: Riccelli Direct, Inc.

Agency: Riccelli Direct, Inc.
President: Richard Riccelli
Writer: Rob Charm

The problem Riccelli Direct had was explaining what they did to potential clients. Recognizing that most other agencies' brochures sounded alike, blowing their own horns, Riccelli hired an outside business writer to work up this piece on the agency—and promoted the fact on the cover. The results were nothing to cover up, generating five new clients for sales of $75,000 at a total cost of just $8,500.

HE MAY ALREADY BE A WINNER

*Richard Riccelli writes junk mail for a living.
But send no money now . . . he'll be happy to bill you later.*

BY ROB CHARM

IN THE COLDEST MONTH, THE MAILBOX IS JAMMED WITH "COLD mail" from magazines. In January, by the dozens, come the big envelopes with messages on the outside. *The New Republic:* "Can you be tough, hard and liberal?" *Harper's:* "The myth of missing children." *Town & Country:* "Sense elegance." *Automobile:* "Win a Corvette." *National Geographic:* "10 pictures you'll never forget." *Playboy:* "50 Beautiful Women...Free."

And that's *subtle* compared with the sweepstakes packages. Big thick envelopes crammed with "You May Already Be A Winner" letters, prize brochures touting houses and yachts, $10,000,000.00 checks [exact to the penny] made out to "Your Name Here," Ed McMahon leering everywhere...

On this winter's morning, Richard Riccelli's mailbox is full of junk mail and he, of course, looks forward to it.

He opens a sweepstakes envelope and a pile of direct mail detritus builds on his carpet. Coupons, stick-em tokens, specimen checks...

"Every year they seem to enclose more pieces," Riccelli says. "I guess they assume you open the envelope and all this stuff falls at your feet; you have to *deal* with it. It's like a spider web. You're involved." He laughs at the vision of some "occupant" who sends back an order in pure self-defense. Anything to get a response is fair play. This, above all, Riccelli appreciates.

He gathers this pile of what some call "direct marketing," some call "direct response," others call "direct mail," but what he, with a smile, calls "junk mail."

Then he goes upstairs to create some more.

YOU, TOO, CAN EARN BIG BUCKS IN DIRECT MAIL....

NEARLY 15,000 MAGA-zines are published in the United States. 400 new ones are launched every year. And every one of them has a circulation director sweating out how to get the damn thing into the hands of more readers.

Their most important weapon is direct mail. A creative, compelling "cold mail" package—the envelope, letter, offer, reply card, and involvement device —that can launch a new magazine, drive an established one, or revive a fading star. But a cold mail package that misses the mark is just like mailing money to the garbage cans of America.

No matter how good the current—or "control"— cold mail package, the circulation director is always searching for a new one that pulls better at less cost. Finding it isn't easy.

Part of the problem is the medium. Anything called "junk mail" doesn't get much respect. It looks easy to create. Its apparent simplicity [see *The Making*

of a Mail Package] has convinced hundreds of would-be's that they, too, can put together a package that pulls. A recent *Writer's Digest* cover story "taught" beginners how to make "big bucks writing direct mail." Circulation directors cringed anticipating what they'd soon see in *their* mailboxes.

"In the last year or so, the field has become very competitive," says David Gianatasio, a reporter for *Adweek.* "Because there've been so many layoffs at [advertising] agencies, you have a lot of freelancers trying direct mail. They aren't making much money. I don't know how good their work is."

A notch above, from a creative standpoint, is the stuff generated by full-service advertising agencies. Although virtually all agencies claim to "do direct marketing," this can often mean nothing more than one of their juniors writing something up, and putting it in the mail. In the hierarchy of ad agencies, direct mail writers are one step up from the mailroom and one step away from the elevator down.

As a result, experienced circulation professionals turn to independent creative specialists who are passionate about the power of direct mail.

Superstars in the field—Bill Jayme, Hank Burnett, Henry Cowen, maybe a dozen more— enjoy incomes in the high six figures. They create cold mail packages for big name magazines or well-bankrolled startups. They command fees in excess of $20,000 plus royalties for a basic package...if you can get them.

"You don't 'hire' them," said the circulation manager of a major national science magazine. "They decide whether they *want* to be hired."

Which means circulation managers are always hunting for breakthrough packages from up-and-coming creatives ready to challenge the big guys.

They're looking for talents like Richard Riccelli. And Riccelli is looking for them. "I figured the best way to be 'discovered' was to beat a few of their controls," Riccelli said. "Response gets response."

never amount to much. As he flipped through the pages, it clicked.

This is what starting a business was all about. Going up against the nay-sayers, all those in-laws and bankers and "experts" so eager to shoot down an entrepreneur's dream.

And starting and building a business was what *Inc.* magazine was all about. Readers are drawn to *Inc.* because in its pages, if no where else, there are people telling that entrepreneur "it *can* be done...and here's how to do it."

Riccelli had an idea.

Take a 9 x 12-inch envelope and run ten of the biggest whoppers pulled from *The Experts Speak.*

"This fellow Lindbergh will *never make it.*" So said Harry Guggenheim, the millionaire aviation enthusiast in 1927...

"*Forget it Louis, no Civil War picture ever made a nickel.*" So said an MGM executive recommending that Louis B. Mayer not bid for the film rights to *Gone With The Wind*...

"*We don't like their sound. Groups of guitars are on the way out.*" So said a Decca recording executive, turning down the Beatles in 1962...

Then Riccelli wrote a headline to run with the quotes: *They said it couldn't be done. But they didn't know you.*

Well, there it was, the perfect message to reach the perfect *Inc.* reader—an entrepreneur trying against all odds, to get a fledgling business off the ground.

the first time in six years, it has a shot of beating *Inc.* magazine's control postcard.

"It's the best package I've seen us do through anyone," says LaPointe. "I wouldn't be surprised if it became our new control."

And that, he says, is the sort of success that should get prizes from one end of the direct marketing business to the other.

"Unfortunately," LaPointe says, "Direct marketing awards are not given on results. They're based on look and feel, because no circulation manager wants to reveal any real numbers."

So Riccelli pulls off the greatest success of his career and ends up facing that old question from Philosophy 101: If a tree falls in a forest...

CONGRATULATIONS...

BUSINESS WAS GOOD THROUGH THE NEXT 12 months. Riccelli produced a variety of efforts for *Inc.* magazine. A new billing and renewal series. A Christmas gift subscription program. Coupon ads for *Inc.'s* videos and books. He created new cold mail packages for *BusinessMonth* and *CFO* magazines. He helped launch *P.S.* a new Patricia Seybold technology newsletter and *SportBoston,* the second of a national network of regional sports magazines. Wraps, blow-ins, television—he even wrote in Chinese to help *World Executive's Digest* sell more subscriptions.

And the money was great. He grossed over $200,000 for the year.

But he wasn't getting a crack at the big national magazines.

So in January, as his mailbox filled with cold mail he didn't create, Riccelli entered his *Inc.* package in the *Folio:* Magazine Publishers of America [MPA] 1990 Circulation Direct Marketing Awards competition.

Two months later, a letter arrives: "Dear Richard, Congratulations. Your entry has been selected as a finalist..."

It was from *Folio:* MPA. They wanted him to come and find out if he won at the awards luncheon in New York in April.

That's right. They were using—how else to look at it?—the classic junk mail come-on.

You may already be a winner.

It worked, too.

ABOUT THE WRITER

Rob Charm has written for *Autoweek, The Boston Globe, Detroit Monthly* and *New England Business* on subjects as diverse as "Domino's" pizza-magnate Tom Monaghan, "Spenser" author Robert Parker, and Detroit "Lions" football team owner, scion William Clay Ford. Charm lives and works in Wellesley, Massachusetts.

Chapter

5

Manufacturing/ Wholesaling

Chrysler Corporation has responded to your needs by developing a quick way to help increase your service traffic during slow periods. It's called "Call Friday"... and it works with a single phone call! For some interesting details on "Call Friday," dial 1-800-445-8341.

For your convenience, we've attached a free phone cord untangler. Connect the ends to your receiver and your phone cord as a reminder that your "straight line" to profits is only a phone call away. Be sure to watch your mailbox for more "Call Friday" information coming soon!

⊕ Mopar
CUSTOMER CARE

Award: Silver
Program: Call Friday

Client: Chrysler Corporation
Manager, Service Marketing: Richard Bentzen

Agency: Ross Roy Communications
Executive Vice President, Executive Creative Director:
  Joseph McNeil
Associate Creative Director, Art: John Sirvinskis
Associate Creative Director, Copy: Danny Freels
Copywriter: Laura Kilpatrick
Art Director: Tom Cerroni
Vice President, Account Supervisor: Don Baldwin
Account Supervisor: Geri Faehner
Administrative Manager: Nancy McPhail
Account Administrator: Kim McCabe
Print Production Manager: Susan Heupenbecker

"Call Friday" is a traffic-building program enabling Chrysler dealers to call and have mail packages offering special service incentives sent to select customers within a week. To enlist participation in the program, a teaser mailing was sent to dealers with sample art, a phone cord detangler highlighting "your straight line to profits," and an 800 number for more information; dealers were addressed in special satellite broadcasts; and a series of follow-up mailings were sent after the broadcast. The resulting customer mailings pulled a 6 percent, with orders averaging $74.62.

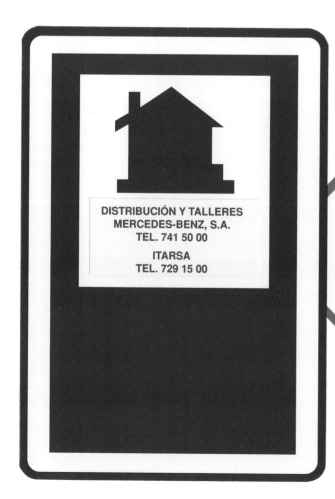

Award: Gold
Program: Mercedes SK's

Client: Mercedes-Benz Espana S.A., *Spain*

Agency: Kobs & Draft Spain
Account Executives: Ignacio Hertogs, Elisabeth Pi
Creative Team: Alfonso Canizares, Carlos Gruber
Creative Director: Rosa Villasante
Production: Pilar Rodriguez

To maintain its position in the large truck category and dramatize its recent recognition as "Truck of the Year," Mercedes sent out this unusual over-sized mailing to owners of older trucks who might need to replace or upgrade. With its large size—and a striking brochure that looks like a truck with an opening on the side—the mailing highlighted Mercedes' "large and special" line. The bottom line? Response of 9 percent with a 3.3 percent conversion, resulting in sales of $30.2 million at a cost per response of just $2.79!

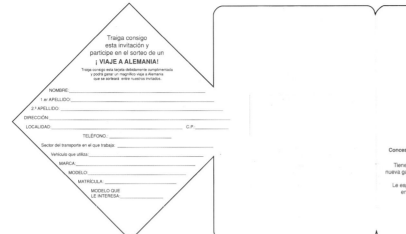

Traiga consigo
esta invitación y
participe en el sorteo de un
¡ VIAJE A ALEMANIA!

Traiga consigo esta tarjeta debidamente cumplimentada
y podrá ganar un magnífico viaje a Alemania
que se sorteará entre nuestros invitados.

NOMBRE:_____
1.er APELLIDO:_____
2.ª APELLIDO:_____
DIRECCIÓN:_____
LOCALIDAD:_____ C.P.:_____
TELÉFONO.: _____
Sector del transporte en el que trabaja: _____
Vehículo que utiliza:_____
MARCA:_____
MODELO:_____
MATRÍCULA: _____
MODELO QUE
LE INTERESA:_____

DISTRIBUCIÓN Y TALLERES
MERCEDES-BENZ, S.A.
TEL. 741 50 00

ITARSA
TEL. 729 15 00

Concesionarios Oficiales Mercedes-Benz para Madrid.

Tienen el placer de invitarle a la presentación de la
nueva gama de camiones especializados Mercedes-Benz.

Le esperamos el día 1 de Diciembre desde las 11 h.
en el Palacio del Negralejo donde deseamos
ofrecerle una atención muy especial.

LE ESPERAMOS EN:

PALACIO DEL NEGRALEJO
Km. 3 Ctra. de San Fernando de Henares
a Mejorada del Campo.

Mercedes-Benz
VEHÍCULOS INDUSTRIALES

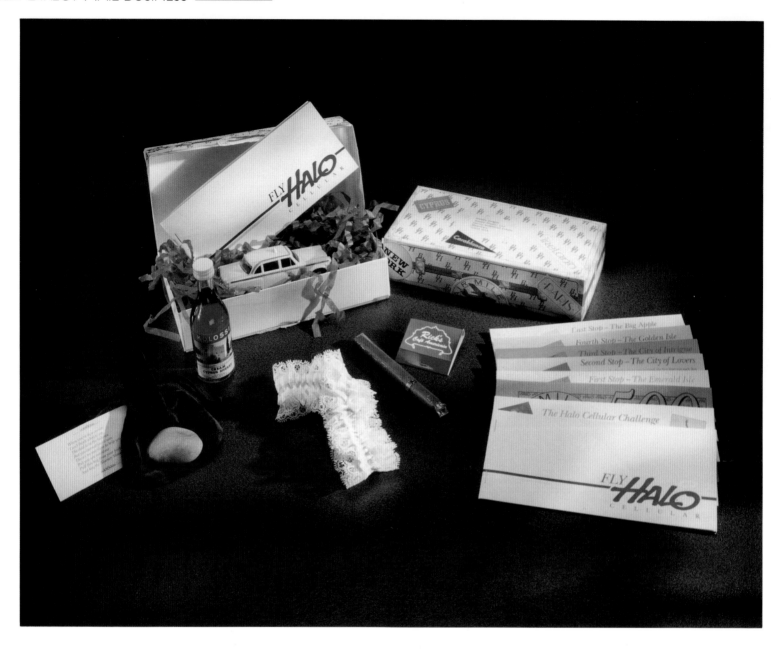

Award: Gold
Program: Steamer Trunk

Client: Bowater Halo, *England*
Marketing Director: Sam Kennedy
List Building and Follow-Up: Jim Trainer

Agency: The Aldersey Taylor Partnership
Creative Director: Jackie Aldersey-Taylor
Copywriter: Robin Aldersey-Taylor
Art Director: Jackie Aldersey-Taylor
Visualisation: Simon Lane
Illustration: Tim Daker
Production: Craig Field

The manufacturer of window profiles, Halo needed to increase sales of their small line of window accessories. Their solution of offering air mile rewards for purchases—and illustrating potential destinations with a steamer trunk box containing representative items—produced a remarkable 73.9 percent response rate, with 60 percent converting, beating the previous campaign by 230 percent.

Award: Silver
Program: Nautila

Client: Butagaz, *France*

Agency: Kobs & Draft France

Butagaz, the leading French propane gas distributor, had come up with a true breakthrough product: Nautila, the first gas tank designed to be buried permanently, not dug up and replaced every ten years. To introduce the product to major home builders, the firm sent out this mailing with the product description appropriately buried—under the pieces of a jigsaw puzzle. The result was a 15 percent response rate, with each respondent potentially worth hundreds of thousands of dollars.

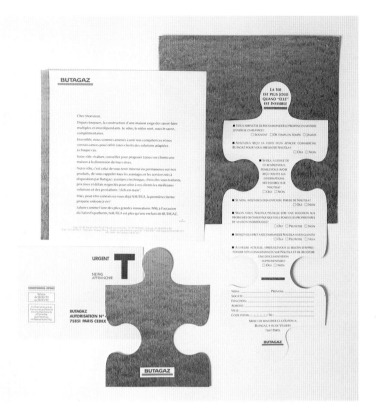

Award: Silver
Program: Free Lunch

Client: Manor Hill Food Corporation

Agency: Trahan, Burden and Charles Direct
Creative Director/Copywriter: Tom DiJulio
Art Director: Philip Tang
Production: Michael Jones
Account Management: Moira McNulty

Manor Hill Food Corporation knew their new Gourmet Beginnings salad bases would be a hit at restaurants and grocery stores—if they could just get buyers to sample them. Rather than deliver samples which might sit unopened in a buyer's office, Manor Hill instead delivered a place setting with an invitation to a Gourmet Beginnings lunch, to be served at the buyer's convenience. The results were especially appetizing: a response rate of 45 percent, at a cost per response of $17.09.

Award: Silver
Program: BHP Press Box

Client: Blaine Hudson Printing

Agency: Merrell Remington Direct (formerly RPM Direct)

Creative Director: A. Kent Merrell
Art Director: Noel Hilden, Jeff Welter, Jack Martin
Copy: Kent Merrell, Greg Hensen

Printing: Blaine Hudson Printing
Assembly: Blaine Hudson Printing

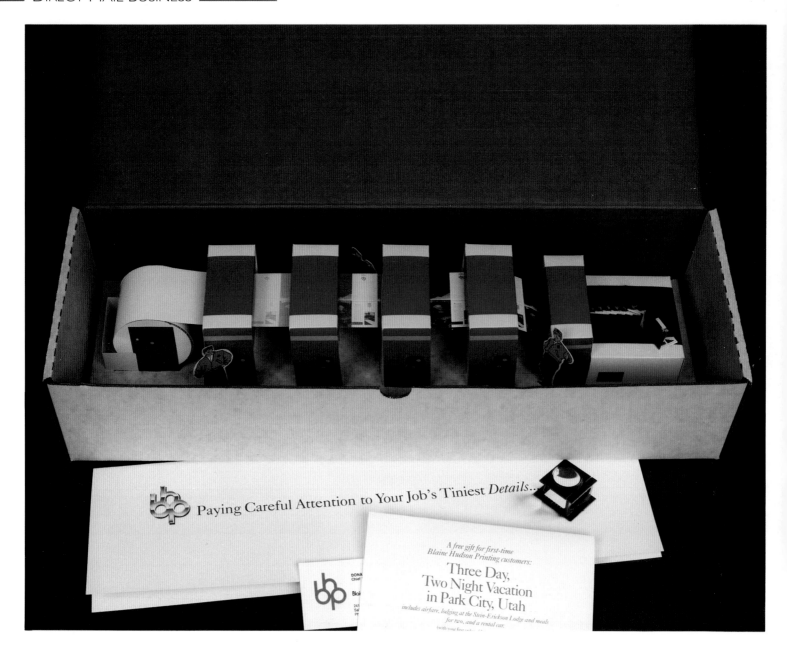

A full-service printing operation, Blaine Hudson sought business from large magazine and catalog publishers. To attract attention and generate leads, they sent out an imposing dimensional mailing featuring this replica of a web press with the headline, "Paying Careful Attention to Your Job's Tiniest Details." It paid off big, with a response rate of 42 percent, a conversion rate of 17 percent, and sales totalling $250,000 to date.

n Telford

Salt Lake City International Airport is just 15 minutes away from the BHP plant, and, as an International airport, it offers non-stop flights into Salt Lake City from virtually anywhere in the United States.

Considered to be the "Crossroads of the West," Salt Lake City is a distribution point for many national corporations who take advantage of its excellent trucking and rail shipping facilities.

Glen Canyon's Rainbow Bridge is one of the majestic, awe-inspiring rock formations and colorful deserts that cover the southern portion of Utah. Visitors from all over the world visit these National Parks each year.

Blaine Hudson Printing has done what printers all long to do. . . create a careful balance between technology, customer service and craftsmanship. You can put this balance to work for you and let Blaine Hudson Printing handle your next printing project, whether it be catalogs, magazines, brochures, manuals, or books.

You'll find that the service and the quality of work we deliver keeps up with the technology.

Rainbow, cutthroat, mackinaw, and brown trout, striped bass, walleye, bluegill, whitefish, and Bonneville cisco can be pulled from over 1000 of Utah's fishable lakes, rivers, streams, and creeks – year-round.

Award: Bronze
Program: NUCREL Grill Promotion

Client: The DuPont Company

Agency: Wunderman Worldwide Detroit
Art Director: David Witkowski
Writer: Lisa Stanczak
Associate Creative Director: Mary Grams Semak
Creative Director: James Turnbull
Account Executive: Ellen Zehler
Account Supervisor: James Risk

To promote the advantages of NUCREL Acid Copolymer among condiment packaging engineers, this clever three-part mailing series included a sample packet of ketchup, a knife to spread mustard, and the top to a Weber grill, which the respondent could claim from a DuPont sales representative. The response rate was tops as well: 100 percent!

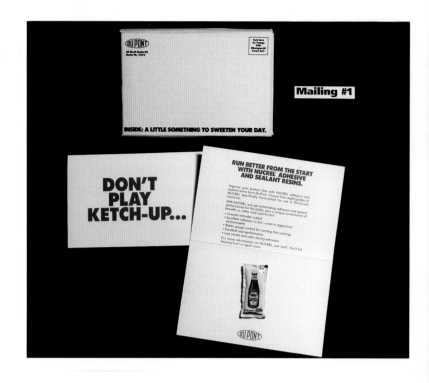

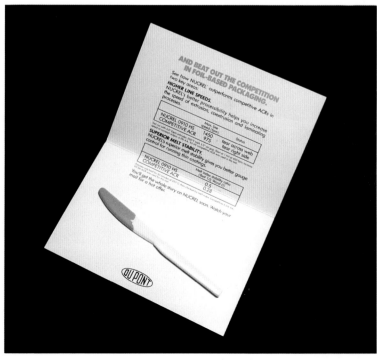

Award: Bronze
Program: Jordan Box

Client: Allied-Signal, Inc.—Bendix Brakes Division

Agency: Orsatti & Parrish
Creative Director: Frank Parrish
Art Director: Paul Tonelli
Copywriters: Frank Parrish, Burr Johnson
Account Supervisor: Mary Courville
Account Manager: Elaine Goetz
Traffic Manager: Bonny Davis

For Bendix Brakes, it was imperative to generate appointments with warehouse distributors, each of whom had resisted all previous efforts. The solution was this dimensional mailing offering an official NBA basketball personally autographed by Michael Jordan—to be delivered only at a sales presentation. The result was the most successful lead generation/sales conversion in Bendix history, with a 53 percent response rate, seven of 53 respondents converting, and revenues from conversion estimated at $11 to 26 million in 1992.

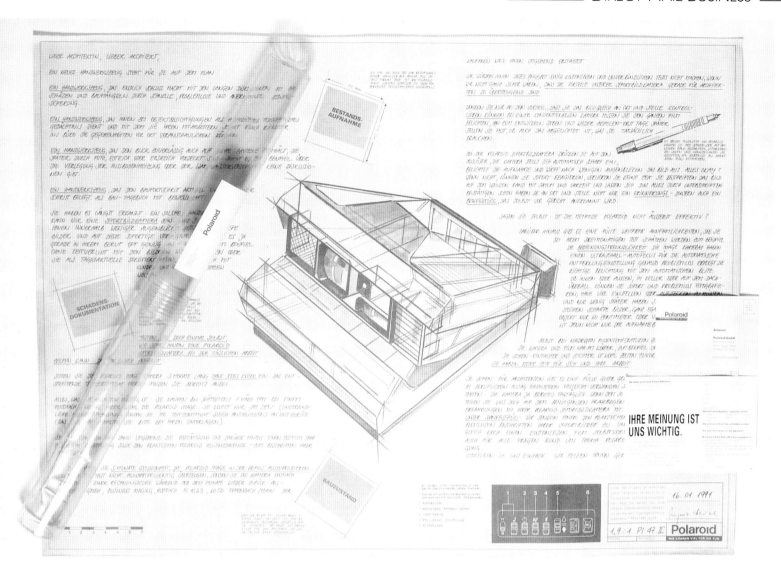

Award: Leader
Program: Architect Mailing

Client: Polaroid GmbH, *Germany*
Senior Product Manager: August Heid

Agency: Ogilvy & Mather Direkt
Creative Director: Sebastian Zuleger
Art Director: Gabi Ehret
Copywriter: Dieter Denk
Management Supervisor: Peter Raesch
Account Executive: Simona Usinger

Like razor blade companies, Polaroid makes its money off its films, not its cameras. To stimulate professional usage among architects, the company sent out this distinctive mailing in a tube like the ones architects use for blueprints, with a letter in the form of an architectural plan detailing the camera's many uses and offering a free trial to non-users or a free gift to users in exchange for feedback. The response scaled new heights, pulling an 11 percent response and a 45.3 percent conversion.

Award: Leader
Program: The Art of Ageing Gracefully

Client: The House of Seagram
Manager, Direct Marketing: Mary Ellen Griffin
Vice President, Direct Marketing and Media: Richard Shaw
Product Manager: Roy Danis
Vice President, Group Marketing Director: Peter Meola

Agency: Bronner Slosberg Humphrey Inc.
Vice President, Account Supervisor: Carol Austin
Associate Account Executive: Fran Dursi
Vice President, Associate Creative Director: Nancy Harhut
Production Manager: Steven Licare
Executive Creative Director: Mike Slosberg
Account Supervisor: Lisa Soule
Senior Art Director: David Squibb
Vice President, Marketing Director: Elizabeth Stearns

Martell Cognac suffered from a low brand awareness level compared to the category leaders—and a high price. To generate awareness and encourage trial of Martell, a series of exceptionally elegant self-mailers was sent to known cognac drinkers, featuring a vellum cover sheet with a Cognac cancellation stamp, a cover note from Patrick Martell, and a special offer of cognac snifters or other premiums, free with proof of purchase. The program achieved an average lift of 152 percent and beat the previous year's creative by 1,640 percent.

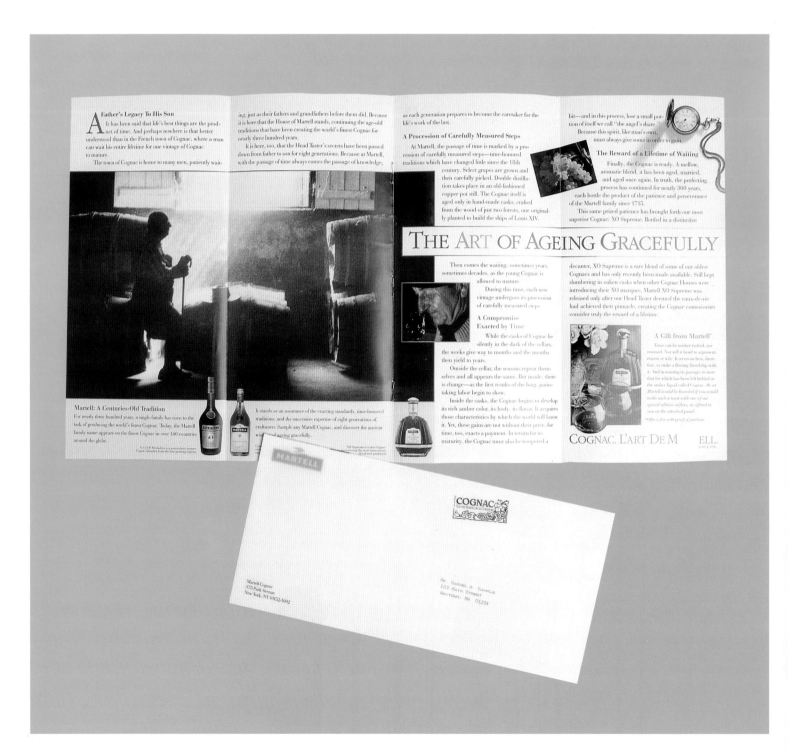

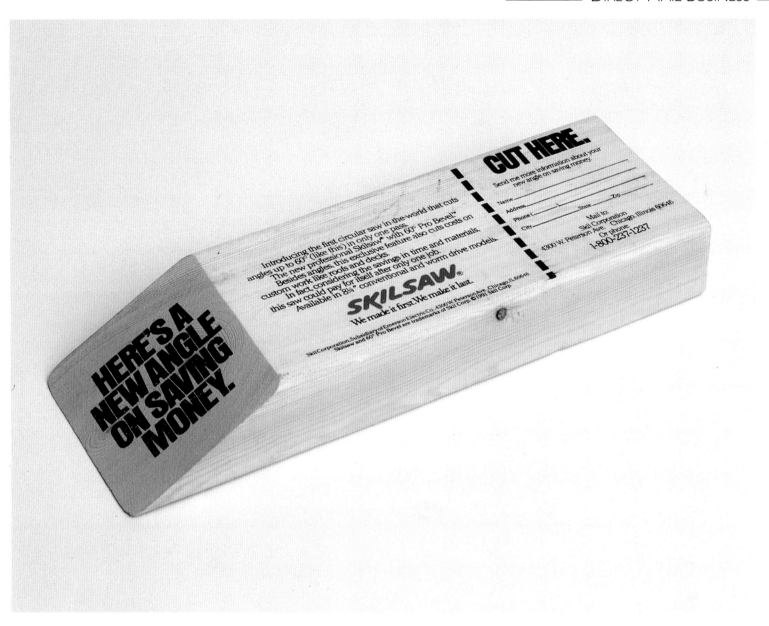

Award: Leader
Program: 2″ × 4″ Mailing

Client: Skil Corporation

Agency: Cramer-Krasselt
Creative Director: Maureen Moore
Writer: Wes Hranchak
Art Director: Doug Githens
Production: Phil Milazzo
Account Team: Brad Tips, Dave Hamel, Ed Hughes

To promote their new circular saw, which could cut a 60 degree angle in one pass instead of the two required by competitive units, Skil sent out this striking mailing to custom home builders. Promising a "new angle on saving money" and an order form that all but demands to be detached, the mailing pulled a 28.5 percent response with a 14 percent conversion.

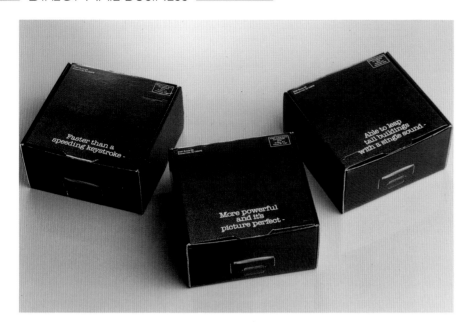

Award: Leader
Program: "More Than Just Typewriters"

Client: AEG Olympia

Agency: Saugatuck Direct
Creative Director/Art Director: Dan Levin
Creative Director/Copywriter: Susan Kurtzman
Production Manager: Kristen Empie
Model Designer: James E. Richardson

The German typewriter manufacturer AEG Olympia wanted to expand their U.S. dealer channels for their new line of high-tech office equipment. To overcome the reluctance dealers had to carry a new line, this series of three dimensional mailings was sent out one week apart, with each box containing a scale model of one of the new office machines and noting that AEG Olympia was now "more than just typewriters." The campaign did the trick, pulling a 4 percent response and 45 percent conversion, generating more than $1.2 million in sales, exceeding revenue expectations by 285 percent.

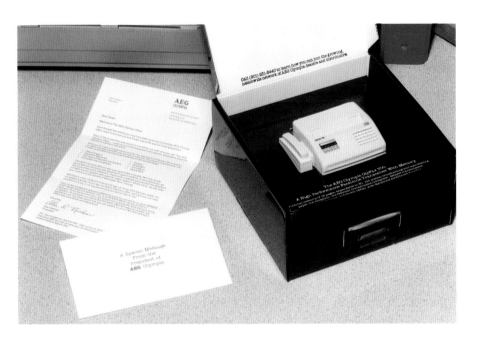

Award: Leader
Program: The Dove

Client: IBM World Trade Corporation, *Malaysia*
Communications Director: Maneha Rasiah
Marketing Reps: C.N. Voon, Sahi Majid

Agency: Ogilvy & Mather Direct
Creative Director: Kurt Crocker
Copywriter: Christopher Yin
Art Director: Vernon Lee
Account Service: Liza Low, Foo Ming Lee

To help their seminar invitation stand apart from the clutter of similar offers from competitors, IBM sent out this oversized mailing with a unique animated pull-tab involvement device that demonstrated how IBM solutions "help your business soar." Like tokens, you can't always explain 'em, but they work, here pulling a 7.1 percent response and a 10 percent conversion, amounting to total sales of more than $5.9 million!

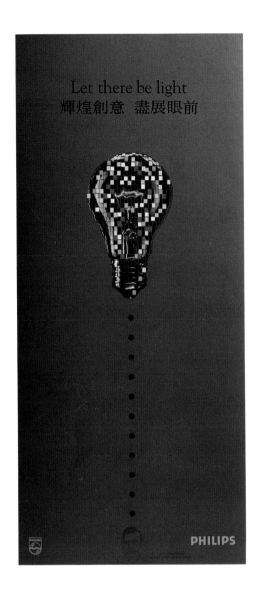

Award: Leader
Program: Opening Night Invitation
Client: Philips Lighting Centre, *Hong Kong*

Agency: Ogilvy & Mather Direct
Account Director: Charles Li
Creative Director: Lisa Lee
Copywriter: Michael Barter
Art Directors: Anthony Sih, Deborah Yarrow

To invite heads of industry and business to the grand opening of the new Philips Lighting Centre displaying their complete product line, this extremely unusual dimensional package was hand delivered to prospects. When the lid of the box was opened, a line of flashing lights lit up, leading from an illustration of company founder Gerard Philips to the invitation itself. The results were, indeed, brilliant, with a 58 percent response rate.

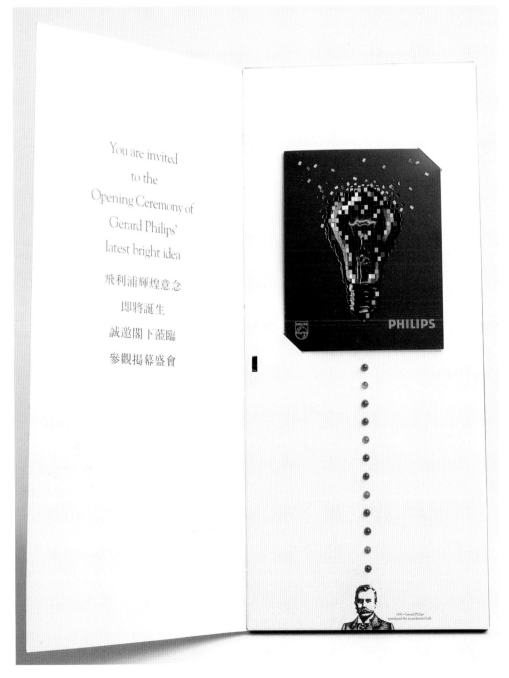

Award: Leader
Program: Triangle

Client: Bell Atlantic
Thinx Product Manager: Frankie Russell
Advertising Manager: Keith Kunberger

Agency: J. Walter Thompson Direct
President: Mitchell Orfuss
Sr. Vice President, Creative Director & Copywriter:
  Mark Hallen
Copywriter: Drake Sparkman
Vice President, Account Director: Audrey Himmelstein
Account Executive: Val Geisler
Director of Production: John DeMaio
Art Director: Liz Ehrlich
Art Director: Domingo Perez

Printer: L.P. Thebault

Bell Atlantic had two problems introducing their
new Thinx PC software: the company had no
recognition in the software market, and the software itself was something no one had ever seen
before: a spreadsheet with images. The solution
was to send out a mailing no one had ever seen
before either: this highly unusual triangular piece,
with a triangular brochure that unfolds to a hexa-
gon. The results stood out as well, with 11
percent of recipients requesting a demo disk.

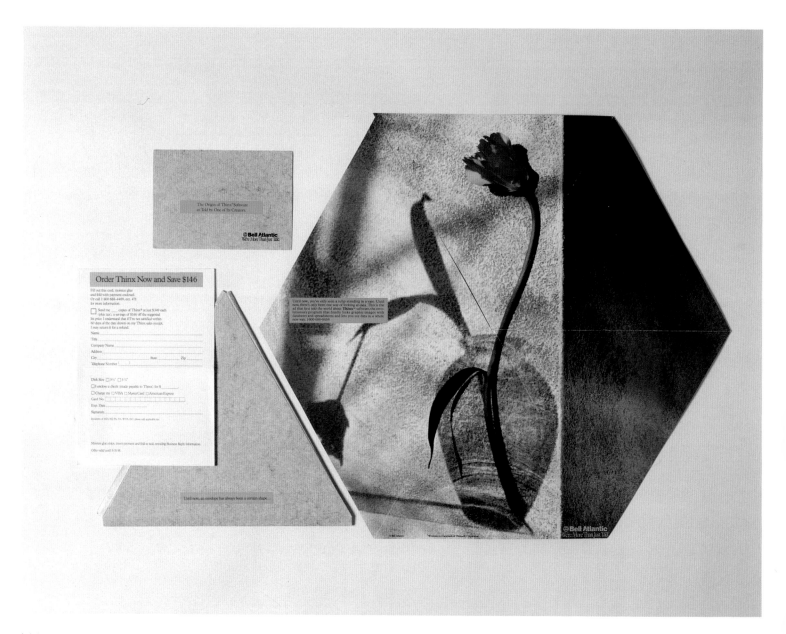

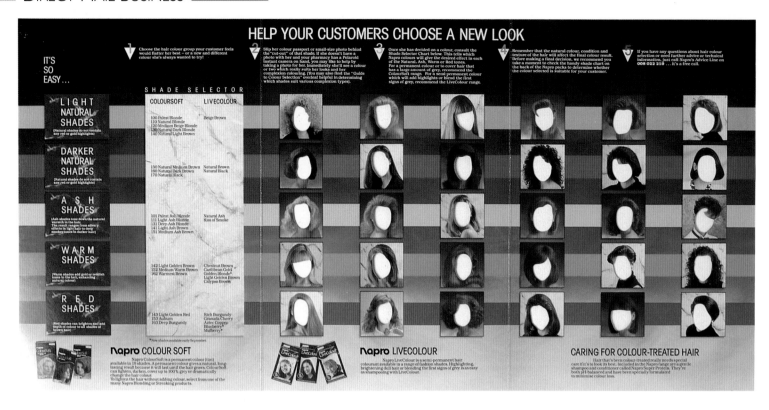

Award: Leader
Program: Napro Pharmacy Mailing
Client: Schwarzkopf Pty. Ltd, *Australia*
Robyn House
Agency: Pinpoint Pty. Ltd.
Kim Harding, Susan Miller, Kirsty Rankin, Miriam Bauers

To increase awareness and recommendation of Napro Home Hair Colouring among pharmacy sales assistants, a mailing was sent out targeting "Hair Color Consultant, XYZ Pharmacy." Inside was a contest entry form and offer of a free die-cut Color Selector Guide, which could help the pharmacy offer a value-added service to customers. The result was a 34.5 response rate.

Award: Gold
Program: The Gulfstream IV Campaign

Client: Gulfstream Aerospace

Agency: Ross Roy Communications
Management Supervisor: Rex B. Smith
Account Supervisor: Julia Francke
Account Supervisor: Scott Turske
Account Administrator: Lisa Nelson
Associate Creative Director: Len Bokuniewicz
Associate Creative Director: Dave Patton
Production Manager: Bill Sperber

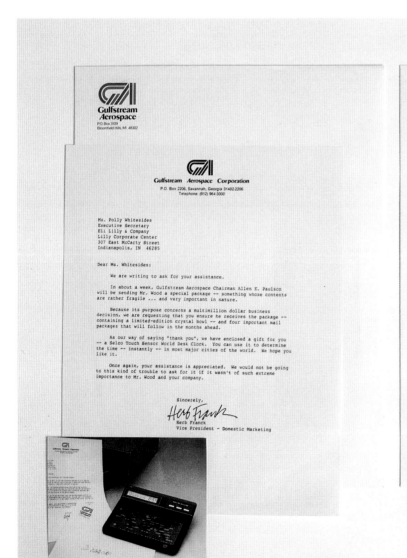

Can direct mail sell a product costing $25 million, like a corporate jet? Gulfstream did it, first by sending the secretaries of Fortune 500 CEO's a mailing inviting their cooperation and enclosing a gift; second, by sending the CEO's a crystal bowl followed by a series of mailings with international candies to fill the bowl; and third, by sending technical mailings offering free rides aboard the jet to the corporations' aviation directors. So far, the campaign has resulted in six sales, totalling a sweet $150 million.

THE CASE FOR THE
GULFSTREAM IV

PART III

THE EAST BLOC

THE CASE FOR THE
GULFSTREAM IV

PART IV

THE PACIFIC RIM

THE CASE FOR THE
GULFSTREAM IV

PART V

THE UNITED STATES

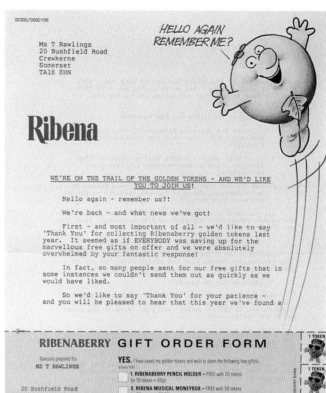

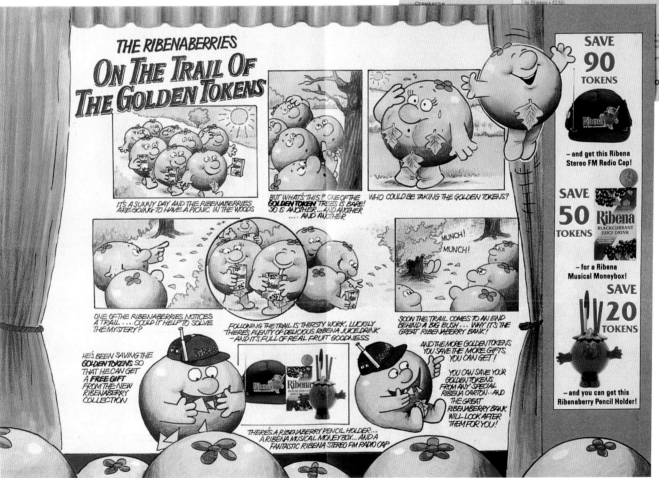

Award: Silver
Program: Ribenaberries

Client: SmithKline Beecham, *England*

Agency: Watson, Ward, Albert, Varndell (WWAV) Limited
Copywriter: Ivan Palmer
Art Director: Mike Wong
Account Management: Leanne Owen

The responders to a previous on-pack promotion from Ribena Soft Drinks had been alienated when the fulfillment of the offer was delayed. To overcome any negative feelings and re-establish brand loyalty, this mailing was sent out, offering new purchase incentives and five free tokens redeemable for prizes. The resulting response rate was a refreshing 33 percent, or 30,000 names.

Award: Bronze
Program: Border

Client: The House of Seagram
Manager, Direct Marketing: Mary Ellen Griffin
Vice President, Direct Marketing and Media: Richard Shaw
Product Director, New Products: Sam Ellias
Sr. Vice President, Director New Products:
   Arthur Shapiro

Agency: Bronner Slosberg Humphrey Inc.
Vice President, Account Supervisor: Carol Austin
Sr. Art Director: Carla Baratta
Associate Account Executive: Fran Dursi
Vice President, Associate Creative Director: Phil Feemster
Vice President, Associate Creative Director: Nancy Harhut
Production Manager: Alison Jones
Account Executive: Jennifer Ogden
Executive Creative Director: Mike Slosberg
Account Supervisor: Lisa Soule
Vice President, Marketing Director: Elizabeth Stearns

To launch a new tequila in a category dominated by a single, long-standing brand, Coyote took full advantage of direct mail to deliver a message with an impact. In this case, it was a brown envelope bearing a Mexican customs stamp and a metered label from Tequila, Mexico, and containing a hand-typed note asking the reader to help find a bottle of Coyote with such clues included as a Coyote bottle label and the brand's unmistakable cork. The best-performing list surpassed breakeven by 247 percent.

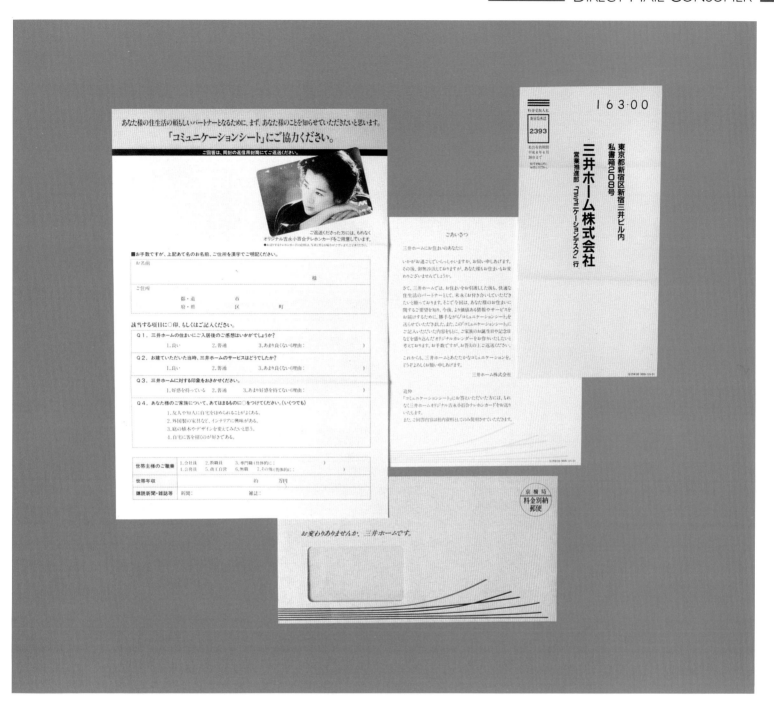

Award: Leader
Program: Customer Loyalty Curriculum

Client: Mitsui Home Co., Ltd., *Japan*

Agency: Dentsu Wunderman Direct, Inc.
Creative Director: Hidehiko Yoshioka
Copywriter: Yuri Hoshiba
Account Director: Miho Shiozaki

In an environment of increased competition and sluggish demand, Mitsui Homes—makers of platform frame houses priced from $150,000 and up—needed to generate renewed demand from previous purchasers and have them bring in new prospects through referrals. The company therefore sent out this series of mailings to open a dialog with their customers, promising a calendar personalized with family anniversaries in exchange for filling out a questionnaire; future mailings suggested purchasing a resort house, a new home with a home office, and a two-generation residence. A comfortable 49.5 percent returned their questionnaires, and 9.9 percent bought new homes.

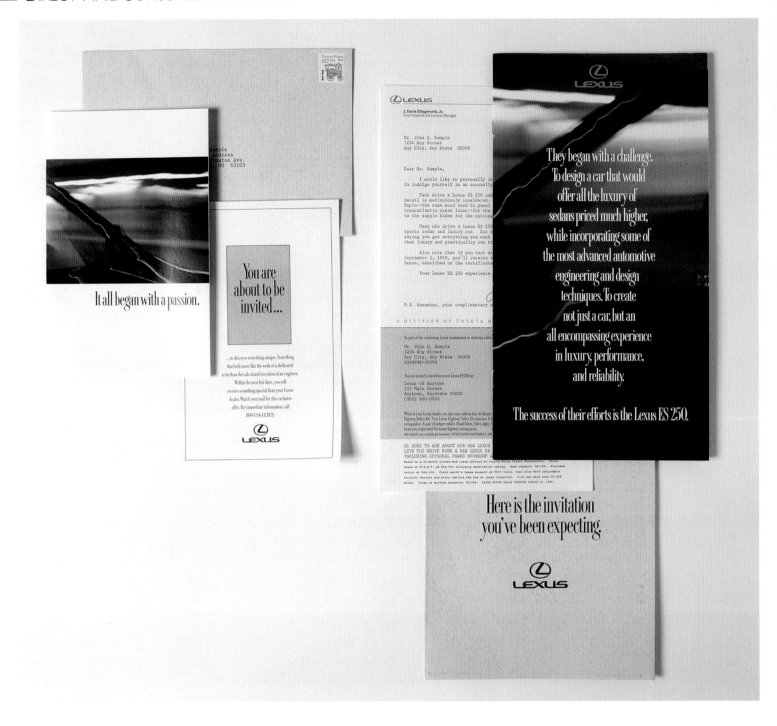

Award: Leader
Program: Passion

Client: Lexus

Agency: Bowes, Dentsu & Partners
Sr. Vice President, Creative Director: Peter Eaton
Art Director: Jeannine Hemmingsen
Copywriters: Steve Means, Richard Wachter
Vice President, Director of Operations: Lindsey Lee
Account Management: Nancy Hittinger, Bob Jensen

Sales of the $25,000 Lexus ES 250 automobile were languishing, as few recognized that the company made a model besides the exemplary $40,000 LS 400. As a result, qualified prospects for the ES 250 were sent this beautiful three-part mailing series, starting with an elegant closed face package announcing an invitation, which was delivered in an extremely unusual elongated envelope soon after. Offering a highway safety kit—or a free oil change—with a test drive, the effort pulled more than 6,400 responses, for total sales of more than $51 million.

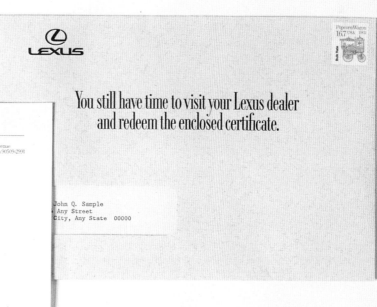

You still have time to visit your Lexus dealer
and redeem the enclosed certificate.

John Q. Sample
Any Street
City, Any State 00000

J. Davis Illingworth, Jr.
Vice President and General Manager

19001 S. Western Avenue
Torrance, California 90509-2991
(213) 781-3200

REMINDER--YOU STILL HAVE TIME TO

TEST DRIVE THE LEXUS ES 250 AND REDEEM THE ENCLOSED

CERTIFICATE FOR TWO YEARS OF

FREE MAINTENANCE

Ms. Jane Q. Sample   May 14, 1990
Optional Address
1234 Any Street
Any City, Any State 00000

Dear Ms. Sample,

    Luxury, reliability, superior safety standards and impressive
performance. These are the appropriate words to describe a Lexus ES 250.

    But words fall short of describing how it feels to be behind the wheel
of this exceptional luxury sports sedan. Which is why we're reminding you to
take a
experi

and at
mainte
test d
additi

P.S.
may us
mainte

A   D

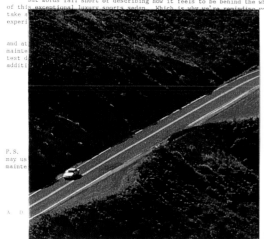

A break in the sky tells you that there's an hour left until dusk.

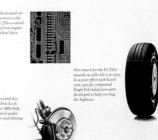

Award: Leader
Program: Lexus Pre-Launch
Client: Toyota Australia, *Australia*
Gerry Forliano

Agency: Ogilvy & Mather Direct
Art Director: Greg Jones
Writer: Tracy Bailey
Creative Director: Michael Kiely
Account Manager: Sally Harper
Database Consultant: Richard Batterly
Finished Art: John Liddle
Production Manager: Brendan Tansey

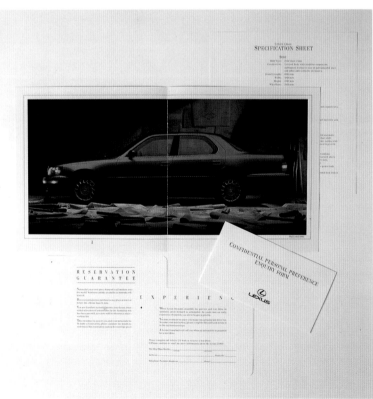

Toyota had a history of manufacturing mass-produced family vehicles, which meant its new upscale Lexus division had no heritage to compete with BMW and Mercedes. To create excitement for the car's introduction and enhance its credibility in the luxury market, these sophisticated mailings were sent out to drivers who had filled out detailed questionnaires at auto shows; the first detailed the car's origin, the second examined its fit and feel, and the third talked performance. The result was a smooth 22 percent, with close to a thousand qualified prospects requesting test drives.

AN AUTOMOBILE WITH SOUL

The interior of a fine automobile is described by the master craftsmen who create them as its "soul."

They mean the emotional part as distinct from the physical attributes; that which touches the senses.

The sensual aroma of soft leather, the feel of finely-polished wood, the exquisite sound of fine music, each element works in harmony to create ambience.

That ambience is unique to the marque as each individual automobile has its own character, its own soul ... that which communicates to the driver the "feeling" in the machine.

Welcome to the soul of Lexus.

SEAMLESS SEAMS

To create harmony within, textures and colours of adjoining and related components must match explicitly.

Whereas conventional car makers use many manufacturing processes to form interior components, each with its own finish characteristics, Lexus uses two.

In places where most would use several moulded components, Lexus uses one.

Naturally there are fewer seams on a Lexus.

Where seams appear, our interior designers employed "zero gap design" techniques to ensure seams are precise and invisible to the human eye.

With the glove box door, for example, where a gap is necessary, a "forced alignment" fitting wedges the closed door accurately in the opening.

TOUCHING THE SENSES

It took two years to find the precise grain of wood for Lexus.

Interior designers scrutinised samples of wood from all over the world.

1

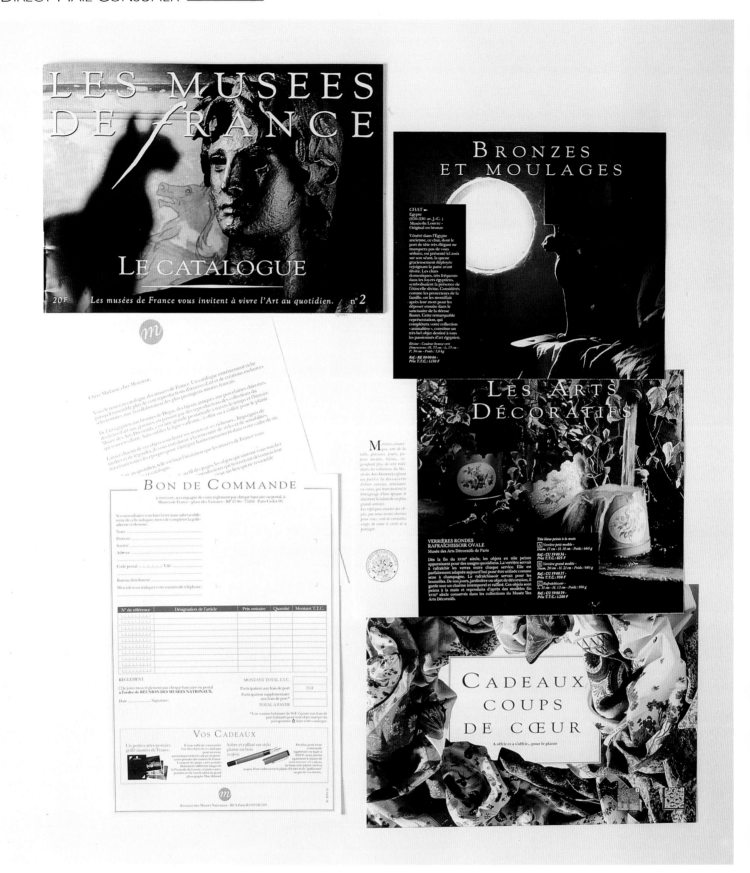

Award: Leader
Program: Catalog

Client: Réunion des Musées Nationaux, *France*
Client Representative: Jean-François Chougnet
Client Representative: Marie-Christine Gerand

Agency: Marboeuf & Associes
Manager: Jacques Marboeuf
Account Director: Brigitte Tournier
Art Director: Jean-Christophe Adam
Art Director: Sandrine Lemmo
Copywriter: Véronika Chiquiar

There was nothing in France like the "Musées of France" program direct-selling copies of masterpieces from 34 French museums, including the Louvre. To validate the economics of the program and minimize the financial risk, a three-stage launch was employed, sending catalogs to museum lists, offering the catalog in print, and sending catalogs to select outside lists. The campaign paid off, pulling up to 11 percent from museum lists, with an average order of $180.

L'art au quotidien

LES MUSÉES NATIONAUX VOUS INVITENT À DÉCOUVRIR UNE SÉLECTION PRESTIGIEUSE
D'OBJETS EXCLUSIFS ET DE REPRODUCTIONS D'ŒUVRES D'ART.

Chère Madame, Cher Monsieur,

Vous avez demandé à recevoir le catalogue
Musées Nationaux, et je vous en remercie.

Dédiée aux amateurs du beau, de l'art et de
événement à plus d'un titre.

En effet, ce catalogue vous propose une sél
d'art et de créations exclusives, provenant des plu

Chaque objet présenté a été sélectionné av
grande diversité de choix.

De l'art égyptien à la sculpture du XIXe siècl
catalogues des grandes expositions, des objets à
ligne des produits du Musée du Louvre, c'est don
travers le temps et l'histoire qui vous est offerte !

Au fil des pages, vous serez séduit par l'élé
visage, la force évocatrice d'un dessin, et le pouv
qui s'intégreront harmonieusement dans votre ca

Une formidable invitation à vivre l'art au quotidien.

Et maintenant, choisissez tranquillement chez vous les reproductions et objets
qui viendront embellir votre intérieur.

Jean-François CHOUGNET
Directeur des Services Commerciaux

· FAIENCES & CERAMIQUES ·

▼ HIPPOPOTAMES BLEUS
Egypte - Moyen Empire
(vers 2000 av. J.-C.)
Musée du Louvre -
Originaux en céramique siliceuse

Outre l'emploi de formes animales
pour traduire une symbolique
religieuse et se protéger des esprits du
mal, les anciens Egyptiens pratiquaient
la chasse à l'hippopotame dans les
marais du Nil. C'est sans doute pour
évoquer ce sport traditionnel – peut-
être déjà empreint de symbolique –
que ces animaux étaient déposés dans
les tombes. Les deux hippopotames
présentés ici sont couleur bleu

turquoise. De taille différente, on peut
apercevoir sur leurs membres la flore
aquatique du Nil et sur leur dos, qui
évoque la surface des eaux, le dessin
de papillons ou de libellules.

Céramique - Couleur bleu turquoise
Grand hippopotame - Dimensions : H. 9,5 cm -
L. 19,5 cm - Poids : 410 g

Réf. : CB 30 00 08 - Prix T.T.C. : 420 F

Petit hippopotame - Dimensions : H. 4,5 cm -
L. 7,5 cm - Poids : 90 g

Réf. : CB 30 00 19 - Prix T.T.C. : 250 F

▼ COUPELLE AUX LOTUS
ET COUPELLE AUX POISSONS
Egypte - Nouvel Empire
Musée du Louvre - Originaux en fritte glaçurée

D'une grande délicatesse et d'un bleu turquoise
lumineux, couleur qui évoque le domaine de la déesse
Hathor, ces deux coupelles seront du plus bel effet
posées sur une nappe ou sur une table basse.

Céramique - Couleur bleu turquoise
Coupelle aux lotus - Diam. 87 mm - Poids : 70 g

Réf. : CB 30 00 17 - Prix T.T.C. : 190 F

Coupelle aux poissons : Diam. 130 mm - Poids : 190 g

Réf. : CB 30 00 16 - Prix T.T.C. : 260 F

Award: Leader
Program: Fioul Performance Elf

Client: Elf France, *France*
Paul Miniconi

Agency: Mediavente Conseil
Account Director: Etienne Hoppenot
Account Executive: Marie Jo Nicolas
Creative Director: Jean Louis Guy
Art Director: Jean Michel Chaubard

Elf France had developed a new home heating
oil with improved performance but a higher price,
a problem in a price-sensitive market. To create
maximum impact for the fuel's introduction, this
unusual vertical mailing was sent out to customer
lists, highlighting the offer of a free cedar tree and
comparing its virtues to that of the new fuel. Responses reached for the sky, with a 23 percent
response rate and sales twice as high as
anticipated.

Award: Leader
Program: For the Light Times

Client: The House of Seagram
Manager, Direct Marketing: Mary Ellen Griffin
Vice President, Direct Marketing and Media: Richard Shaw
Senior Product Manager: Gil Solnin
Vice President, Group Marketing Director: Angelo Vassallo

Agency: Bronner Slosberg Humphrey Inc.
Vice President, Account Supervisor: Carol Austin
Vice President, Associate Creative Director: Phil Feemster
Production Manager: Katherine Holzman
Account Executive: Jennifer Ogden
Executive Creative Director: Mike Slosberg

Seagram's Mount Royal Light was something totally new: a full-bodied Canadian whisky with ⅓ less calories and ⅓ less alcohol. To generate awareness and promote trial, this mailing was sent out to whisky drinkers, promising an "important product disclosure enclosed" and offering a $3 instant redeemable check with purchase. The response was anything but light, with an average 15.8 percent redemption rate that surpassed breakeven by 277 percent and beat the previous year's control by 658 percent.

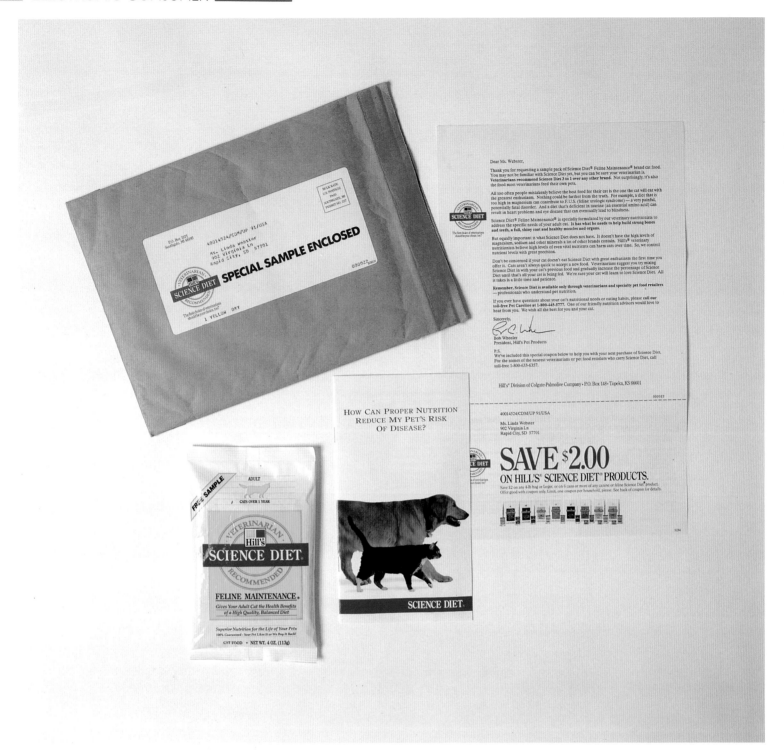

Award: Bronze
Program: Winter '91 DR TV

Client: Hill's Pet Products
Group Marketing Manager, Pet Channel: Jan Karnes

Agency: Wunderman Worldwide Detroit
Sr. VP, Account Director: Bob Fane
VP, Creative Director/Copy: Fred Stafford
VP, Associate Creative Director/Art: Bob Wilson
Agency Producer: Greg Marsh

Science Diet was the number one selling brand in the specialty market of premium-priced, health-oriented pet food, but its high price had caused the brand to lose market share. The solution was this multi-media campaign offering a free product sample and stressing Hill's unique claim of being recommended by veterinarians 3 to 1 over any other pet food. The campaign beat the previous effort by 325 percent, pulling more than 600,000 responses at a cost per response of just $1. What's more, 22 percent converted, for total sales exceeding $19.6 million.

"THREE TO ONE" — DIRECT RESPONSE TV

BETTY: With so many pet foods to choose from, which one do you trust to keep your pet healthy?

Listen to the following message and I'll be back with an important free offer.

MAN (VO): A lot of pet foods promise good health, but just one has the unsurpassed nutrition, quality ingredients . . .

and proven performance that is recommended by veterinarians for good health . . .

above all the rest: Hill's Science Diet.

Science Diet is recommended by veterinarians 3 to 1 over any other brand . . .

and fed by most veterinarians to their own pets. Science Diet.

Because the first choice of veterinarians should be your choice, too.

BETTY: I'd like to send you a free sample of the food veterinarians recommend 3 to 1 over any other. Science Diet.

BETTY (VO): Call 1-800-368-7200 and receive this free sample pack with canine or feline formula.

BETTY: Science Diet. Because the first choice of veterinarians is my choice.

And it should be your choice, too.

Award: Bronze
Program: Tek Direct

Client: Tektronix Inc.

Agency: KVO Advertising & Public Relations
Art Director: Dave Withers
Copywriters: Carl Guess/Jack Challem

Printer: Graphic Arts Center

Tektronix sells electronic test and measurement instruments, accessories, and training classes that range in price from $25 to $6,000. To sell their lower cost products cost effectively, provide a channel for existing customers to order and re-order supplies—and enhance relationship building—the company sent out a Tek Direct catalog to its house list. The catalog produced total sales of $2.6 million, reflecting a .53 percent response rate, which beat previous efforts by 8 percent.

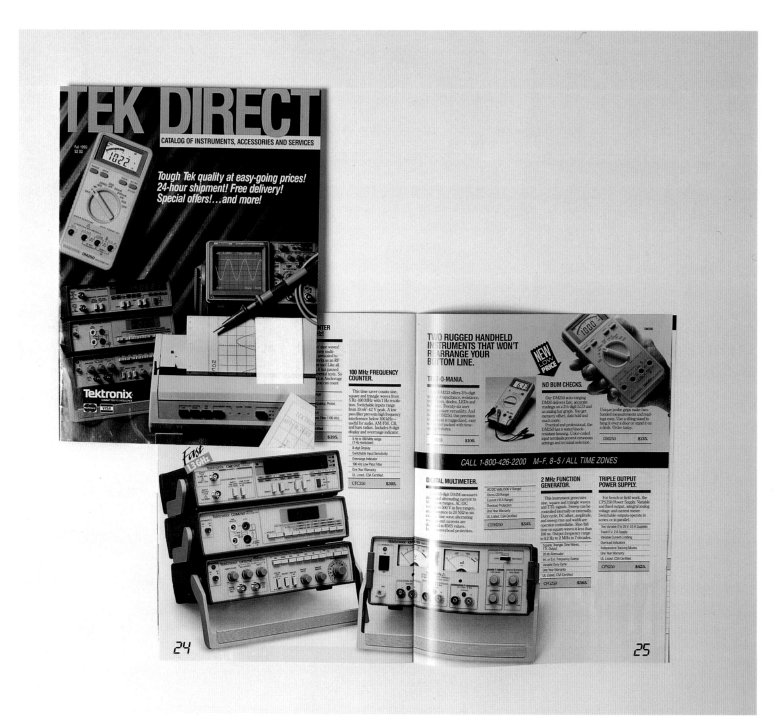

Award: Leader
Program: Generic

Client: California Walnut Commission
Dennis A. Balint

Agency: Proad O&M Direct
Managing Director: Dimitris Paximadis
Promotion Director: Panayotis Papageorgiou
Direct Services Manager: Nicos Kemos
Account Handler: Ginie Koutroubas
Art Director: Dina Karatzas

Direct response was employed to create awareness and promote trial of California walnuts in Greece, with a television and print campaign aimed at consumers soliciting entries for a contest—and a direct mail package inviting participation from key outlet owners. The campaign increased sales by up to 310 percent from the previous year.

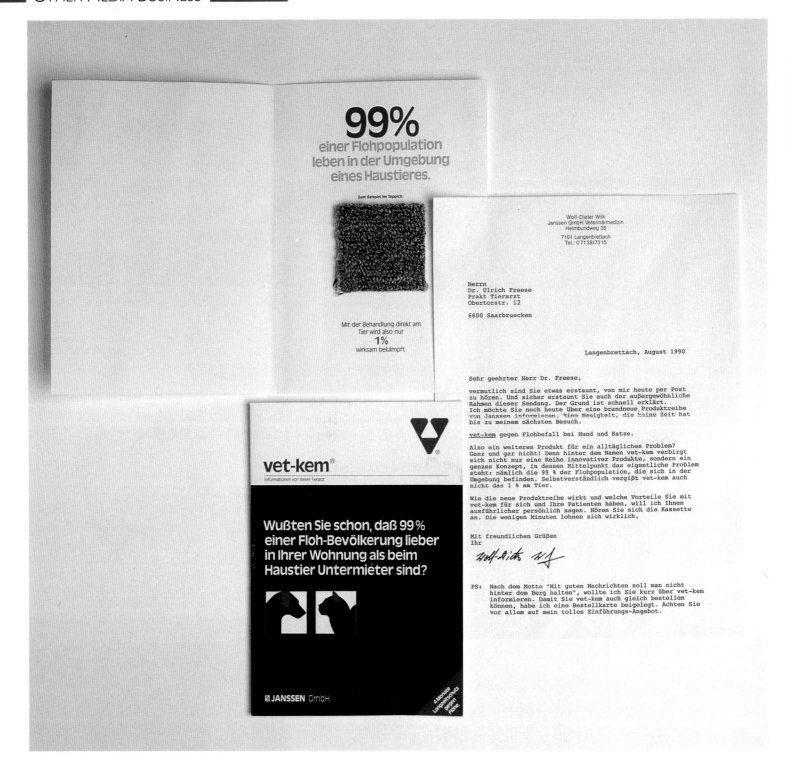

Award: Silver
Program: Vet Kem Introduction

Client: Janssen GmbH, *Germany*

Agency: DMB & B Dialog
Concept: Manfred Dorfer, Andrea Karras
Copy: Bernd Klyne
Art: Yasmin Markus, Silke Peters

Janssen Pharma felt their new Vet Kem anti-flea powder for cats and dogs, a parity product, wouldn't be successful enough to merit distribution through its expensive sales force. So they sent these high-impact mailings directly to veterinarians, including a personal audio tape from their sales rep and a swatch of rug under the headline, "What conventional flea treatment likes to sweep under the carpet." The result was nothing to hide either: the Vet Kem introduction broke all Janssen records, surpassing the annual sales target in just one month and becoming the new category leader.

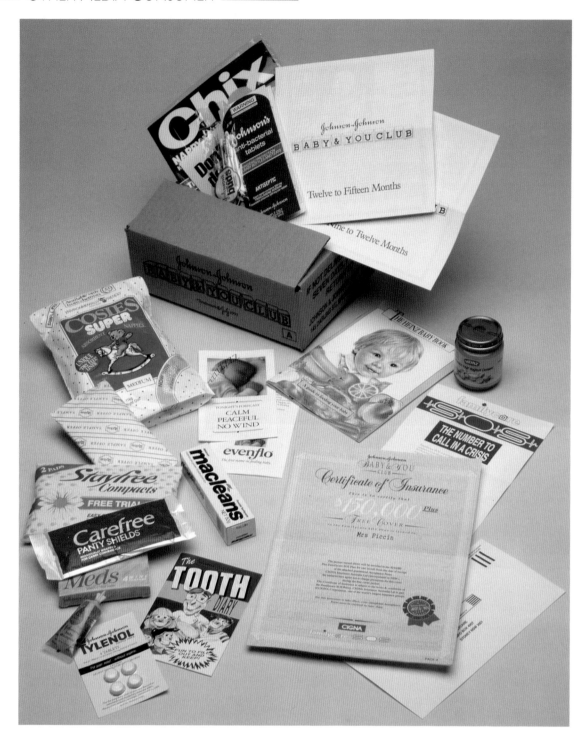

Award: Leader
Program: Baby and You

Client: Johnson & Johnson, *Australia*
Mark Clout

Agency: Pinpoint Pty. Ltd.
Kim Harding, Susan Miller, David Ojerholm
  Diana Begg, Miriam Bauers

To encourage product trial and establish brand loyalty while preempting the competition, Johnson & Johnson distributed a supply of Gift Packs to key contacts in Australian hospitals. Given free to new mothers, these packs were filled with Johnson & Johnson and non-competing samples, as well as a membership form to join the "Baby and You" Club, where members received quarterly mailings containing advice, samples, and special offers. So far, the program has achieved a 45.6 percent conversion, at a cost per response of just $1.76.

Chapter

Store Retailing

Award: Gold
Program: John Deere Competitive Owners

Client: John Deere

Agency: Yeck Brothers Company
Creative: Darrell T. Hare
Art Director: Al Krohn
Account Executive: Robert A. Yeck
Account Coordinator: Ed Mayes

Winning over customers loyal to other brands of farm equipment was no problem for John Deere when they sent out this intriguing four-part mailing series, offering free premiums for a visit to the dealer. The campaign pulled a 29 percent response at a cost of just $110 per response, with an 11 percent conversion rate.

This antique parts truck can be yours free

Award: Silver
Program: Tourism Trade Presentations

Client: EXPO '92, *Spain*

Agency: Ogilvy & Mather Direct
Account Director: John Arnott-Lynn
Account Supervisor: Marta Gómez
Account Executive: Sofía de Altolaguirre
Copywriter: Cristina Jaudenes
Art Director: Adolfo López

To boost attendance at EXPO '92 in Seville, Spain, this ambitious mailing series was sent out to the tourism trade in Europe. The first mailing contained a "pre-invitation" from the Spanish Ambassador, the second a handsome ceramic plate with a formal invitation, and the third a dossier of brochures with a map, entertainment program, and promotional video tape. In all, the campaign elicited more than 1,000 responses, with a response rate of 57 percent in Spain and 40 percent across Europe.

DIRECT ACCESS

Visitors to EXPO'92 will have a number of ways of reaching the exhibition grounds.

Firstly, the site is within easy walking distance of Seville's city centre. Extensive car and bus parking has been built close to the exhibition entrance gates or visitors can take an air-conditioned taxi right to the door.

By rail, inter-city trains from Málaga or Madrid (particularly the new high speed trains), and local trains from Seville's Santa Justa station, will take passengers to the site's railway terminal.

By river, boats will bring visitors from the city centre to the EXPO'92 site in a few minutes.

And by cable-car. Visitors will board air-conditioned cabins in town and cross the river onto the site. The 135 cabins, each holding eight people, provide a panoramic view of the site in cool comfort.

There's also an elevated monorail, running for 3 kms around EXPO'92, passing through the International Pavilion area and the Lake. With six ultra-modern trains, each with ten carriages, 16 million passengers are expected to ride it during the Exposition.

In addition, a continuous bus service will take visitors around the perimeter of EXPO'92 stopping close to points of major interest.

Finally, for special occasions, EXPO'92 has a modern heliport.

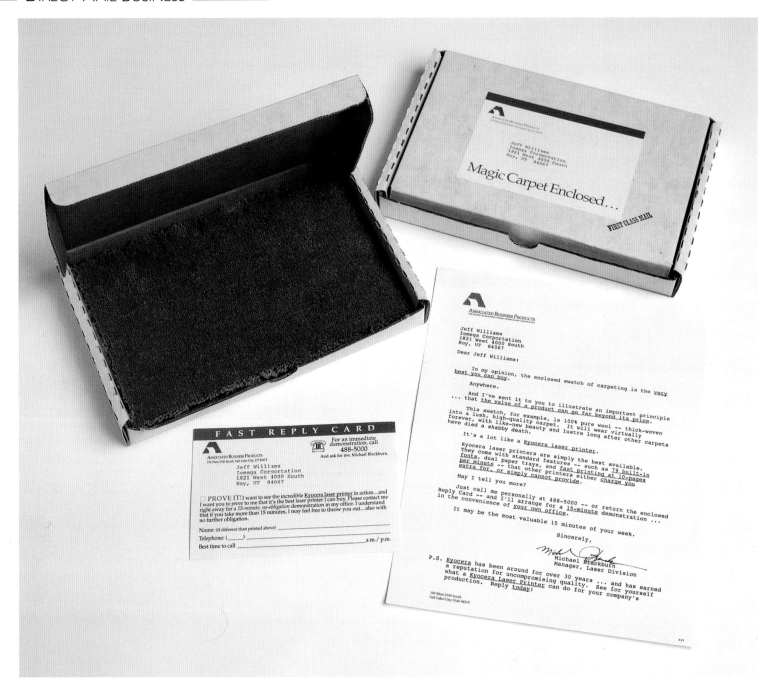

Award: Leader
Program: Smart Investments

Client: Associated Business Products
Sales Manager: Michael Blackburn

Agency: Smith Harrison Direct
Creative Director: Peter D. Harrison
Account Executive: Steve Cuno

Kyocera laser printers had a higher price tag than their competitors but a lower cost-per-page. To illustrate this long-term advantage, this mailing series was sent to office managers, featuring objects that had appreciated in value, including a piece of plush wool carpet, a baseball card, and a Batman comic book. Showing once again how involvement devices can involve even resistant professionals, the series pulled a 14 percent response, with a 21 percent conversion rate, for sales of more than $100,000 on a budget of just $6928!

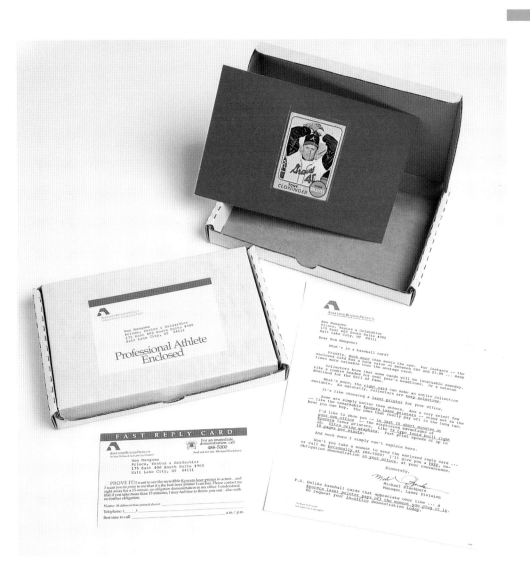

Award: Gold

Client: Citroen, *France*
Client Representative: Pascale Beauchot

Agency: Marboeuf & Associes
Manager: Jacques Marboeuf
Account Director: Benoît Martin
Art Director: Jean-Christophe Adam
Copywriter: Pascal Fonquernie
Account Coordinator: Dominique Decouais

To increase market share and overcome consumer inertia during the Gulf War, Citroen offered a 24-hour test drive—and this chocolate sampler, equating a taste of the world's best chocolates with a test of one of the world's best cars. The campaign pulled a 10 percent response with 34 percent conversion, for total sales of $1 million. This beat the previous campaign by 5 percent.

Award: Silver
Program: Grand Opening Self-Mailer

Client: Sears, Roebuck and Co.
Ned Pierron, Jim Sturrock, Mike Buxton

Agency: Ogilvy & Mather Direct
Creative Director: Tim Claffey
Art Director: Johanne Duprat
Copywriter: Jacki Gelb
Account Service: Lisa Watson, Sandy Markus
Production: Linda Basnik, Kellie Gorsche

While Sears had great strength in such areas as tools and appliances, the retailer had traditionally been weak in its women's clothing offerings. To announce the grand opening of a women's store at Sears and project its fashionable new image, these two beautifully designed mailers were sent out, displaying the new wares and offering time-limited dollars-off coupons to encourage a visit. The mailers resulted in sales of more than $2.7 million, at a cost per response of $6.72.

EN RANGE ROVER, LA VILLE EST DESERTE

Award: Bronze
Program: Direct Mail

Client: Land Rover, *France*

Agency: Kobs & Draft France

Who said a self-mailer can't generate leads for a high-end product? Not Land Rover in France, which supplied dealers with these simple but elegant mailers to send out to prospects. Presenting the Range Rover 4 × 4 as "automobile paradise," the remarkably short copy notes, "In a RANGE ROVER, the city is deserted…the road is too short…nature is peaceful." And the results are exceptional: a 9 percent response, producing 2,250 leads and yielding $4 million in sales.

Award: Leader
Program: EckerdCare

Client: Eckerd Drug Company
Director of Advertising: Betsi O'Neill
Manager, Database Marketing & Research: Mark Warren
Manager of Advertising & Marketing Services:
    Julie Gardner
Advertising Specialist: Sandy Krand

Agency: W. B. Doner & Company
Creative Director: Sande Riesett
Copywriters: Sandy Coleman, Jeff Rassmussen
    Dave Spivey
Art Director: Debbie Piccolino-Saag
Printing: Webcraft
Managing Director: Tony Everett
Account Supervisor: Holly Rich
Assistant Account Executive: Kathryn Brock

The Eckerd chain of drug stores was under attack from discount competitors. The company therefore decided to target three high usage groups—seniors, parents of children under four, and diabetics—and mail out a series of these informative newsletters, highlighting recent health tips of concern to each group, offering discount coupons, and identifying the location of the nearest Eckerd store. Each mailing cost just 30¢, with five mailings to each prospect a year, a small investment on customers who spend $300–$500 on prescriptions a year.

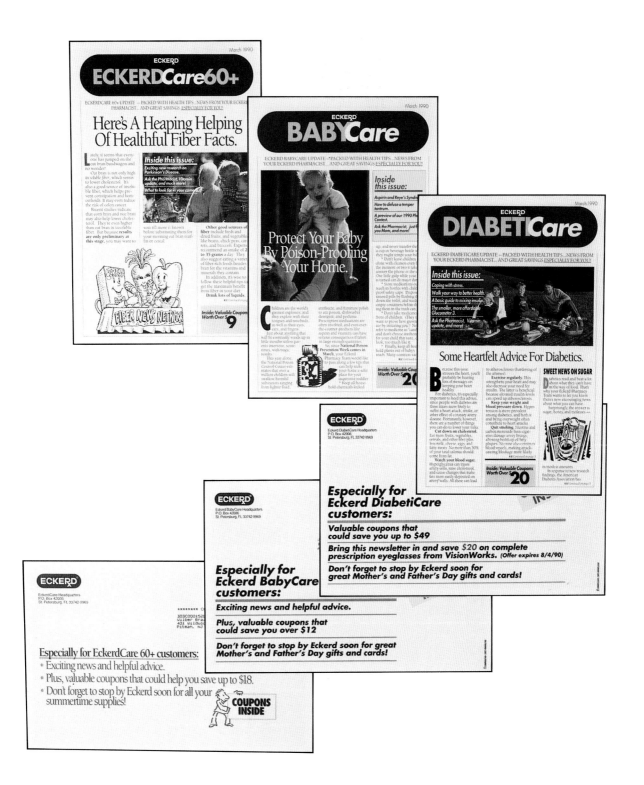

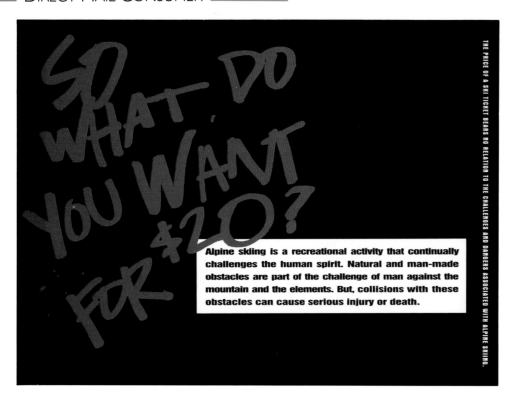

So What, Do You Want For $20?

THE PRICE OF A SKI TICKET BEARS NO RELATION TO THE CHALLENGES AND DANGERS ASSOCIATED WITH ALPINE SKIING.

Alpine skiing is a recreational activity that continually challenges the human spirit. Natural and man-made obstacles are part of the challenge of man against the mountain and the elements. But, collisions with these obstacles can cause serious injury or death.

$20 Mid-week Lift Ticket*

Mount Snow just eliminated one of the biggest obstacles in skiing— the price. Simply present a current college ID and we'll give you a day on the slopes for just $20.

Now at least the cost of skiing won't wipe you out.

Catch the daily Peter Pan/ Mount Snow ski express: round trip transportation and lift ticket from just $34.95. Call 1-800-237-8747, ext. 270.

Mount Snow

Mount Snow, Vermont 05356 (802) 464-8501

*Offer good Monday through Friday, non-holiday. For ski report, call (802) 464-2151.

Bulk Rate
U.S. Postage
PAID
Mount Snow Ltd. .

Award: Leader
Program: College Mailer

Client: Mount Snow Resort

Agency: Orsatti & Parrish
Creative Director: Frank Parrish
Art Director: Robert Levers
Copywriter: Martin Stadtmeuller
Management Supervisor: NancyJane Goldston
Account Manager: Elaine McCarthy

Vermont's Mount Snow family ski resort had come to believe that poor weekday traffic was a fact of life, until they mailed out this simple but engaging post card, targeted to college students located within 90 minutes of the resort. Offering a special $20 lift ticket during the week, the promotion was an enormous success with the students, who had high disposable income, few responsibilities, and a flexible schedule. Midweek lift ticket sales increased 770 percent, for a total of $950,000, while incremental sales of lodging, equipment rentals, and food amounted to more than $2.1 million—all for just $21,059 for the entire mailing, including postage.

Award: Leader
Program: Gordon's Gold Card

Client: Gordon's

Agency: Raphel Marketing
Creative: Murray Raphel
Copywriter: Neil Raphel

The Atlantic City Central Business District where Gordon's shops were located was rapidly deteriorating, with customers migrating to suburban malls. Discovering that just 500 shoppers produced more than 75 percent of the store's sales, Gordon's set up a Gold Card frequent shoppers club offering monthly mailings of special offers, free birthday gifts, free lunches, and awarding bonus points for purchases. Not only did the program help Gordon's keep their previous volume, but they posted a gain in a year when 15 percent of neighboring shops went out of business!

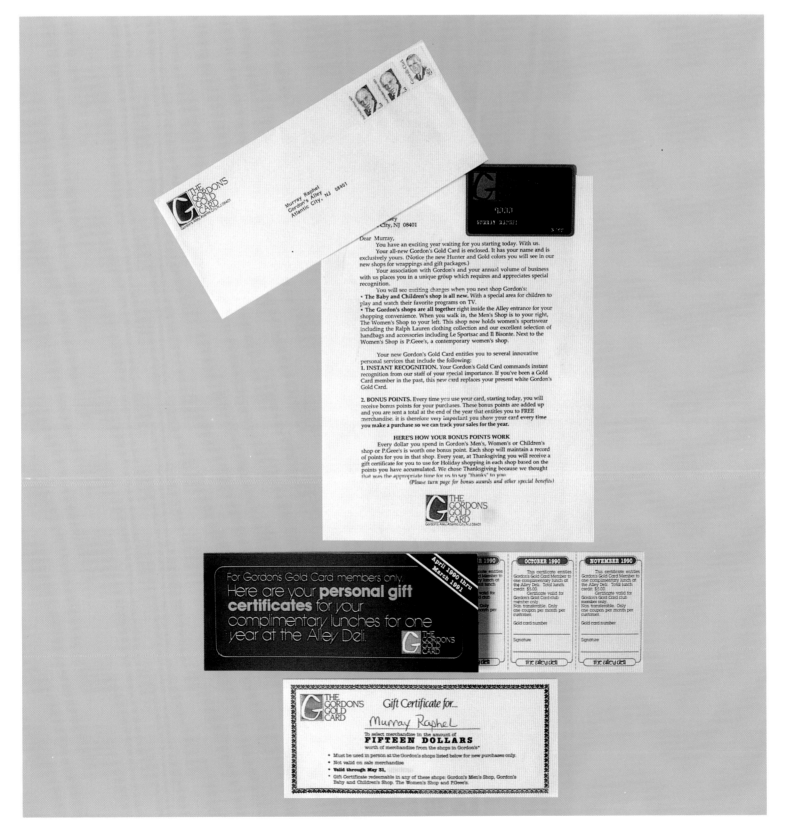

Award: Silver
Program: TV Spot

Client: Jos. A. Bank

Agency: W. B. Doner & Company
Creative Director: John Parlato
Copywriter: John Parlato/Neil Rogers
Art Director: Greg Simonton
Agency Producer: Janet Mockard
President: Jim Dale
Executive VP: David Sackey
VP, Account Director: John Havrilla
VP, Account Supervisor: Nancy Knox
Account Executive: Jodie Deyke

To demonstrate the value and quality of its classic men's suits, Jos. A. Bank challenged viewers to call and distinguish the Bank suit from one selling for $200 more; the right answer earned a certificate worth $50 off the next suit purchase at Banks. Running for two weeks, this spot increased sales by 38.5 percent and led to incremental sales of $58,000, resulting in total sales over six weeks of $330,000.

"Two Suits/Number" :30

STEVE: Two classic men's suits.

Both imported Australian wool.

Both superbly crafted.

But one sells for around $500.
The other's made by Joseph A. Bank.
And sells for just $310.

Can you tell which is which?

You can?

Well, call and tell us which
one is the Joseph Bank suit.
If you're right, we'll give you a certificate
for fifty dollars off your next men's or
women's Joseph Bank suit. Call.

It's this one. This one right here.

B&Q invites home movers to walk out with more than they've paid for.

(WHEN THEY WALK IN WITH THIS CARD)

10% DISCOUNT

VALID FOR ONE TRIP TO B&Q

The cost of moving home isn't far short of daylight robbery.

But happily, filling a trolley at B&Q is nothing less than a steal.

Simply rip off this Discount Card. And you'll save 10% off everything you buy. It's valid for any purchase, large or small. Whether you need to fill a small hole with a tube of polyfilla — or a large space with a fitted kitchen.

And remember, for only £25, you can tool yourself up with a 10% Discount Card that lasts a whole year.

You can use it at 260 B&Q Supercentres nationwide. You'll find over 25,000 different products.

Our Garden Centres offer more than 2,000 varieties of plants and shrubs. And we're open 12 hours a day, Monday to Saturday and many stores are open Sundays too.

We'll even take your order over the phone, and deliver to your door — absolutely free.

So pick up the card, and stroll into your local B&Q. And see what you can get away with.

B&Q SUPERCENTRES NEAR YOU: ABINGDON ALPERTON ASHFORD BANBURY BASINGSTOKE BEXHILL BLETCHLEY BOGNOR REGIS BOURNEMOUTH BRAINTREE BRIGHTON BURY ST EDMUNDS CANTERBURY CHINGFORD CHISWICK CHRISTCHURCH CLACTON COLCHESTER CRAWLEY CROYDON DAGENHAM DARTFORD DOVER DUNSTABLE EASTBOURNE EASTLEIGH ELTHAM ENFIELD FAREHAM FARNBOROUGH GILLINGHAM GRANTHAM GRAYS GREENFORD HARLOW HASTINGS HAVANT HAYES HEMEL HEMPSTEAD HIGH WYCOMBE HITCHIN ILFORD IPSWICH ISLE OF WIGHT LARKFIELD LEATHERHEAD MAIDSTONE MARGATE MITCHAM NEW MALDEN NEWBURY NEWHAVEN NORWICH OXFORD PETERBOROUGH POOLE PORTSMOUTH READING ROMFORD SALISBURY SHOREHAM SIDCUP SOUTHAMPTON SOUTHEND STANMORE STAPLES CORNER STEVENAGE STRATFORD STROOD SURBITON SUTTON SWINDON TONBRIDGE TOTTENHAM WALTHAM FOREST WATFORD WELWYN WEST NORWOOD WEST THURROCK WEYMOUTH WHETSTONE WHITSTABLE WIMBLEDON WISBECH WORTHING

Award: Bronze
Program: *House & Home* Magazine Ad

Client: B&Q PLC, *England*
Peter Milne, Helen Leslie

Agency: Kobs & Draft London
Creative Director: Iona Stern
Art Director: Brian Ennals
Copywriter: Tony Allison
Photography: Julian de Havilland
Creative Services Manager: Karen McCallie
Art Buyer: Pip Drummond
Account Director: Andrew Haigh
Sr. Account Manager: Richard Duncan

The Do-It-Yourself hardware store chain B&Q needed to identify their key market, home improvers and movers, but very few up-to-date lists existed in the UK. That's why they ran this full-page ad, with a tipped-on, one-time 10% discount card, in the quarterly magazine sent to people recently registering with their local Electricity Board. The promotion produced more than 27,000 responses—and sales of more than £2 million.

Award: Gold
Program: Green Bottles

Client: The Victoria Wine Company, Ltd., *England*

Agency: Brann Direct Marketing
Art Director: Caroline Damon
Copywriters: Ken Muir, Richard Madden
Account Handling: Fiona Senior, Alistair Wright
  Martin Davies, Deborah Langley

In the UK, there is little or no loyalty to wine merchants or liquor stores. Thus Victoria Wine sent out a mailing asking store managers to sign up their most loyal customers in the Green Bottles service, where members would receive four mailings a year, with special features on wine and spirits as well as coupons redeemable on higher priced merchandise. The response rate was a heady 33 percent with a 28 percent conversion rate.

An A–Z of Much-Used Terms

Appellation d'Origine Contrôlée
(Often shortened to 'AOC' or 'AC')
The official quality mark awarded to French wines. It's a guarantee that everything the label tells you about the region, the grape variety and the production method, is true.

Brut
This means 'even drier than extra-dry', and it's mostly seen on Champagne and Sparkling Wine labels.

Crémant
Like Champagne, but with fewer bubbles. Try a bottle of Mumm Crémant de Cramant, and you'll see what we mean.

Demi-Sec
Literally 'medium dry' – but often surprisingly sweet. To be sure, look for the Victoria Wine white wine selector code (see 'Understanding Our Own Language of Labels' overleaf).

Doux
French for sweet – though, once again, look for the Victoria Wine white wine selector code to make doubly sure.

Estate-bottled
Bottled on the premises where the wine was made. Look for the words 'Mise en bouteille au château' on a bottle of French wine.

Fino
Means a pale, dry sherry – fun enough on its own, though try it chilled with black olives and spicy *tortillas*... Mmm!

Grand Cru
French term meaning 'top quality'. You'll see it most often on bottles of fine Burgundy.

Hock
This is a name we British invented to describe any German wine made along the Rhine. (Appropriately enough, it was Queen Victoria's favourite drink.) The name probably comes from the village of Hochheim, an important wine-producing centre in the Rhine region.

Island Malt
Malt whisky from the Scottish Islands. Often more intense in flavour than the sweeter, softer malts of Speyside or the Northern Highlands. Try our 10-year old Isle of Jura, and judge for yourself.

Kabinett
A light, not too sweet quality German wine. Our Kabinett, Bornheimer Adelberg and Kabinett Mainzer Domherr are particularly good examples. Kabinett is a QmP quality wine (see **Qualitätswein** below).

Lager
The name given to beer that's been 'lagered' (stored and left to mature) at around 0°C. The best lagers, like Becks Bier, are left to mature for at least three months.

Mousseux
[pron: moose-oh]
French for 'fizzy'.

Négociant
The French term for a merchant or shipper who buys in wine from growers and prepares it for sale by maturing, blending, then bottling it. You'll see the word most often on bottles of Burgundy. There, the individual estates are so small that blending is very common. This ensures that wines like our own Louis Jadot are of a consistently high quality.

Oloroso
A style of full-bodied sherry – usually sweet.

Pils
Short for *Pilsener*. Once, Pils Beer had to come from Pilsen, in the province of Bohemia, Czechoslovakia. But now, Pils is used to describe many top quality lagers, such as Germany's Löwenbräu Pils.

Qualitätswein
The official German quality mark for wine. For a guarantee of *really* special quality, look for the words **Qualitätswein mit Prädikat** – often shortened to **QmP**.

Ruby
The youngest kind of Port; sweet, red and fiery: like our own Conference Fine Old Ruby Port.

Single Malt
When you see this on a bottle of Whisky, you know it's the product of just one distillery. Each single malt has a character of its very own – get to know it, and you've found a friend for life.

Spätlese
[pron: spate-laser]
A German term meaning 'late harvested'. It's a sign that the wine's likely to be slightly sweet, like our own Urziger Schwarzlay Riesling Spätlese '88. Spätlese is a QmP quality wine. (see **Qualitätswein** above)

Trocken
German for 'dry'. **Halbtrocken** means medium-dry – though if it's a very sweet wine you're after, look out for the words **Auslese, Beerenauslese** and **Trockenbeerenauslese**, indicating increasing degrees of sweetness.

Ugni Blanc
This is the French name for the variety of grape the Italians call 'Trebbiano'. It's grown in southern France and Tuscany and is used to make fresh, dry white wines – including our own sparkling Blanc de Blancs.

Vin de pays
The term used to describe a French 'country wine' which, for one reason or another, doesn't fall under any official regional classification. It's often a sign of an exciting wine – at a very reasonable price. Try our dry white Vin de Pays des Côtes de Gascogne, and judge for yourself.

Wood aged
Means that a wine has spent time ageing in a wood (usually oak) barrel. The wine absorbs flavours from the wood, making the taste sensation much more rewarding.

Xerez (Or Jerez)
[pron: herrez(th)]
The name of the town in Andalucía where Sherry comes from. (As usual, we stole the name, but got the pronunciation slightly wrong!)

Y'quem
[pron: ee-kemm]
A very expensive word to find on a label! In 1986, Christie's Auction House sold a bottle of 1794 Château d'Yquem white Bordeaux for a record £36,000. We regret that this particular vintage is *not* available at your local Victoria Wine.

Zinfandel
The native grape variety of California. Why not celebrate July 4th with some Red Inglenook Zinfandel from the sunny Napa Valley?

You might like to cut along this line to make yourself a handy pocket guide...

A Helpful Guide to Serving and Savouring Wines, Beers and Spirits

To chill or not to chill?

There's no need to rush out and buy a thermometer. All the same, there's little doubt that wine and beer is more enjoyable when it's served at the right temperature.

🍷 *Red Wine* – Room temperature, though remember: they invented that phrase *before* central heating...

🍷 *White Wine* – Two hours in the 'fridge is about right – or better still, use an ice bucket.

🍺 *Lager* – Much the same as for white wine. Don't be tempted to over-chill a premium lager – you've paid for the taste, after all!

🍺 *Ales (Bitter, Mild, Stout)* – Remember: ales are brewed to be served straight from a pub's cellar. So make sure they're just slightly cooler than room temperature when you serve them.

Choosing the right glasses

We'd be the last to suggest you have to stand on ceremony when serving your favourite wine, beer or spirits. But by using the right glasses, you'll be able to enjoy the wonderful flavours of your favourite drinks to the full.

🥂 *Champagne* – A fluted glass is best. Why let all those beautiful bubbles escape?

🍷 *Still Wines* – Any bowl-shaped glass that curves in towards the top will do – though some people prefer a larger glass for red than for white.

🥃 *Brandy and other liqueurs* – A proper brandy glass not only looks good, the globe shape also helps you capture the remarkable bouquet of a fine liqueur.

Award: Bronze
Program: We've Got Your Shoes

Client: i.e., a division of Nike
Advertising Manager: Nancy Monsarrat

Agency: Herring/Newman
Group Director: Karen G. Ridings
Account Supervisor: Jill Eenigenburg
Account Executive: Julie Engel
Account Coordinator: Claire Celeste Simecek
Creative Director: Gini Lawson
Art Director: Darby Roach
Copywriter: Dennis Globus
Designer: Deb Hobson
Media Director: Pamela Plowman

Model: Jennifer Rubin
Data Processing: Olympic Data
Color: Color Control
Printing: Impression Northwest
Lettershop: Mailhandlers

To generate traffic and increase brand awareness of i.e. women's casual shoes from Nike, a sweepstakes was created featuring wardrobe prizes instead of the usual cash and cars, and these two mailings were sent out to prospects. Both mailings displayed a ransom note that read, "We've got your shoes," and enclosed a sweepstakes entry form to be brought to the retailers—while the box, mailed to a more responsive audience, even included one shoelace. The results beat the previous control by 600 percent.

Chapter

7

Non-Store
Retailing

Award: Bronze
Program: Beach Head Program

Client: Wunderman Marketing Direto, *Brazil*

Agency: Wunderman Marketing Direto
Creative Director: Jayme Serva

As a self-promotion piece, Wunderman Brazil sent out this holiday greeting card allowing respondents to choose a greeting to send in return. This simple but effective demonstration of direct response pulled almost 1,400 leads, for a 92 percent response rate, and cost the agency just $3,500.

Award: Silver
Program: Regal Bribe

Client: Kraft/General Foods International
Gevalia Kaffe Import Service: Gerald Maxson

Agency: Wunderman Worldwide (New York)
Art Director: Jane Walsh
Copywriter: Mary Ann Donovan
Production Manager: Peter Cifuni
Account Supervisor: Lisa Arkovitz

To acquire new members for the Gevalia Kaffe gourmet coffee club, a handsome and functional coffee canister was offered as a premium and featured on an envelope with a photo of the canister and an irresistible pull-to-open tab at the lid. Results were stimulating to be sure, with a 5.5 percent overall response rate, beating the control by 57 percent.

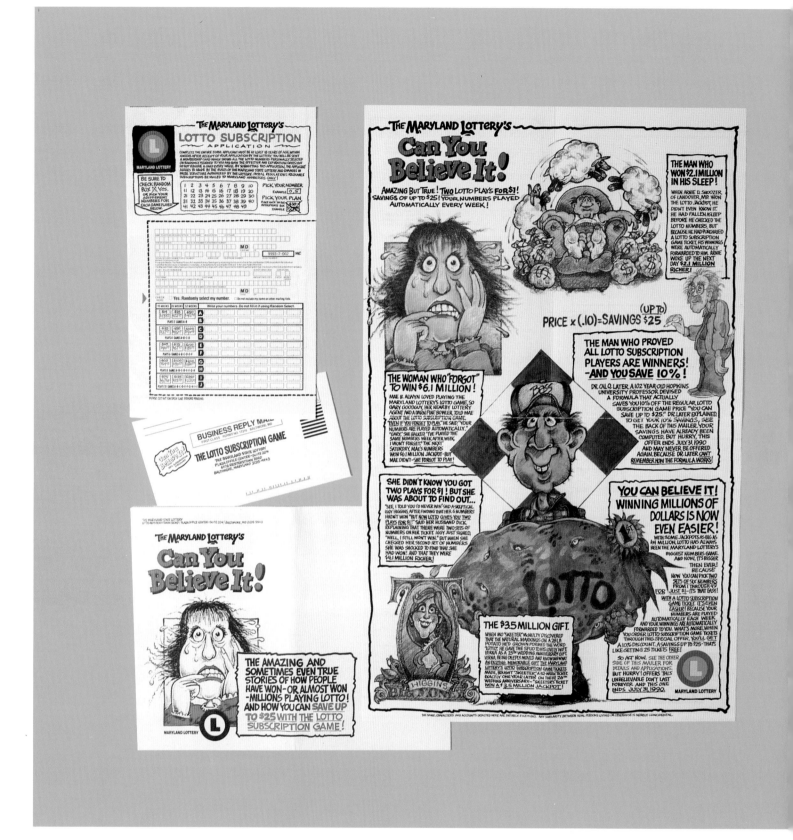

Award: Silver
Program: Can You Believe It!

Client: Maryland Lottery
Director of Advertising & Promotions: Tom Skarzynski

Agency: Trahan, Burden & Charles Direct
Creative Director/Copywriter: Tom DiJulio
Art Director: Philip Tang
Illustrations: Tom Burden
Lettering: Ray Sheffler
Production: Tracey Kuhns

One of the biggest problems confronting any state lottery is the fluctuation of levels of play depending on the size of the weekly jackpot. To guarantee a more consistent level of play, this direct mail piece sold a subscription game at a 10 percent discount and with a new 2-plays-for-$1 structure. The result was a 17 percent response rate, resulting in total sales of more than $918,000 with an average sale of $75.

Award: Bronze
Program: Just the Ticket

Client: Baltimore Orioles
Vice President of Sales: Lou Michaelson

Agency: Trahan, Burden & Charles Direct
Creative Director/Copywriter: Tom DiJulio
Art Director: Philip Tang
Production: Michael Jones, Tracey Kuhns
Account Management: Jill Swain

To increase season ticket sales during the Orioles' historic last season in Memorial Stadium, a direct mail piece was created suggesting a Season Ticket Mini-Plan as the perfect holiday gift. The effort generated more than $400,000 in revenue, for a return on investment of an astonishing 1,233 percent.

Award: Silver
Program: Catalog

Client: Art Institute of Chicago
Director of Retail Marketing: Marija Raudys
Merchandiser: Mary Douthit

Agency: Vroom, Inc.
Creative Director: Jacques Vroom
Merchandise Consultant: Margaret Ann Cullum
Account Executive: Cathy Rentzel
Production Coordinator: Sally Sloan
Design/Art Director: Michael Landon
Photographer: Steve Murai
Copywriter: Anita Williams

Color Separations: Offset Separations Corporation
Printer: Lehigh Press

The Art Institute of Chicago had had only moderate success marketing gifts, books, and visual arts through their previous catalogs. Then they sent out this striking effort, offering half the prior number of items to reduce visual clutter—and printed in an unusual size to stand apart from other holiday gift books. The response was striking as well, producing a 48 percent net sales increase over previous efforts.

THE ART INSTITUTE OF CHICAGO

CHRISTMAS SURPRISES
Christmas Surprises, An Antique Revolving Picture Book by Ernest Nister. Victorian Christmas delights are revealed through the poetry and literally moving pictures of this classic revival. Clothbound, 20 pages. 8" x 8".
26A $16.95.

WOODEN ANIMAL TWISTS
Create 64 different animals by twisting cubes and changing heads, bodies and feet. Beechwood, non-toxic finish. 2½" high. Imported.
Set of 2. 26B $18.

HUMPTY DUMPTY & CHESHIRE CAT
Classic storybook characters. Printed suede cloth stuffed with natural kapok and non-toxic beans. Humpty Dumpty, 5" high. 26C $13.50.
Cheshire Cat, 5" x 11".
26D $15.50.

ARTS IN PLAY LOTTO GAME
Lotto and memory game uses musical instruments, theatrical

Members of The Art Institute of Chicago

BABAR BOOK AND STUFFED TOY
The Art of Babar, The Work of Jean and Laurent de Brunhoff by Nicholas Fox Weber. 192 pages, 312 illustrations.
26E $39.95; Silk-screened hand puppet. Suede cloth, non-toxic. 12" tall with cardboard stand. 26F $
Set of book and puppet. 26G $59.95.

SPIRAL EARRINGS
Adaptation from an ancient garment pin (8th-6th century B.C.) in our Department of European Decorative Arts, Sculpture and Classical Art. Antiqued 22K gold-plated pewter. ⅞" diameter.
Pierced. 21B; Clip. 21C $26.

FROG NECKLACE
Carnelian, fossil, and 22K gold-plate beads. It is a replica of a Central American gold frog (1000-1500 A.D.) from our Department of Africa, Oceania and the Americas. Necklace approx. 20" long.
Frog 1¼". 21A $135.

RAM'S HEAD EARRINGS
Adapted from 3rd century B.C. Greek earring from our Department of European Decorative Arts, Sculpture and Classical Art. 22K gold plate. 1" diameter.
Pierced. 21D. Clip. 21E $26.

SILVER AND ONYX EARRINGS
Handmade by silversmiths in Taxco, Mexico. The simple contemporary design is crafted from sterling silver and black onyx. Approximately 1" x 1".
Pierced. 21F; Clip. 21G $78.

NAVAJO BANGLE BRACELET
Sterling silver bracelet completely handmade by Navajo artist Vernon Tahe. 3" diameter. 21H $84.

SILVER GRAPE EARRINGS AND PIN
Hand-cut and hand-fabricated, these sterling silver pieces are of classic native design, crafted by artisans of Old Mexico. Surprisingly lightweight, these dimensional pieces are a glorious celebration of the silversmith's skill. Clip earrings, 2½"w x 1"l. 21J $64.
Pin, 2½" x 2¼". 21K $84.

21

Order Toll Free 1-800-621-9337

THE ART INSTITUTE OF CHICAGO

ED PASCHKE: PAINTINGS

Published by The Art Institute of Chicago, this catalogue of Paschke's work surveys the career of one of Chicago's most celebrated artists. Accompanies exhibition of the same name (October 13, 1990, through January 2, 1991). 156 pages, 63 color and 30 black-and-white illustrations. 10" x 10". Clothbound. 18A $35. Paperbound. 18B $24.95.

SENUFO NECKLACE

Carnelian and turquoise combine with 22K gold plate. Adapted from a West African brass casting said to be used by a diviner to give advice. From our Department of Africa, Oceania, and the Americas. 23" long. 18C $130.

THORNE ROOM MODEL

An Art Institute exclusive. Easy to-make paper model of an 18th-century French boudoir. Finished piece 8½" x 9" x 7". 18D $7.95; 2 or more, 18E $6.95 each.

MINIATURE ROOMS: THE THORNE ROOMS AT THE ART INSTITUTE OF CHICAGO

Our catalogue of the 68 miniature rooms. Photographs of meticulously crafted interiors with narrative text. 168 pages, 140 color and 11 black-and-white illustrations. 8" x 11". Clothbound. 18F $35. Paperbound. 18G Regularly $19.95, Now $14.95.

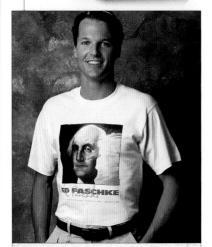

ED PASCHKE T-SHIRT

This exclusive t-shirt depicts a full-color reproduction of the painting Prima Vere, 1986, by Ed Paschke (American, b. 1939). 100% heavyweight cotton. L 18H; XL 18J $15 each.

18

"BAKUBA" SCARF

An adaptation from a ceremonial skirt of the Bakuba People in Central Zaire. From our Department of Textiles. Wool challis. 16" x 62". Imported. Brown. 19B; Olive. 19C $48 each.

MASTER PAINTINGS IN THE ART INSTITUTE OF CHICAGO

An informative reference to significant works from European and American artists in the Art Institute's permanent collections. Selected by James N. Wood, Director, and Katharine C. Lee, Deputy Director. Extraordinary examples of French Impressionists are represented. Includes discussion of the museum's history and growth since its founding in 1871. 169 pages, 149 color illustrations. 11" x 11". 19A $35.

HOPPER CALENDAR

Nighthawks, 1942, by Edward Hopper (American, 1882-1967) captures the inherent loneliness of urban settings on the cover. 12 other images inside. 12" x 12". Imported. 19D $9.95.

BYŌBU CALENDAR

Japanese screens from the Art Institute. 24 color illustrations; 16½" x 24" open. Imported. 19F $11.95; 2 or more, 19G $10.95 each.

SEURAT PUZZLE

From one of the favorite Impressionist paintings of the museum, Sunday Afternoon on the Island of La Grande Jatte, Georges Seurat (French, 1859-1891). 500-piece puzzle. 14" x 18". Imported. 19E $12.95.

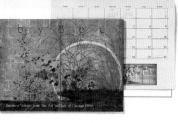

19

Award: Bronze
Program: Holiday 1990 Catalog
Client: Pleasant Company

Agency: In-house

Direct Marketing Team:
Vice President Marketing & Merchandising: Tamara Hauck
Director—Direct Marketing: Lynn Pitman
Direct Marketing Programs Manager: Frances Kruse
Circulation Manager: Alyce Amirian
Catalog Mail Supervisor: Sharon Drews

Catalog Creative:

Creative Director: Pleasant T. Rowland
Designers: Myland McRevey, Karn Litsheim
Printer: R.R. Donnelley, The American Girls Collection®
  Webcrafters, Inc., The New Baby Collection™
Color Separator: Scan Graphics, The American Girls
  Collection
  Northwestern Colorgraphics, The New Baby
  Collection

To introduce a new product line designed for a younger audience than its existing collection, the Pleasant Company created a special insert section in its regular catalog, reaching customers in a cost efficient manner while maintaining the integrity of each distinct product line. Total sales exceeded $18 million and beat the previous catalog by 6 percent.

KIRSTEN'S WINTER STORY
9

In Changes for Kirsten, *the Minnesota winter seems very long to Kirsten and her family, who are crowded in their tiny log cabin. Kirsten looks forward to the days she's allowed outside to help her brother Lars with his trap line. One day she brings home a baby raccoon she's found in the woods, and trouble begins. The raccoon gets loose and starts a fire that destroys the Larsons' home. The future seems bleak until Kirsten and Lars make a frightening but important discovery in the woods.*

♥ **CHANGES FOR KIRSTEN**
by Janet Shaw; With color illustrations
Paperback Book; 65 pages KWP $5.95
Hardcover Book; 65 pages KWH $12.95

♥ **WINTER SKIRT AND BLOUSE**
Kirsten's winter outfit was inspired by a festival costume from the "old country." The white *blouse* has full peasant sleeves and a button at the keyhole opening of the neckline. The black

... *EL* **UNDERWEAR**
... nds blow across the prairie,
... into her flannel underwear. The
... down almost to her knees, and
... quilted border on the *petticoat*
... nth. To keep her toes toasty,
... f black and white striped *socks*.

*... istorically accurate reproductions appropriate
... er.*

♥ **CARPETBAG**
Practical pioneers used scraps of carpet and sewed them into roomy satchels to hold their belongings. Scraps of leather were used for handles just like the ones on this *carpetbag*. *KWA-L $18*

♥ **WINTER PASTIMES**
On long winter days in the cramped cabin, Kirsten would play with her little *thaumatrope*, spinning the disk so the bird would hop into its cage—an optical illusion that's as fun today as it was in 1854. *Paper dolls* helped fill the long hours inside, too. They were a treat for pioneer girls who had few playthings. And on days when Kirsten worked the trap line with Lars, she would strap on her *snowshoes* and walk for miles on top of the deep snow. *KWA-F $18*

KIRSTEN'S SCHOOL STORY
4

New
School Furniture!
Page 38.

In Kirsten Learns a Lesson, *Kirsten has a hard time in her new American school because she doesn't speak English very well. Miss Winston, her new teacher, is strict and not very understanding. Things get worse when Miss Winston comes to live with the Larson family. Kirsten's only escape is playing with her secret friend Singing Bird, the Indian girl. When Singing Bird suggests running away forever, Kirsten must decide where she belongs. Kirsten learns some important lessons in school, but she learns something even more important about herself.*

♥ **KIRSTEN LEARNS A LESSON**
by Janet Shaw; With color illustrations
Paperback Book; 69 pages KSP $5.95
Hardcover Book; 69 pages KSH $12.95
Audio Cassette KST $8.95

♥ **SCHOOL DRESS WITH SHAWL**
Mrs. Larson probably made Kirsten's red print *school dress* out of leftover material from her own—the first mother-daughter styles! Since girls didn't wear jackets, Kirsten has a plaid *shawl* that you can tie around her so she won't get cold on her long walk to school across the prairie. Her outfit includes dark blue woven *hair ribbons. KSO $20*

♥ **PIONEER SCHOOL LUNCH**
Pack a lunch for Kirsten in this charming oval wooden box. In Sweden, it's called a *tine* (tee-na). Kirsten's father might have carved and decorated hers with its traditional wood-burned design.
Pioneer food was simple but hearty. For lunch, give Kirsten a piece of *bread*, a *sausage*, a wedge of *cheese*, and a juicy wild *apple*. Kirsten's make-believe food is tucked in the tine with a woven *napkin. KSA-L $18*

Accessory kits are historically accurate reproductions appropriate for children 8 and over.

♥ **SLATE BAG AND SUPPLIES**
Pencils and paper were scarce in early country schools, so Kirsten did her lessons on a *slate*. When you play school with her, you'll see that the *slate pencil* really works, so it comes with a *wiper*, too. A *ruler* completes the school supplies that come in her brown calico *slate bag*.
Read a tiny version of the original *book* that Kirsten used when she learned to read English.
When Kirsten does a good job in school, you can give her the *Rewards of Merit* just like she earned in the story. These were the report cards for girls and boys back then. *KSA-B $18*

SAMANTHA'S SCHOOL STORY

New School Furniture! Page 39.

*S*amantha goes to Miss Crampton's Academy, a private school for proper young ladies. In Samantha Learns a Lesson, everyone at school is buzzing about the upcoming speaking contest. Samantha is working hard to win the gold medal, but she has something else on her mind, too. She's worried about Nellie, the poor servant girl who has become her friend. She's trying to teach Nellie to read so the boys and girls at her school will stop calling her "dummy" and "ragbag." Samantha sets up a school and becomes Nellie's teacher. But Nellie teaches Samantha some very important lessons, too.

SAMANTHA LEARNS A LESSON
by Susan S. Adler; With color illustrations
Paperback Book; 61 pages SSP $5.95
Hardcover Book; 61 pages SSH $12.95
Audio Cassette SST $8.95

BUSTER BROWN DRESS
Samantha wore her gray Buster Brown *dress* with its snappy black bow tie to school at Miss Crampton's Academy. It's made of fine flannel and has a pleated skirt and placket front that are top-stitched in white. Six buttons march smartly down the front, and white collar and cuffs add the finishing touches. It comes with a wide black satin *hair ribbon* which Samantha had to keep perky even during afternoon exercise classes. SSO $20

TEA TIN LUNCHBOX
Each morning Mrs. Hawkins, the co[...] a lunch for Samantha in a shiny *bra[...]* was originally filled with tea. Her lu[...] and ladylike—half of a watercress s[...] deviled *egg*, a perfect *peach*, and a g[...] *cookie*. Tuck the proper embroidered [...] in with the make-believe food before [...] lid on. SSA-L $18

Accessory kits are historically accurate reproductio[...] for children 8 and over.

BOOK STRAP AND SUPPLIES
A *book strap* was the practical "modern" way for girls to carry their books in 1904. Put Samantha's school supplies under the two straps and fasten the buckles tightly.
  Samantha's wooden *pencil box* has a top that slides off. Inside you'll find two *pencils* and

SAMANTHA'S SUMMER STORY

*I*n Samantha Saves the Day, it's summer at Piney Point, Grandmary's home in the mountains. Agnes and Agatha, the mischievous twins, have come to visit Samantha. The three girls love to explore. In the attic they find a sketchbook made long ago by Samantha's mother. Using it as their map, the girls head off on a secret excursion that almost turns to disaster.

SAMANTHA SAVES THE DAY
by Valerie Tripp; With color illustrations
Paperback Book; 65 pages SAP $5.95
Hardcover Book; 65 pages SAH $12.95

MIDDY DRESS WITH TAM
Every Victorian girl had a *middy dress*, a most popular style in 1904. Samantha's is trimmed in black braid with an anchor, a crest, and stars on the back of the big square collar. A shiny brass *bo's'n's whistle* hangs on a cord around her neck. With the middy Samantha wears a sailor's *tam* for an outfit that's truly shipshape! SAO $22

HIGH BUTTON SHOES
High button shoes in black and white are a stylish part of Samantha's wardrobe. SAO-B $8

NATURE PARAPHERNALIA
For the Victorians, vacations were a time to learn about the outdoors as well as to have fun there. On sunny days at Piney Point Samantha loaded up her *pack basket* and took a nature hike into the Adirondack Mountains. She chased *butterflies* with her *net* and picked wildflowers like these *black-eyed Susans*. Back at the lodge you can help her study the butterflies with her *magnifying glass* and dry the flowers she picked in her wooden *flower press*. You can press real flowers in it, too. SAA-N $22

Accessory kits are historically accurate reproductions appropriate for children 8 and over.

SUMMER AMUSEMENTS
Even rainy days were fun at Piney Point, if there weren't too many of them! Samantha stitched pine needles into a little *tuffet* as a spicy-scented memento of her vacation to take back home at the end of summer. Rainy days were perfect for painting, too. Samantha would take out her *paint set* with its palette, brush, and six tubes of watercolors and paint pictures just like her mother had done in her *sketchbook* when she was a girl at Piney Point long ago. There are blank pages for you to paint in, too. SAA-S $22

MOLLY'S CHRISTMAS STORY 29

In Molly's Surprise, the McIntires face a disappointing Christmas. Dad is off at war in England, Molly's grandparents can't come for the holidays, and it looks like there won't be any exciting presents. Worst of all, the family hasn't heard from Dad for a long time, and they're worried. But Molly decides they should make their own merry Christmas—a Christmas filled with the kind of unexpected surprises that Dad would make. Thanks to Molly, the best surprise of all is waiting for the McIntire family on Christmas morning.

Because the snowball cannot be shipped in cold weather, a comparable product will be substituted from November 1 to March 15.

★ MOLLY'S SURPRISE
by Valerie Tripp; With color illustrations
Paperback Book; 65 pages MCP $5.95

'S STOCKING
...riped Christmas *stocking* next ...ulging with surprises! A wooden ...yo that really works, a *flip book* ...ctures of Mickey Mouse and ...wo white *barrettes* for Molly's ...ne, and a *paint set*. Lots of tiny ...u and Molly to play with on ...and all year long. *MCA-S $16*

★ MOLLY'S CHRISTMAS BOX
There are always surprises at Christmas and some of the best ones come in the mail. Open Molly's big *box* and find two presents inside. A miniature *snowball* and the *doll* of Molly's dreams dressed as a Red Cross nurse in apron, cape, and cap. *MCA-D $16*

Accessory kits are historically accurate reproductions appropriate for children 8 and over.

MOLLY'S WINTER STORY 33

In Changes for Molly, Dad is coming home from the war and Molly can hardly wait to see him. She's especially excited because he'll arrive in time to see her tap-dance as Miss Victory in the big Red Cross show. Molly wants to look sophisticated so Dad will know how much she's grown up while he's been away, but her hair is all wrong. When she finally finds a way to have glorious curls, everything seems to be perfect. Then Molly gets sick . . .

★ CHANGES FOR MOLLY
by Valerie Tripp; With color illustrations
Paperback Book; 67 pages MWP $5.95
Hardcover Book; 67 pages MWH $12.95

★ SLICKER AND RAIN HAT
Keep Molly warm and dry in her bright yellow *slicker* and matching *hat*. The raincoat closes up the front with fireman's clasps, and buckles on the sleeves keep her snug. *MWO $18*

★ UMBRELLA AND GALOSHES
Perfect for puddle-jumping are these bright red vinyl *boots* that zip up the sides and a big red *umbrella* that opens wide. *MWO-A $14*

★ MOLLY'S UNDIES
A cotton knit *undershirt* and matching *panties*, a ruffled *slip*, and a pair of red and white *argyle knee socks* make up Molly's underwear set. It comes with *bobby pins* just like Molly used to set her hair with. *MWA-U $14*

Accessory kits are historically accurate reproductions appropriate for children 8 and over.

★ WINTER ACTIVITIES
Molly had lots of after-school activities to do all winter long. When it was too cold outside, she played with her *kaleidoscope* or with her set of Army nurse *paper dolls*. But she especially loved to go to tap dance class so she could wear her sparkly *Miss Victory costume* with its matching *pants* and shiny star *headband*! *MWA-F $22*

★ PLAID SUITCASE
Molly carried this handy plaid *suitcase* trimmed in green vinyl when she went to Miss LaVonda's dance class. Open the clasp and there's a pocket inside the lid that's a perfect place for her star headband. *MWA-L $16*

Award: Leader
Program: Fall 1990 Mail Order Catalog

Client: Laurel Burch Gallerie By Mail

Agency: In-house
Design: Michael Patrick Cronan, Cronan Design
  Tony Farrell, Laurel Burch, Inc.

Photography: Gerald Bybee, Bybee Studios
Separations: Color Tech
Printing: Foote & Davies
Lists: Susan Rice, Direct Media West
  Michael Hayden, Millard Group
Merge Purge: Triplex
Insert: Veronica Gaynor, Webcraft
Sales & Circulation: Janice Nelson, Laurel Burch, Inc.
Catalog Manager: David Rudd

To increase catalog sales of jewelry, accessories, clothing, and other products bearing the designs of San Francisco artist Laurel Burch, it was decided to feature more of the artist's own thoughts on her pieces. Thus this unusually shaped catalog was sent out, with a welcome message, collection essays, and anecdotes from the artist. The result beat the previous catalog by 43 percent for rental lists and 68 percent for the house list.

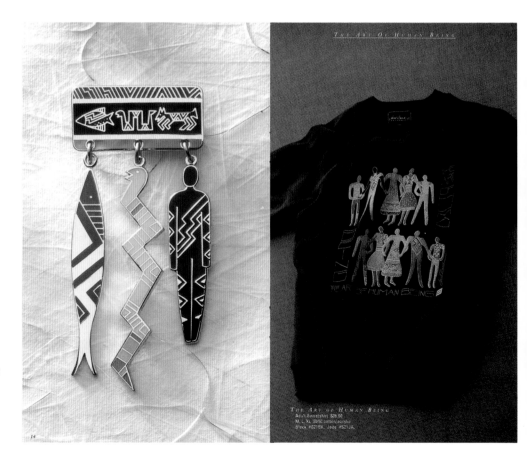

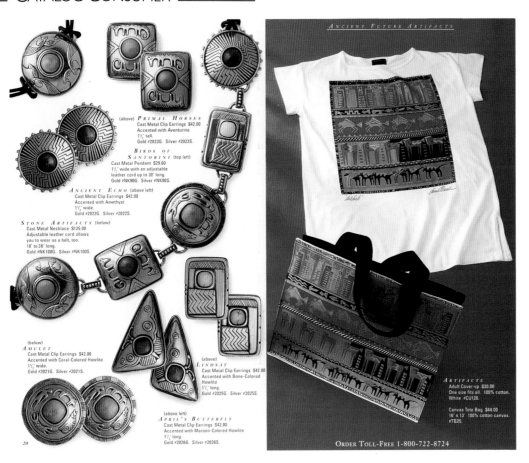

(above) **PRIMAL HORSES**
Cast Metal Clip Earrings $42.00
Accented with Aventurine
1½" tall.
Gold #2023G. Silver #2023S.

BIRDS OF SANTORINI (top left)
Cast Metal Pendant $29.00
1½" wide with an adjustable
leather cord up to 30" long.
Gold #NK90G. Silver #NK90S.

ANCIENT ECHO (above left)
Cast Metal Clip Earrings $42.00
Accented with Amethyst
1½" wide.
Gold #2022G. Silver #2022S.

STONE ARTIFACTS (below)
Cast Metal Necklace $125.00
Adjustable leather cord allows
you to wear as a belt, too.
18" to 36" long.
Gold #NK100G. Silver #NK100S.

(below)
AMULET
Cast Metal Clip Earrings $42.00
Accented with Coral-Colored Howlite
1½" wide.
Gold #2021G. Silver #2021S.

(above)
LINDSAY
Cast Metal Clip Earrings $42.00
Accented with Bone-Colored
Howlite
1½" long.
Gold #2025G. Silver #2025S.

(above left)
APRIL'S BUTTERFLY
Cast Metal Clip Earrings $42.00
Accented with Maroon-Colored Howlite
1½" long.
Gold #2026G. Silver #2026S.

ARTIFACTS
Adult Cover-up $30.00
One size fits all. 100% cotton.
White #CU120.

Canvas Tote Bag. $44.00
16" x 13". 100% cotton canvas.
#TB25.

ORDER TOLL-FREE 1-800-722-8724

20

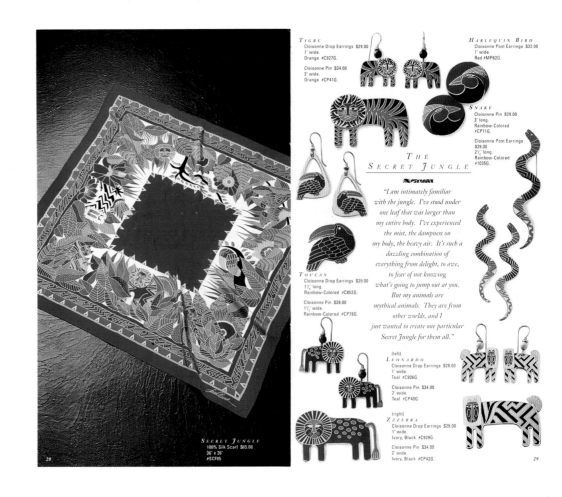

SECRET JUNGLE
100% Silk Scarf. $65.00
36" x 36".
#SCF05

28

TIGRE
Cloisonne Drop Earrings $29.00
1" wide.
Orange #C927G.

Cloisonne Pin $34.00
2" wide.
Orange #CP41G.

HARLEQUIN BIRD
Cloisonne Post Earrings $32.00
1" wide.
Red #MP62G.

SNAKE
Cloisonne Pin $29.00
3" long.
Rainbow-Colored
#CP71G.

Cloisonne Post Earrings
$29.00
2½" long.
Rainbow-Colored
#1035G.

THE SECRET JUNGLE

*"I am intimately familiar
with the jungle. I've stood under
one leaf that was larger than
my entire body. I've experienced
the mist, the dampness on
my body, the heavy air. It's such a
dazzling combination of
everything from delight, to awe,
to fear of not knowing
what's going to jump out at you.
But my animals are
mythical animals. They are from
other worlds, and I
just wanted to create one particular
Secret Jungle for them all."*

TOUCAN
Cloisonne Drop Earrings $29.00
1½" long.
Rainbow-Colored #C852G.

Cloisonne Pin $28.00
1½" wide.
Rainbow-Colored #CP78G.

(left)
LEONARDO
Cloisonne Drop Earrings $29.00
1" wide.
Teal #C926G.

Cloisonne Pin $34.00
2" wide.
Teal #CP40G.

(right)
ZZZEBRA
Cloisonne Drop Earrings $29.00
1" wide.
Ivory, Black #C929G.

Cloisonne Pin $34.00
2" wide.
Ivory, Black #CP42G.

29

Award: Leader
Program: 1990 Christmas Book

Client: Neiman Marcus Mail Order

Agency: In-house

Sr. Vice President, General Merchandise Manager:
  Pat Morgan
Executive Artistic Director: Eddie Nunns
Production Director: Lisa Jilek
Sr. Copywriter: Pat Stehr

Selling items priced from $15 to $250,000, the
Neiman Marcus catalog has become one of the
most eagerly awaited holiday traditions. The 1990
Christmas Book was no exception, offering cus-
tomized his and hers caricature chairs, an
authentic gypsy wagon, and a pair of Napoleon's
reading glasses. The catalog pulled a response rate
above 5 percent—and sold each and every one
of these extraordinary items!

The
1990 Christmas Book

Neiman Marcus

122A,B

122C

122A,B The true seer's ball was, by legend, such as this:
pure, unblemished, full lead crystal. The Baccarat of France,
the perfect ball, about 4 inches in diameter, is a classic objet
d'art. Stand is optional. From The Galleries.
122A. Baccarat "Sirius" crystal ball, 375.00.
122B. Stand, 45.00.

122C Send someone a tangible wish for their success with
the Prosperity Pouch. A compilation of signs, symbols, and
talismans, fifteen in all, gathered from many cultures far and
wide. Augmented by eight pictorial cards and packed in a
green cloth pouch decorated with a golden "Fu" character
— in Chinese tradition the Fu represents the five blessings
of happiness, good luck, wealth, longevity, and peace.
An NM® introduction. From The Galleries.
122C. The Prosperity Pouch, 35.00.

122

The Ultimate RV

Our RV is a "Romany vardo" — not a modern "recreational vehicle," but
a one-of-a-kind antique gypsy caravan over 150 years old, once both
home and transportation to an important English gypsy. Less elaborate forms of
this beautifully preserved vardo are still seen in Western Europe and Britain.

Intricate and elegant inside and out, this wagon is carved and decorated with fox-
heads, grapes, eagles, roses, medallions. Bright colors, gilding, oil-painted ceilings,
French plate glass mirrors, tile fireplace, silvered brass appointments, storage drawers and cupboards, a pull-out bed for three are only part of the enchantment at
this museum on wheels. It's also ingeniously and practically built. The carved fox-
heads, for example, are rain-spouts. There are a larger number of shock absorbers
than usual to provide cushioning for the considerable amount of antique glasswork.
Five shuttered windows let in the light to sparkle on the fantasy interior.

The inside is 4 feet wide, 8 feet long, 6½ feet high. Overall the caravan is 6 x 12
x 12', with a weight of 2500 pounds. Some restoration has been done through the
years, but in the authentic and original style, from newly iron-shod wooden wheels
to meticulous revival of the painting and gilding.

If you travel with the vardo, be sure to purchase a fine, heavy cob horse of at
least 14 hands, used to working in harness and heavy traffic. Otherwise, park it
permanently as a unique studio, party cabaña, or guest house. We can guarantee
it to bring out the gypsy in your soul.

123A. Antique gypsy wagon, 85,000 (X).* For full information,
call 1-800-NEIMANS. Subject to prior sale.

123A

123

Pooling Resources

130A,B A pool cue by Bill Stroud has been called "The Excalibur of Cues." Mr. Stroud creates his cues by hand and computer, and will not release any less than perfect. The phenomenal cues may be used in either pool or billiards. Each cue is one of a kind, and made to order. Allow 8 weeks. Shown at left is a cue in Canadian and bird's-eye maple, .999 fine silver-inlaid ebony. The cue at right is Canadian and bird's-eye maple inlaid with ebony and pink ivory wood, and .999 fine silver. Prices start at 2500.00. Items shown are subject to prior sale. For special orders, call 1-800-NEIMANS.
130A. Ebony/silver cue, 5000.00.
130B. Ebony/pink wood cue, 2500.00.

130C Handmade, personalized acrylic pool balls coated with tough, clear polymer. Specify name (20 spaces max.), allow 6 weeks. With wooden rack. Mail Order.
130C. 16-ball set, 225.00.

130D Portable pool. Miniature balls, cues, rack, wooden table, all in a 19½ x 14½ x 3" leatherette attaché case. By Cambor Enterprises, Inc. Mail Order only.
130D. Portable pool, 130.00.

131A The Parthenon of pool tables, a work of art created for Neiman Marcus by Ron Blatt of Blatt Billiards. As with all his tables, this is completely handmade — and he only makes one at a time. The composition is: solid, heavy stock maple frame with 1" diamond-honed Italian slate bed, hand selected Canadian maple top rails, West German gum rubber rail cushions, 20-oz. nylon/wool cloth (22 colors available), automatic gully-style ball return, handsewn leather-covered #3 pocket irons, black ebonized wood rails and trim hand rubbed to a high gloss, brushed-finish ⅛" thick seamless stainless steel legs, ¼" thick brushed-finish stainless steel side apron trims. In professional 8' or tournament 9' sizes. Allow 5 to 6 months to complete. NOTE: specifications subject to change without notice. Mail Order only.
131A. Pool table, 40,000.00 (X).* Subject to prior sale. For full information or to special order, call 1-800-NEIMANS.

131

His and Hers 1990

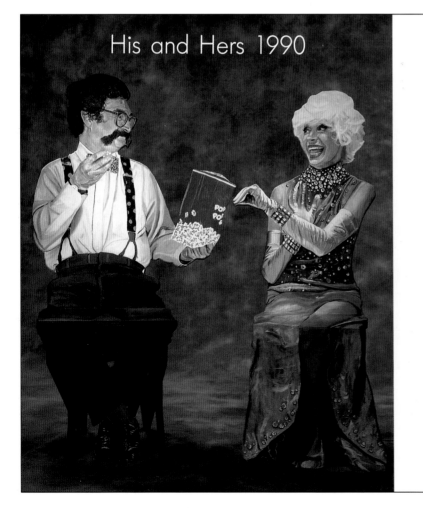

Elect someone to a seat of honor . . . a permanent chairperson. Artist Philip Grace combines the magic of trompe l'oeil with his finely-tuned eye for portraiture, creating chairs that are portraits, painted with oils on wood in the technique of the Old Masters. Choose realism or fantasy — as you see the person, or as they would like to see themselves. With your chairperson, even dinner alone is an event. The experience of seeing two of these very life-like portraits "interacting" may have you convinced you saw them move. No party could resist an ice-break of such memorable proportions with chairpersons in attendance. So ladies and gentlemen, be seated, for the 1990 NM® His and Hers gifts. The best seats in the house.

108A. Single chair, complete with preliminary photography session at your home or business by Philip Grace, 6000.00. Allow 8 weeks for delivery. Call 1-800-NEIMANS for information.

Note: Our sincere thanks to the gracious Carol Channing and the urbane Mr. Gene Shalit for their "sit-in" as our models. At their requests, for appearing in this book, donations have been made to Bennington College in Vermont, and Cambridge School in Maryland.

Fabulous Fur — Precious Jewels

46A-D One of a kind. The coat made from the 1990 top bundle of rare Black Willow® minks. Designed exclusively for NM® by Giuliana Teso. The full, swing silhouette, which dips slightly longer in back, is formed by tiers of intricate skin-on-skin construction. The 2-button neck converts from funnel to roll. Fur origin: USA. From the Fur Salon.

46A. Black Willow® coat, subject to prior sale, 50,000.00.
46B. The same style in natural wild-type mink, 19,500.00.
46C. In natural ranch, 19,500.00.
46D. In natural Lunaraine®, 19,500.00.

47A,B One-of-a-kind designs, created exclusively for Neiman Marcus in Valenza, Italy. The butterfly brooch contains 24 cts. of diamonds, 12 cts. of sapphires, 11 cts. of emeralds, and 22 cts. of rubies. The dome ring contains 4 cts. of diamonds, 4 cts. of rubies, 3.5 cts. of sapphires, and 4 cts. of emeralds. Both in settings of 18-kt. yellow gold. Precious Jewels Salon. Items subject to prior sale.

47A. The brooch, 250,000.00.
47B. The ring, 70,000.00.

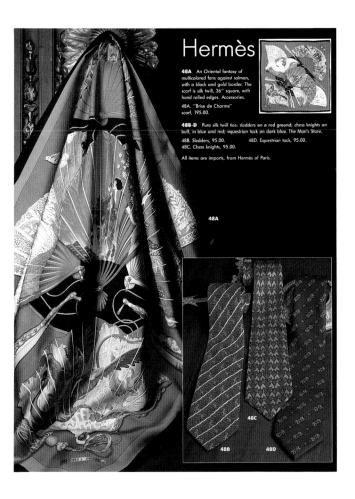

Hermès

48A An Oriental fantasy of multicolored fans against salmon, with a black and gold border. The scarf is silk twill, 36" square, with hand rolled edges. Accessories.

48A. "Brise de Charme" scarf, 195.00.

48B-D Pure silk twill ties: sledders on a red ground; chess knights on buff, in blue and red; equestrian tack on dark blue. The Man's Store.

48B. Sledders, 95.00.   48D. Equestrian tack, 95.00.
48C. Chess knights, 95.00.

All items are imports, from Hermès of Paris.

Napoleon Bonaparte was known to entertain on a lavish scale — yet his most important spectacles were probably these: his reading glasses. Not surprisingly needed, as he was a prolific writer, and a chronicler of the most minute details.

These were possibly his "state spectacles," as they have exquisitely wrought folding frames of 18-kt. yellow gold fitted with 2½ sphere lenses of glass thought to be from Venice. The spectacles were made by the eminent firm of Joliot Freres, circa 1815. Therefore, undoubtedly used in Napoleon's last years.

Their handmade case of burgundy leather is 5" long to accommodate the 4½" folded size of the glasses. An unprecedented find, and a prize for the collector of Napoleonic effects, these spectacles were for generations in the possession of the esteemed family of Prince Murat, Napoleon's brother-in-law.

117A. The spectacles and case, with provenance and certificate of authentication, 90,000.00. Subject to prior sale. Precious Jewels Salon.

Note: shown larger than actual size for detail.

Napoleon's Spectacles

Classic Menagerie

26A,B In celebration of the Chinese New Year of the Goat, 1991, NM®'s exclusive full lead crystal reclining goat from Baccarat. Those born under this sign are thought to be elegant, well-liked, gentle, and generous. From France, 3¾″ long. The Galleries.
26A. Baccarat goat, 155.00.
26B. Stand, 15.00.

26C A wee porcelain cat, 3½″ long x 2½″ high, is from the Bête Noir collection of Chase, Ltd. Hand painted, with black background, blue dragonfly, green foliage, purple and blue flowers, and a goldfish on its back. Weighted to serve as a decorative paperweight. Available from The Galleries.
26C. Paperweight cat, 125.00.

26D For those collecting a school of Lalique's diminutive full lead crystal angelfish, an introduction of the new colors; yellow, grenadine, clear turquoise, and Cap Ferrat blue. Each about 2 x 2¼″. The Galleries.
26D. Lalique angelfish, each, 89.00.

26E Baccarat captures the vitality and lovability of the shaggy little Yorkshire terrier — a breed with a heart bigger than its body. Full lead crystal, 4¼ x 3″. The Galleries.
26E. Baccarat "Yorkie," 150.00.

26A,B

26C

26D

26E

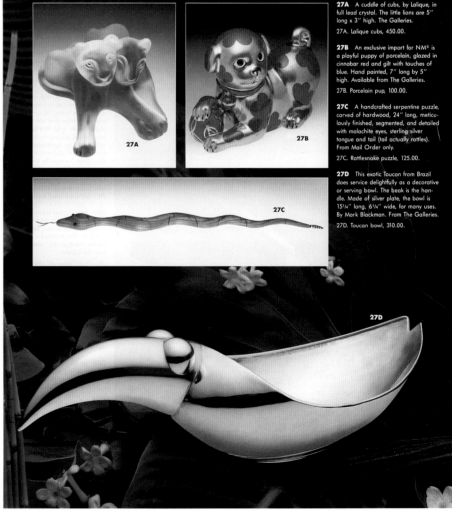

27A

27B

27C

27D

27A A cuddle of cubs, by Lalique, in full lead crystal. The little lions are 5″ long x 3″ high. The Galleries.
27A. Lalique cubs, 450.00.

27B An exclusive import for NM® is a playful puppy of porcelain, glazed in cinnabar red and gilt with touches of blue. Hand painted, 7″ long by 5″ high. Available from The Galleries.
27B. Porcelain pup, 100.00.

27C A handcrafted serpentine puzzle, carved of hardwood, 24″ long, meticulously finished, segmented, and detailed with malachite eyes, sterling silver tongue and tail (tail actually rattles). From Mail Order only.
27C. Rattlesnake puzzle, 125.00.

27D This exotic Toucan from Brazil does service delightfully as a decorative or serving bowl. The beak is the handle. Made of silver plate, the bowl is 15¼″ long, 6¼″ wide, for many uses. By Mark Blackman. From The Galleries.
27D. Toucan bowl, 310.00.

Award: Leader
Program: 1990 Holiday Catalog

Client: Windsor Vineyards
VP, Marketing: Donna Elias

Agency: Brix Direct
Account Executive: Cathy Clifton
Creative Director/Writer: Eileen Haas
Art Direction/Design: Sally Landis, Lisa Luke
   Karen Holmes

Photography: Ming Photography
Color Separator: Spectrum Color
Printer: World Color Press

Battling the neo-prohibitionist sentiments and health consciousness at work in the U.S., this Windsor Vineyards catalog mailed to the house file was careful to position wine as a natural, wholesome component of civilized life. The positioning worked, with revenue per order beating last year's catalog by 7.5 percent and exceeding expectations by 28 percent.

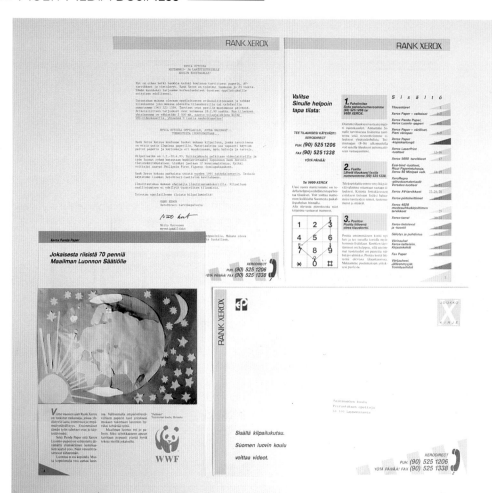

Award: Bronze
Program: Xerox Art

Client: Rank Xerox, *Finland*

Product Manager: Jukka Laitinen
Sales Manager: Niilo Kutvonen
Director, Sales: Matti Haila

Agency: Ogilvy & Mather Direct
Creative Director: Leena Vento
Copywriter: Sirkka-Liisa Pohja
Art Director: Ari Arva

To target medium and small offices using laser printers and copiers—as well as art teachers not favorably disposed toward a large American company like Rank Xerox—the firm sent out with its new catalog the announcement of an art competition inviting schools to submit work created using Rank Xerox supplies, with the winning school receiving free video equipment. The result beat the previous year's effort by 45 percent and pulled a 10 percent response, generating $640,000 in sales.

Award: Leader
Program: Regal Bribe

Client: Kraft/General Foods International
Gevalia Kaffe Import Service: Gerald Maxson

Agency: Wunderman Worldwide (New York)
Art Director: Jane Walsh
Copywriter: Mary Ann Donovan
Production Manager: Peter Cifuni
Account Supervisor: Lisa Arkovitz

To acquire new, quality members for the Gevalia Kaffe gourmet coffee club, this elegant campaign promised the "regal bribe" of a handsome and functional ceramic coffee canister with the introductory shipment. The bribe and the campaign worked, pulling responses as high as 5.5 percent, and beating the previous campaign by 60 percent.

The Leonard J. Raymond Collegiate ECHO Competition

Named for one of the founding fathers of direct response, the Leonard J. Raymond Collegiate ECHO Competition gives college students the chance to develop an actual campaign for an existing company.

Entries are judged on each student team's understanding of the marketing objectives as well as the quality of its research, marketing strategy, media plan, and creative strategy and execution.

Winners receive all-expense-paid trips to DMA's annual conference and other industry functions plus partial scholarships to Northwestern University's Graduate Program in Direct Marketing.

The 1991 competition challenged entrants to devise a campaign introducing Spiegel's new line of leisure wear for men, women, and children, RTW—Ready–To–Wind–Down.

Student teams were to create an integrated campaign using direct response, image advertising, and other brand-building techniques. They had a $1 million budget for a six-month campaign, and could use any or all media, singly or in combination.

In addition, teams were to prepare an assessment of the most viable demographic segment(s) to target from the range of ages 18–50 plus, including a complete competitive environment analysis.

GOLD AWARD

LOUISIANA STATE UNIVERSITY

Faculty Advisor
Dr. Alan Fletcher, Manship School of Journalism
Team Members
Elizabeth Ardoin '91
Michelle Lee '91
Rebecca Spustek '91
Charlotte Wilkerson '91

Louisiana State's Gold-Echo-winning entry employed the brand theme, "Escape to RTW," positioning the line as an alternative to everyday stress with its style, comfort, and convenient catalog shopping. Creative executions in print and mail expanded the theme to promise, "Escape the Boundaries," "Escape the Ordinary," and "Escape to Freedom."

SILVER AWARD

JAMES MADISON UNIVERSITY

Faculty Advisor
Dr. Harold Teer, Jr., Department of Marketing & HRM
Team Members
Elizabeth Lee Cotner '91
Tina Hill '91
Susan Watts '91
Suzanne Wolfe '91

This team from James Madison University developed a campaign under the theme, "Casual Clothes Busy People Can Relax In," which included a mailing package with a heat-sensitive "stressometer" involvement device, and print ads highlighting the line's comfort as well as the convenience of catalog shopping from Spiegel.

BRONZE AWARD

LOUISIANA STATE UNIVERSITY

Faculty Advisor
Dr. Alan Fletcher, Manship School of Journalism
Team Members
Jana Kae James '91
Michele R. LaFrance '91
Suzanne Olinde '91
Carla Taylor '91

This team from LSU won the bronze with a campaign built around the theme, "Experience the weekend...seven days a week with Spiegel's RTW." Included was a mail package featuring a closed-face, handwritten OE and a post-it note with the reminder to call for a free catalog.

HONORABLE MENTION — *Best Creative Plan*

JAMES MADISON UNIVERSITY

Faculty Advisor
Dr. Harold Teer, Jr., Department of Marketing & HRM
Team Members
Elizabeth Lee Cotner '91
Tina Hill '91
Susan Watts '91
Suzanne Wolfe '91

HONORABLE MENTION — *Best Marketing Plan*

STATE UNIVERSITY OF NEW YORK AT PLATTSBURGH

Faculty Advisor
Dr. Nancy Church
Team Member
Michael Kavanaugh

UNIVERSITY OF TENNESSEE AT KNOXVILLE

Faculty Advisor
Professor DeForrest Jackson, Advertising Department
Team Members
Cedric Alford
James Cox
Dara Johnson
Jill Peters

HONORABLE MENTION — *Best Budget/Financial Projections*

NORTHWESTERN UNIVERSITY

Faculty Advisor
Professor Ron Jacobs, Medill School of Journalism
Team Members
Christiane Brown
Julia Haabestad
Sara Russo
Craig Safir

HONORABLE MENTION — *Most Innovative Campaign Concept*

UNIVERSITY OF TENNESSEE AT KNOXVILLE

Faculty Advisor
Professor DeForrest Jackson, Advertising Department
Team Members
Laura Davis
Debra Goans
M. Todd Mills
Daniel Moore

NORTHWESTERN UNIVERSITY

Faculty Advisor
Professor Ron Jacobs, Medill School of Journalism
Team Members
Emily Kellam
Jill Rodkin
Amy Scallan
Julie Schonberger

APPENDIX ▌

1992 DMA Board of Directors

EXECUTIVE COMMITTEE

Chairman
Jerome W. Pickholz
Chairman & CEO
Ogilvy & Mather Direct

Vice Chairman/Chairman-Elect
Alan M. Glazer
President & CEO
Bedford Fair Industries, Ltd.

Treasurer
John F. Temple
President & CEO
Guideposts Associates, Inc.

Secretary
Vachel Pennebaker
Vice President
Circulation/Market Analysis
Sears, Roebuck and Co.

Jonah Gitlitz
President & CEO
Direct Marketing Association, Inc.

Immediate Past Chairman
John A. Cleary
President
Donnelley Marketing, Inc.

Richard N. Cabela
Chairman
Cabela's Inc.

M. Virginia Daly
President
Daly Direct Marketing

Allen W. Dyon
Vice President & CEO
Allstate Enterprises, Inc.

Michael T. McSweeney
President & CEO
DIMAC Corporation

Francis P. Pandolfi
President & CEO
Times Mirror Magazines, Inc.

Barrie M. Spelling
Vice President-Central Europe
Colgate-Palmolive Company

BOARD OF DIRECTORS

Jock Bickert
Chief Executive Officer
NDL/The Lifestyle Selector

Claude de la Forest Divonne
International President
Le Redoute Catalogue

Robert M. Edmund
President
Edmund Scientific Company

David W. Florence
President
Direct Media, Inc.

Vickie K. Hagen
Vice President and General Manager
Gourmet Foods Division
Omaha Steaks International

Max L. Hart
Director of Direct Mail
Disabled American Veterans

Fred P. Hochberg
President
Lillian Vernon Corporation

Richard Hochhauser
President
Harte-Hanks Direct Marketing

Rudolph G. Johnstone
Senior Vice President
Envelope Division
Westvaco Corporation

Peg Kuman
President
The Power Line

Graeme Livingstone-Wallace
Counsellor
Visual Communications
Nestec Ltd.

Sheila Martin
President
Triplex Direct Marketing Corporation

Jack E. Rosenfeld
President & CEO
Hanover Direct, Inc.

Thomas O. Ryder
President
Publishing and Direct Marketing Group
American Express TRS

Edmund Schooler
Executive Vice President
Inmac Corporation

Emily Soell
Vice Chairman, Chief Creative Officer
RAPP COLLINS MARCOA

Karl A. Steigerwald
Vice President
Information Services & Marketing
Spiegel, Inc.

William J. Totten
President
U.S. Books and Home Entertainment Division
The Reader's Digest Association, Inc.

Merrill R. Tutton
President
Consumer Communications Services
AT&T

George S. Wiedemann
President
Grey Direct

H. Robert Wientzen
Manager Promotion & Marketing Services
The Proctor & Gamble Company

John D. Yeck
Partner
Yeck Brothers Group

FORMER CHAIRMEN

1988
Stephen E. Toman
Executive Vice President-Reference
Grolier Inc.

1989
Richard C. Wolter
President
Columbia House

1990
James D. McQuaid
President & CEO
Metromail Corporation

APPENDIX ■ ■

Agency Directory

Action I/S
72 Stranoveden
DK-2900 Hellerup
Denmark

The Aldersey Taylor Partnership
Penhill Offices, Colesbourne
Cheltenham, Gloucestershire GL53 9NS
United Kingdom

Amherst Direct Marketing Ltd.
Cissbury House, 14 West Ave.
Worthing, West Sussex BN11 5LW
England

Ball Direct Marketing
11/F, Vicwood Plaza
199 Des Voeux Road Central
Hong Kong

Bowes, Dentsu & Partners
4751 Wilshire Blvd., Suite 201
Los Angeles, CA 90010

Brann Direct Marketing
Phoenix Way
Cirencester, Gloucestershire GL7 1RY
England

Brix Direct
655 Bryant
San Francisco, CA 94107

Bronner Slosberg Humphrey Inc.
695 Atlantic Ave.
Boston, MA 02111

Leo Burnett U.S.A.
35 West Wacker Dr.
Chicago, IL 60601

Cabot Direct Marketing
One Constitution Plaza
Boston, MA 02129

Carlson Frequency Marketing
12555 State Highway 55
Minneapolis, MN 55440

Chapman Direct Advertising
230 Park Ave. South, 8th Floor
New York, NY 10003

Chapter One Direct Plc.
Green Lane
Tewkesbury, Gloucestershire GL20 8EZ
England

Cramer-Krasselt
225 N. Michigan Ave.
Chicago, IL 60601

Creative Communications
10940 Whiterim Dr.
Potomac, MD 20854

Creative Marketing Management
1521 Elliot Place, NW
Washington, D.C. 20007

d.a.p. associates
280 Summer St.
Boston, MA 02210-1182

Dentsu Wunderman Direct, Inc.
3F Dentsu-kosan Bldg. No. 3, 16-7
Ginza 2-chome, Chuo-ku
Tokyo 104
Japan

DiMark
105 Terry Dr., Suite 118
Newtown, PA 18940

DMB & B Dialog
Schaumain Kai 87
Frankfurt/Main D-6000
Germany

DMCA Direct
One Corporate Woods Dr.
Bridgeton, MO 63044-3838

W. B. Doner & Company
2305 North Charles St.
Baltimore, MD 21218

Drake Beam Morin, Inc.
100 Park Ave.
New York, NY 10017

A. Eicoff & Company
401 North Michigan Ave.
Chicago, IL 60611

Epsilon
50 Cambridge St.
Burlington, MA 01803

Grey Direct Marketing Group, Inc.
875 Third Ave.
New York, NY 10022

Grey Response Marketing (Pty.) Ltd.
Box 1438 ParkLands
Johannesburg, TVL 2121
South Africa

Griffin Creative Group
4900 Rivergrade Rd., Bldg. 500
Irwindale, CA 91706

Herring/Newman
414 Olive Way
Seattle, WA 98101

Hodgins Design, Inc.
1208 St. Paul St.
Baltimore, MD 21202

Ingalls, Quinn & Johnson
855 Boylston St.
Boston, MA 02116

Jordan-Savage Direct
233 West Central St.
Natick, MA 01760

Kern/Mathai
11601 Wilshire Blvd.
Suite 1111
Los Angeles, CA 90025

Kobs & Draft Advertising Chicago
142 East Ontario
Chicago, IL 60611

Kobs & Draft Advertising France
177 rue Armand Silvestre
Courbevoie 92400
France

Kobs & Draft Advertising London
141 Westbourne Terrace
London W2 6JR
England

Kobs & Draft Advertising Spain
Capitan Haya 49
Madrid 2802
Spain

KVO Advertising & Public Relations
15220 NW Greenbrier Parkway, #300
Beaverton, OR 97006

Lintas: Marketing Communications
11100 Santa Monica Blvd., Suite 600
Los Angeles, CA 90025

Look Creative Group
A Department of Prodigy Services
445 Hamilton Ave.
White Plains, NY 10601

Irma S. Mann, Strategic Marketing, Inc.
360 Newbury St.
Boston, MA 02115

Marboeuf & Associes
24, rue Eugene-Flachat
Paris 75017
France

The Martin Agency
500 N. Allen
Richmond, VA 23231

Mediavente Conseil
7, rue de Monceau
Paris 75008
France

Merrell Remington Direct
(formerly RPM Direct)
1847 West 2300 South
Salt Lake City, UT 84119

Mullen Advertising
36 Essex St.
Wenham, MA 01984

Ogilvy & Mather Direct Australia
132 Arthur St., 7th Floor
North Sydney, N.S.W. 2029
Australia

Ogilvy & Mather Direct Barcelona
Avda. Tibidabo, 32
Barcelona 08022
Spain

Ogilvy & Mather Direct Denmark
Martinsvej 7
DK-1926 Frederiksberg C
Denmark

Ogilvy & Mather Direct Finland
Aleksanterinkatu 19
00100 Helsinki
Finland

Ogilvy & Mather Direct Hong Kong
X7/F., Mount Parker House
Taikoo Shing
Hong Kong

Ogilvy & Mather Direct Madrid
Capitan Haya 1, 3rd Floor
Madrid 28020
Spain

Ogilvy & Mather Direct Malaysia
6th Floor, Wisma MCIS, Jalan Barat
Petaling Jaya, Selangor 46200
Malaysia

Ogilvy & Mather Direct New York
309 West 49th St.
New York, NY 10019

Ogilvy & Mather Direct New Zealand
Pete Marwick House, 10th Floor
135 Victoria St.
Wellington 1, P.O. Box 27240
New Zealand

Ogilvy & Mather Direkt Germany
Geleitsstrasse 14
6000 Frankfurt/Main 70
Hessen
Germany

Orsatti & Parrish
101 Arch St.
Boston, MA 02110

Pinpoint Pty. Ltd.
Unit 17-19, Waterview Wharf
37 Nicholson St.
East Balmain, N.S.W. 2041
Australia

Proad O&M Direct
314-316 Sygrou Ave
Athens 17673
Greece

Raphel Marketing
Gordon's Alley
Atlantic City, NJ 08401

Riccelli Direct, Inc.
2 Training Field Rd.
West Newbury, MA 01955

Ross Roy Communications
100 Bloomfield Hills Parkway
Bloomfield Hills, MI 48304

Russ Reid Company
2 North Lake Ave., Suite 600
Pasadena, CA 91101

Saugatuck Direct
18 Kings Highway North
Westport, CT 07880

Shain/Colavito/Pensabene Direct, Inc.
655 Third Ave.
New York, NY 10017

Smith Harrison Direct
175 W. 200 South
Suite 2000
Salt Lake City, UT 84101

The Stenrich Group, Inc.
10128 West Broad St., Suite J
Glen Allen, VA 23060

Sudler & Hennessey
The Denison, 15th Floor
65 Berry St.
North Sydney, NSW 2060
Australia

J. Walter Thompson Direct
420 Lexington Ave., Suite 610
New York, NY 10017

Trahan, Burden & Charles Direct
1030 North Charles St.
Baltimore, MD 21201

Vroom
2200 N. Lamar #205
Dallas, TX 75202

Watson, Ward, Albert, Varndell (WWAV) Limited
31 St. Petersburgh Place
London W2 4LA
England

Wunderman Marketing Direto
Av. Brigadeiro Faria Lima 21
Sao Paulo 01451
Brazil

Wunderman Worldwide Detroit
200 Renaissance Center, Suite 1000
Detroit, MI 48243

Wunderman Worldwide Limited London
Greater London House, Hampstead Road
London NW1 7QP
England

Wunderman Worldwide New York
675 Avenue of the Americas
New York, NY 10010

Yeck Brothers
2222 Arbor Blvd.
Dayton, OH 45439

INDEX ∎

Agencies

INDEX ▮▮

Clients